Aberdeenshire Library and Information Service
www.aberdeenshire.gov.uk/libraries
Renewals Hotline 01224 661511

HEADQUARTERS
- 7 FEB 2011
HEADQUARTERS
03 JUN 2015
14. JUN 11
11 JUL 2018
19 SEP 2007
- 6 MAY 2008
21 JUL 2012
- 6 APR 2009
HEADQUARTERS
27 JUL 2009
05 SEP 2013
19 DEC 2013
HEADQUARTERS
24 FEB 2012
ABERDEENSHIRE LIBRARIES
20 NOV 2009
20 AUG 2010
18 NOV 2014
WITHDRAWN FROM LIBRARY

GUILIANO, Mireille

French women for all seasons

D1351432
2556545

BY THE SAME AUTHOR

French Women Don't Get Fat

French Women for All Seasons

Mireille Guiliano

Chatto & Windus
LONDON

Published by Chatto & Windus 2006

First published in the United States of America by Knopf in 2006

2 4 6 8 10 9 7 5 3 1

Copyright © 2006 by Mireille Guiliano

"French Women Don't Get Fat" is a trademark of Mireille Guiliano

Mireille Guiliano has asserted her right under the Copyright, Designs and Patents Act 1988 to be identified as the author of this work

This book is sold subject to the condition that it shall not, by way of trade or otherwise, be lent, resold, hired out, or otherwise circulated without the publisher's prior consent in any form of binding or cover other than that in which it is published and without a similar condition, including this condition being imposed on the subsequent purchaser

First published in Great Britain in 2006 by
Chatto & Windus
Random House, 20 Vauxhall Bridge Road,
London, SW1V 2SA

www.randomhouse.co.uk

Addresses for companies within The Random House Group Limited can be found at: www.randomhouse.co.uk/offices.htm

A CIP catalogue record for this book is available from the British Library

ISBN 0701180609
ISBN 9780701180607 (from Jan 07)

The R [illegible] to ensure
that [illegible] hat have
been legall[illegible] ed forests. Our

ex

ABERDEENSHIRE LIBRARY AND INFORMATION SERVICES	
2556545	
HJ	492839
613.042	£12.99
AD	PORP

Live in each season as it passes; breathe the air, drink the drink, taste the fruit, and resign yourself to the influences of each. Let them be your only diet drink and botanical medicines.

—Henry David Thoreau

CONTENTS

Ouverture: A Tale of Two Cities, a Matter of Taste 3

1. *J'ai oublié de vous dire*: Something I Forgot to Mention 15

2. *Au printemps*: Spring into Life 37

3. *En été*: Summertime Smiles 101

4. *En automne*: Fall Ahead 153

5. *En hiver*: Winter Pleasures 207

Entr'acte: The French Eat *What*? 257

6. Wine Is Food 278

7. *Recevoir*: Entertaining *à la Française* 319

À Bientôt: A Little French Lesson 360

Index 380

FRENCH WOMEN FOR ALL SEASONS

OUVERTURE: A TALE OF TWO CITIES, A MATTER OF TASTE

"It was the best of times, it was the worst of times." Thus Charles Dickens began his *Tale of Two Cities* a century and a half ago. The cities he imagined were Paris and London. The countries he was contrasting were revolutionary France and late eighteenth-century England. Two opposing worlds, two points of view. And two divergent destinies. When I wrote *French Women Don't Get Fat*, I had in mind two disparate worlds of eating: the French and the American. Also, to a lesser extent, two cities: Paris and New York. What I did not realize at the time was that I was in fact writing a tale of two global cultures increasingly without borders. For better and worse, where you live no longer dictates how you eat. It's up to you.

In our ever more complex world, it is still possible to have our cake *and* eat it, too, to enjoy our days to the full in many ways while embracing a time-tested, back-to-basics approach to life—one filled with quality, sensitivity, seasonal foods, and pleasure. I don't want to live in the past, but I do want to learn from it, and I believe that the culture of moderation, painstaking attention to taste, and healthy eating and living that I absorbed growing up in France can be adapted to today's world and pursued just about anywhere. This is not to say I don't understand or appreciate firsthand the challenges women these days face: the pressures of too much to do in too little time, of mega portions, and industrially produced food often eaten on the run.

On the one hand, there was the culture of moderation and painstaking attention to taste and healthy eating that I had absorbed growing up in France, later adapting and updating it to twenty-first century living: a back-to-basics approach to life, filled with quality foods and pleasure—but free of diets. This lifestyle has stood the test of time and can be pursued just about anywhere.

For a long time, this clash of cultural and lifestyle perspectives and outcomes took shape in my mind as a contrast between, on the one hand, fundamental elements of French culture and, on the other, behaviours I learned in America. But with the appearance of *French Women Don't Get Fat* in language after language, I have come to understand that what I thought of as a national divide is really only an emblem for a conflict of two world orders. While I certainly don't think I have all the solutions to this conflict, or any highly specialized expertise, I try not to take myself too seriously—I still have more experiences and secrets (and many more recipes and weekly menus) to share that will help people enjoy a better quality of life—and almost certainly lose weight.

Last autumn a French reporter followed me through the Union Square Greenmarket in New York, where we encountered a class of eight-year-olds with their teacher. The kids were participating in a programme called Spoons Across America, a not-for-profit organization dedicated to educating children, teachers, and families about the benefits of healthy eating and the value of supporting local farmers and sharing meals around the family table. As it was autumn, apples of many varieties were abundantly available. But when the reporter, half kidding, picked up an apple and asked one little boy what it was, the child drew a blank. Forget the variety; he did not know it was an apple. This city kid had apparently never seen an apple in real life. It gives one pause. I would bet, though, that he could recognize the packaged apple pie at the McDonald's just opposite the Greenmarket.

The world where I grew up—and my experience of apples—in Alsace-Lorraine could not have been further from this little boy's in New York City. As I recall it, all our neighbours had at least one fruit tree, and we had numerous apple trees in our garden. Come apple-picking time, my job was to place the different varieties we grew into little flat crates called *cagettes*, which we put into the cold cellar for winter storage—a centuries-old practice now mostly gone. What sweet and glorious aromas filled that cellar when I deposited all those baskets! (Tellingly, in French the word for smell, *sentir*, also means feel.) Today I recall the apple smell even more powerfully than the old footage of that autumn ritual I carry around in my head. And, of course, the harvest meant my mother would once again make an apple pie, *une tarte aux pommes alsacienne*.

In our garden we also had bushes of *groseilles*, tart redcurrants that are a regional speciality. My mother and I loved to make pies with these tiny berries. The season for redcurrants is short and we quickly made jam (*confiture*) or jelly (*gelée*) or pies, and sometimes a sauce (*coulis*). And oh, how we looked forward to this once-a-year treat, which somehow exemplifies for me the French woman's psychological pleasure in food. It is the anticipation and joy that we gain from a pleasure we cannot take for granted and know we will soon lose. Tasting such seasonal bounty heightens our awareness of what we put into our mouths and contrasts with routine, mindless eating that provides little pleasure and often unwanted pounds or kilos.

These days, an image I carry around with me is of two airports. It's fitting, since airports are now the crossroads of the world, the most common interface of one culture with another. At O'Hare International, in Chicago, on the way to an appearance on the *Oprah* show, I witnessed a surreal spectacle I wish I had videotaped. People all around me in the terminal were gulping down hamburgers, fries, and pizza and knocking back big tubs of cola or coffee as they tapped away on their laptops, talked on their mobile phones, and flipped through newspapers. Most remarkable: it was 10 a.m. Why were they even eating? I asked myself. Breakfast? Early lunch? Or just a way to pass the time? It looked more like stuffing than eating, actually. And most of the people I saw were significantly overweight. Plus, I could not detect pleasure on a single face. On my way back to New York, it was equally disturbing to see the airport bars doing a brisk business at 3 p.m. Here and there, however, one could spot people not of this place: American abstainers from the madness, or perhaps visitors just passing through? Anyway, these people reminded me of the French approach.

The airport-cum-food court may be a sign of the times, but not quite yet in France. At Charles de Gaulle (or Roissy, as the French call it), the busiest hub on the Continent, when French people eat, they still generally sit down with a knife and fork at enclosed cafeterias or restaurants. There are small stand-up bars for those who want a quick croissant or perhaps a *jambon beurre* and a cup of coffee. But have you seen a typical French cup of coffee? Three sips, four max. No *frappuccino gargantuoso con lateria* or whatever (though Starbucks has followed McDonald's as a global brand). In France, if you want milk, you order a *crème* or even a *grand crème*—add a few more sips. The airports may still reflect the traditional differences for the most part, but they also show that infiltration is taking place in both directions. Things in France aren't yet set up to accommodate the contemporary culture of excess, but where there's a will, there's a way: in the odd corner you do find people engaging in alien habits, with two sandwiches, an iPod and a magazine feeding them all at once; but they are the exception.

Ever since that eye-opening day in Chicago, whenever I see such scenes, I think of a quote by Brillat-Savarin, the eighteenth-century "modern" gastronome, well known for his writings and meditations on the physiology of taste and for his famous dictum: "We are what we eat". But he also wrote even more revealingly: "The destiny of a nation depends on how it feeds itself."

Even Paris, famed as the world capital of slender women, isn't immune to the growing culture of excess and the global breakdown in traditional ways of eating. Some readers have gone so far as to send me "gotcha" letters informing me that, while in France, they actually saw a fat French woman! *Vraiment*. I never said they don't exist. While the vast majority are not fat, there is indeed an—*excusez-moi!*—growing minority of the *bouboule* (overweight and dumpy), many of whom are not far from becoming obese. How could it be? Fast food chains arrived years ago on the boulevard Saint-Germain and the Champs-Élysées. French women are not immune to the primal urges for the sweet and salty that make fast food appealing. But even more important, they are not exempt from the pressures of living and working in a globalized world that erodes traditional local values and speeds up the pace of life, leaving less time for savouring food as our parents did. As eating becomes less and less a family affair, mothers and fathers neglect to teach their children the right way to eat. Bad habits rush to fill the void. There's even a public service ad campaign in France with the slogan *L'Obésité Tue* (obesity kills). Make no mistake: overeating is an approaching global epidemic (already arrived in many countries). Unless we get our act together, in one generation the French will be as dangerously overweight as many Americans and will fit perfectly into a contemporary airport movie.

If the threat were not real, *French Women Don't Get Fat* would have been a curiosity instead of a phenomenon when it was published in France in 2005. My native land, it seemed, wanted to be reminded of its own traditional habits almost as much as my adoptive homeland wanted to be introduced to them. In the twenty-first century, we can no longer expect to receive lifestyle as an inheritance; it has become a matter of active choice. There is no *cordon sanitaire* to keep Pizza Hut Poppers out of France.

On the other hand, there is also virtually nothing barring you from importing what is beneficial from the classic French lifestyle and finding ways of making it work where you live. Long ago, I made the connection that a serious interest in food, this pillar of the French way of life, is the main reason why, overwhelmingly and by tradition, French women don't get fat. My first book was addressed to the untold legions of diet victims, people all over the world, whom I urged to reject the twin hoaxes of (1) deprivation as the key to weight loss and (2) indulgence being to blame for weight gain. Pleasure has proved itself to be the most powerful and lasting motivation, even more compelling than the dream of dropping a dress size. Actually it was just common sense reborn—if we can only harness the pleasure principle, we can lose weight, as French women have done for generations; all we need is to learn a sense of proportion and cultivate our appreciation of taste. Do that and we should never feel deprived. In *French Women Don't Get Fat* I asked for a commitment of months, not weeks. But the promise in return was results that last—no yo-yoing (the pitfall of any quick-fix diet). My aim was to lead people to become effortlessly slender beings, alert and devoted to pleasure. I am hardly a champion of France in all things, just in some. And it's not out of some precious snobbery that I reject many of the things on supermarket shelves. When foods are bursting with natural taste—as opposed to being artificially flavoured, laden with fat and salt, or just plain tasteless—the experience of eating them is more satisfying and we can content ourselves with less. And so, when French women exult over some perfectly ripe melon, they are making a spectacle not just of themselves but of their capacity to register real degrees of difference—a talent nurtured by a culture in which things are harvested in season and bought fresh. This capacity, more than anything else, is their secret weapon in not getting fat. The pleasure of quality more than offsets the temptation of unlimited quantity.

French DNA is not necessary for the experience. French women don't have thousands of extra little taste receptors that allow them to distinguish Jacques Torres's chocolate from Cadbury's. They do, however, have a lifetime of exposure to and cultivated appreciation of the good stuff. This is something we can all develop. Helping to cultivate that knack—which requires an awareness of what each season has to offer—and thereby learn to reap all the invigorating benefits is one of my main purposes in writing this book.

Cost? Yes, as I've admitted, better things generally—though not always—cost more. But I am not asking readers to buy a ticket to the French Riviera. Many of the pleasures I suggest are inexpensive, from walking or cycling to avoiding built-in transportation costs by buying local produce in season. The French do spend more per capita on food than, for instance, Americans or the British. But by eating better, you eat less. And the French have a lower per capita income to begin with. If it's a matter of your health, body image, and peace of mind, isn't it worth digging a little deeper? Everyone blows money on something, usually something less important than food. It's a question of conditioning and priorities—of which you may find you share more with the French than you realized.

Quality exists on the palate of the person, who must teach herself to distinguish it. Education is crucial. People need to understand what they are putting into their bodies. What are the consequences of drinking 250 or 300 millilitres of orange juice in the morning? Most fruit juices are high in sugar. And even something as simple as bottled water requires attention. All bottled waters are not created equal. Read the label. Some of the best-selling brands have high levels of sodium, which people with high blood pressure or heart disease should avoid, and many mineral-rich waters have high calcium levels, which should be a red alert to those susceptible to kidney stones.

Cooking is also education—it raises your awareness of what you are feeding your body and when, sharpens your taste buds and can help you develop the sort of relationship with food that inhibits overeating. Anybody can learn to cook. (Involving children in cooking, and taking them food shopping in a market to see real ingredients and buy what's fresh, can make a huge difference in their lives.) Cooking doesn't have to be difficult or time-consuming when the ingredients are fresh and good—the best preparations are the simplest. The recipes in this book overwhelmingly adhere to my philosophy of pure and simple, and always pleasure. (Once in a while, pure and simple is not the goal, though pleasure still is. Who doesn't enjoy ordering something in a restaurant that took someone else hours and hours to prepare?)

Of course, quality of life, French or otherwise, requires more than good food. *Joie de vivre* is in direct proportion to how much pleasure you know how to derive from *every* aspect of living. As I will describe, the French *art de vivre* offers examples of delicious experience beyond just the gastronomic. Everything from how we move to how we groom ourselves or how we greet each day has the potential for unlocking pleasure and making life feel fuller. There is, after all, more to life than not getting fat.

I have heard amazing stories (*merci beaucoup*) of successful self-transformation, changes of hearts and minds, as well as bodies, inspired by *French Women Don't Get Fat*. *Voilà*, the secret of pleasure in a nutshell: change the way you think, and the way you eat will follow. Change the way you eat, and your weight will take care of itself. Conversely, let a diet book dictate how, what, where and when you eat, and you will learn nothing, only postpone the inevitable relapse.

In my first book I laid out the basics for a do-it-yourself turnaround, a path to weight loss and a happy equilibrium, that weight at which one feels *bien dans sa peau* (comfortable in one's skin). Now we proceed *peu à peu* (little by little), so that you are reborn for life, not just for the bikini season.

This new book is a guide to a deeper understanding of the basics I presented in the first. It is also a source of suggestions to take you through one year, and years to come of continually inventing and embracing pleasurable experience—the key to the good life as the French enjoy it. As always, I provide not templates but food for thought: I'll let you in to secrets of my own and of other French women, with tips, and recipes, and menus (as well as insights on wine and cheese, *bien sûr*), but what you make of it is uniquely your own.

Here, then, is a continuation of the French lessons we began in *French Women Don't Get Fat*, in things my family and the saviour of my youth, Dr. Miracle, taught me. I am perpetually adapting them to suit our busy lives. Nothing here, taken as always in moderation, will make you fat, but the express aim is rounding out your life (as opposed to your bottom). It is about embracing the seasons and seasonality and making eating and savouring life a more intense experience. It's learning the way to find pleasure in all things. I offer a new framework in which to contemplate some of the timeless principles of French women, as well as new ideas—the goal being to promote a more holistic approach to living. You're bound to pick up slimming pointers, but if your immediate concern is weight loss, why not start with the first book in order to achieve your point of stable equilibrium (a healthy weight that satisfies you)? While making no claims to literary genius, I do know that you can't enjoy Proust until you have made the time commitment and picked up sufficient vocabulary and grammar to savour the reading experience.

In *French Women Don't Get Fat* I introduced readers to the basic elements of *joie de vivre*; here we take up *l'art de vivre*, the finer points of living to the full. It may be that after this next level you'll be able to teach some French women a thing or two. In the nineteenth century, American painters came to Barbizon to learn about art from the world's undisputed masters. A generation later it was the French painters seeking to learn from the Americans. As long as the lamp of French women remains lit, it hardly matters what nationality is holding it aloft. This is no more a tale of two cities.

I

J'AI OUBLIÉ DE VOUS DIRE: SOMETHING I FORGOT TO MENTION

"J'ai oublié de vous dire" ("I forgot to tell you") was an expression of my mother's that I remember from a very young age. It seemed *Mamie* was always forgetting to tell you something important she had remembered only after you had left the room or hung up the phone. For instance: "Oh, and I forgot to tell you, if you don't beat your egg whites to firm peaks, your soufflé will collapse!"

Before my first book was launched in France, a Parisian friend had a dinner party with French ladies, some of whom had read the English version, eager to know what beans I had spilled. One of them, Michèle, who hadn't read a word, pressed me to declare what I had written. But before I could say anything, Claudette, another guest, said with mischievous nonchalance, "Oh, she has told them absolutely everything about how we eat without getting fat!" I laughed, a bit uneasy to see Michèle getting quite *énervée* (agitated). Finally she said, "How dare you give away OUR secrets to the world?" I am not making this up, and it wasn't a totally isolated incident in the company of French women. "We are all in this together," I said. "I was only trying to help a few troubled souls." Nothing would calm her down until I muttered, "Don't worry, *j'ai oublié de leur dire* [I forgot to tell them]. . . . I have not given away *all* our secrets." I didn't, however, take a vow of silence.

PITFALLS OF THE "ELEVATOR" SPEECH

We live in a world far more complex than our parents' and grandparents', but in some ways our world is more superficial. People, my fellow New Yorkers not least, want short answers and quick solutions, and in their multi-tasking universe they can't spare the attention to think deeply or focus for too long on any one problem—even a problem as immediate as their own excess weight.

The "elevator" speech—a form invented and perfected in Manhattan—is the notion that in a world where time is money and attention spans are short, you have only thirty seconds to sell your new idea. Depending on where you are this is roughly equivalent to the time required to take the lift up ten floors, during which you are holding a decision maker captive. "If you can't get your idea across in a few sentences, you haven't refined your thinking"; so goes the prevailing business-speak. Well, I suppose that's true for many simple innovations, from double-sided tape (excellent invention) to multi-coloured umbrella hats (beats me). Some ideas, even good ones, really need only thirty seconds.

There are, however, somewhat more involved propositions that don't lend themselves to this format. What thirty-second version of a political philosophy would you subscribe to? Diets, on the other hand, being consumer products, must toe the line of brevity. For instance, "It's all about carb restriction" or "It's not what you eat but when you eat it." People wanted me to sum up in thirty seconds my own programme for life, which I have always presented as emphatically as I could as a non-diet with a holistic approach. The "elevator" synopsis of *French Women Don't Get Fat* includes mention of rediscovering the pleasures of eating and cooking. "Eat three meals a day; keep portions small; eat seasonal fruits and vegetables; drink lots of water; savour wine; walk more; and have occasional treats." But, that's so general it can apply to many books and is rightly called common sense. Reduced to a set of bullet points, the whole really is much less than the sum of its parts. A lifestyle, or way of life, however, is a set of behaviours by which you adopt lasting principles and embody certain values. No one on its own, or even listed together, gives a complete picture, any more than a plot summary could give you a whole book. A book is a thing to be read and absorbed over time. By contrast, a diet is not a lifestyle (heaven forbid!) any more than a diet book (really just an instructional manual) is, properly speaking, a book to be savoured and enjoyed.

To read a book is, at least for a time, to try on a different way of thinking, a way of seeing and, in this case, a way of eating, moving, and living. A complete turnaround in the way you eat, move, and live properly takes six months to a year. It's admittedly more of an investment of time than plugging numbers into a calorie chart—I may well have neglected to make clear in the first book the need for patience and perseverance. (Prescribing pleasures, not deprivations, I guess I assumed pleasures pay their own way—don't they?) Results, as many readers have reported, do come in direct proportion to application: the more you think about change, the more things you wind up changing; the more things you change, the better your whole life becomes. Sort of the opposite of the never-ending cycle of diets: a brief interval of unpleasantness in exchange for a brief respite from your woes. If you really want to drop a quick five kilos just for a few weeks—I don't advise it—a diet, though never healthful, may serve you fine. But if you want to drop the weight permanently and enjoy life while keeping it off, keep on reading. This book promises deeper understanding of my philosophy and therefore even more pleasures, a level of mastery where weight management and other benefits become pretty much effortless.

But before we get into some lengthier chapter presentations, here are some afterthoughts, reaffirmations, and a few more secrets that "I forgot to tell you."

FRENCH WOMEN LIVE LONGER

A few years ago, the oldest person in the world died. She was 122 years old and lived in the south of France, in Arles, the big old town that passes for a city in Provence. Much about her life has been scrutinized and verified: she ate a traditional

French-Mediterranean diet, local seasonal fruits and vegetables, olives, olive oil, a moderate amount of freshly killed meats and fowl, and fish. Her fat intake was mainly of good fat, though doubtless she enjoyed her cheeses and the occasional pat of butter. Eating locally grown produce, she would have ingested relatively little in the way of pesticides, pollutants, and preservatives and certainly no genetically modified foods. I don't know that she drank my Magical Leek Soup, but she surely ate leeks. She enjoyed a daily glass or two of the local wine, which is almost exclusively red; she also liked a taste of port before meals. She did not eat fast food. She did not eat good food quickly. She ate three meals a day at a pace suited to savouring them. Walking and cycling were her primary means of transportation (the latter till age one hundred), and she lived by the clock of Provence, where deadlines exist in only the laxest sense and there are long midday breaks for lunch and perhaps a nap. (When my husband, Edward, and I are in Provence, we have three wall clocks. One is set to New York time, one to Paris time; the third is set to Provence time [literally the same as Paris's but not really]. We never added batteries to that clock as a reminder that it never seems necessary to keep track of the local time exactly. Come to think of it, the New York clock is probably the most stressful thing we have in that house.)

Oh, and I forgot to mention, this long-lived woman was never fat.

We cannot all turn the clock back a century, move to Provence, and live the life of Jeanne Louise Calment, into our hundreds. To be honest, though a long life sounds good, I would not want to live hers. I like mine. But her example offers a great lesson—indeed, many lessons—from which any of us can profit. For although she was alone in the *Guinness Book of World Records*, her life as a French woman of her generation was not atypical.

According to the World Health Organization, French women have the highest life expectancy in the western world and, excluding Japan, the highest worldwide. Today a French woman can expect to reach the age of 82.8. One of the reasons is simple: despite alarming trends in the opposite direction, French women overall still don't get fat. And the greatest risk factors for mortality in the developed world are the diseases associated with obesity. If she had been fat, Jeanne Louise Calment could not have been riding her bike at age one hundred, even in the unlikely event that she had lived to see that age.

Medical science has made remarkable strides in extending the human lifespan by successfully treating many infectious agents and life-threatening cancers and managing chronic conditions such as diabetes. But in those countries where the benefits of modern medicine are most readily available, the lifestyle choices are often fighting against the benefits of science.

Most of us would prefer not to be fat. But do we have the time and the means to take as good care of ourselves as did Jeanne Louise Calment? Our lives may in many ways be far more complicated than the traditional French life, but it's well to remember that all those French women living past eighty today were born into the difficulties of the Depression and survived the occupation of their country during the Second World War and regular shortages of basic necessities. You think you've got stress! It wasn't all picking cherries in the Vaucluse for them either. The example of French women teaches that good habits can help us endure stress and, if properly instilled, can be maintained under the most adverse circumstances. French women traditionally live, as the expression goes, *entre deux âges* (between two ages, or of ambiguous age). Your actual number of years upon the earth is one thing, but after a certain point it is the condition of your mind and body that will dictate your physical and mental age and, by extension, how you feel. (We are not like trees, whose cross sections reveal indisputable rings of truth.) Short-term, French women don't get fat. Consequently, long-term, French women stay young, living not just longer but better.

THE 50 PER CENT SOLUTION

If, as one critic commented on *French Women Don't Get Fat*, it's "all about portion size"—it's not, really, but *if*—then change is indeed a tall order. It's generally known that Americans on average eat 10 to 30 per cent more than we need to every day. This is not such a surprising result of an increasingly knowledge-based economy, in which the jobs of many individuals involve sitting all day. It is simple deductive reasoning to connect this situation with the fact that Americans are also on average 30 per cent above their ideal weight—and their British cousins are fast catching up, too. It was a sixteenth-century Frenchman, Montaigne, who rightly observed that gluttony is the source of all our infirmities. In the land where there's honour in being able to eat the most hot dogs, what is one to do?

Portion control is more an art than a discipline, one grounded in a useful bit of self-deception. I have written about the power of incrementalism, cutting back portions over weeks and months as you introduce new variety. Though very simple, the method sometimes requires a scale and can be a bit too unstructured for some.

One trick I use to control my intake is to ask myself if I can live with half the amount being offered; indeed, will I be just as happy eating half as much? I put this approach into play in a variety of ways, from splitting a dessert with my husband to counting the number of pieces of bread I eat in a restaurant. (Bread is one of my "offenders", a food I'm particularly vulnerable to overeating, and I can mindlessly eat three or four slices if I don't pay attention.) I use this simple alternative regularly, especially when not sure about the "hidden" ingredients of what I've been served or when the portion I've been offered is obviously large. I eat half. Slowly, of course, chewing well. I then ask myself whether I'm content, and therefore whether continuing would be a matter of pleasure or merely routine.

Contentment with most foods, in terms of taste, is to be found in the first few bites. It's your brain that tells your stomach what's enough, not vice versa. After that, another psychological phenomenon kicks in: that of literally filling ourselves, which evolution perhaps favours as a hedge against starvation, making it a pleasant feeling (at least until you're totally bloated) and therefore a natural impulse.

Often I do continue eating, but I have only half of the half that's left. Then, after pausing, I consider half of what's left again. Edward calls this my Zeno's Paradox of portion control. To paraphrase the ancient principle, if you continue eating only half of what's on your plate each time, you will never eat the whole thing. That's a theoretical explanation. I'm content to call it the 50 Per Cent Solution and think more practically about why it works. The act of stopping and reflecting slows down consumption, allowing the brain to catch up with the stomach and release the hormone that tells us, "Mmm, that was good, but I've had enough." Contentment is largely a matter of the clock—not just how much you ingest but also what you've eaten during a given interval.

If you implement the 50 Per Cent Solution routinely, your sense of a satisfying portion is bound to shrink. I've been doing it so long it even works on a banana.

Bananas are a welcome staple, available year-round since they grow in tropical climes not subject to the seasons of our temperate zone. Certainly in winter they fill out the relative dearth of fresh fruit. And they are good for you: low in saturated fat, cholesterol, and sodium and a good source of dietary fibre, vitamin C, potassium, manganese, and vitamin B_6. Most of their calories, though, come from sugars, which increase with ripeness, so they are a potential "offender" and must be eaten with care. When they are perfectly ripe, bananas are a peerless "dessert" fruit.

I've noticed two things about bananas over the years. First, they are on average twice as large as they were in my youth. Second, you peel it, you'll eat it—often in very big bites, making it disappear in no time. So applying the 50 Per Cent Solution, I cut the banana in half before peeling it, then wrap the exposed end of one half in plastic. I set that aside for another time, perhaps for breakfast the next day or a later dessert. With a bit of practice, half a twenty-first-century banana makes a most satisfying dessert, especially when you treat it as you would a piece of cake or pie. I don't eat it with my fingers. I peel it and set it out on a plate and eat it with a knife and fork. I savour each bite, and I put down my fork between bites. Eating slowly enlarges the experience, alerting my brain to the banana consumption in process. (Hint: A sliver of banana tastes just as much like banana as a big chunk. Eat the smallest bite that lets you register taste. Then have another.) Lots of people I know would make that half banana vanish in twenty seconds, but how much satisfaction are they getting? I'd bet I derive more by consuming my half mindfully over the course of a few minutes. Try it.

The principle works with liquid nutrition as well. As I'll describe later at greater length, wine is food, but a food whose great benefits can be negated by immoderate consumption—too much of a good thing. Wine is also my business, an indispensable part of my life and lifestyle. And as everyone knows, French women enjoy it without getting fat. Red wines are rich in the flavonoid called resveratrol, a superpotent antioxidant also found in blueberries. But actually all wines are good for you, and one of the most complex, Champagne, has a few distinctive trace elements and uniquely salubrious effects.

But how much is good for you? Doctors, French and otherwise suggest 125 to 175 millilitres (one or two small glasses) a day, depending on your size, but with food, *bien sûr.* Open a typical 750-millilitre bottle, however, and *voilà*, you are looking at six glasses. What to do? When we are at home, Edward and I rigorously apply the 50 Per Cent Solution, because we know that after that first or second glass, it can be deliciously simple to pour a third or more, after which the health benefit is shot. (Okay, the *occasional* third glass won't kill you, but it's still not part of a healthy lifestyle.) So here's how it works.

We started out buying some half bottles (375 millilitres) and kept the empties. Now, when we open a new bottle of wine for dinner, the first thing we do is pour half the contents into an empty half bottle and cork it immediately. The wine has seen air for perhaps fifteen seconds. Recapped and usually refrigerated, it will last in top form for days, weeks, and even months.

So we always have one of several capped half bottles on hand for future meals. At dinner, a half bottle is good for about three or four small glasses, total. But remember, wine should be sipped and tasted. A wine glass should never be more than half to two-thirds full: to taste it properly, you need room to swirl it, expose it to the air to soften it, and you want the empty part of the glass trapping the bouquet. Enter the 50 Per Cent Solution yet again: we drink a half glass at a time, each of us perhaps enjoying two refills from the half bottle. (It is amazing how easy it is to fool ourselves. Three half-glass pours are far more psychologically fulfilling and pleasurable, without a feeling of restraint, than a glass and a half or a single pour into a very large glass.)

The greatest and most memorable wine I've ever experienced was a rare Burgundy served to me in a 50-millilitre portion—and I remember it to this day! Over the years Edward and I have been fortunate to acquire some pretty decent bottles, and using the half-bottle trick, we have not been shy about opening them, knowing that each can be savoured on more than one occasion.

And here's one more example of using the 50 Per Cent Solution in managing portions. I suspect we all know someone who "adds coffee to their sugar". I know at least two women who routinely add four of those little packets of sugar to each of the several cups of coffee they have every day. And that's for a normal cup. We all need our stimulants, but there are so many better ones than sugar.

With a sweet tooth like mine, I am lucky to have learned from Dr. Miracle to take my coffee without sugar. Order coffee or tea in America, however, and you automatically get a sugar bowl with it. So let the sugar in your coffee lead me to another subject deserving more attention than I gave it in *French Women Don't Get Fat.*

THE INCIDENTAL SWEETNESS OF AMERICAN LIFE

This marvellous anthropological expression I owe to Adam Gopnik, who uses it in his book *Through the Children's Gate*, the story of his family's move back home to New York after years of living in Paris. Everybody, and especially the kids, found so many things in America too sweet. It's true, the French have a much lower tolerance for sweetness than most other people. Like saltiness, bitterness, sourness, and what some taste physiologists describe as *umami* (savouriness), sweetness is a broad taste sensation that obscures more particular and subtler tastes (and we French try to be all about the subtlety).

Dessert in France is much likelier to be cheese or fruit

than pastry (saving room for a final chocolate square or some bite-sized biscuits and the like, called *petits fours*), the point being to clear the palate—or the table, if we follow the derivation from the Old French, *desservir*. At any rate, the idea never was to drown the taste buds in sweetness and fat. Actually, before the nineteenth century, when sugar became cheap and widely available, truly sweet desserts as most Americans now recognize them would have been strictly for the rich or else a special occasion or holiday treat, not an everyday thing.

Unfortunately, America's problem (and to be fair, it's not just America's problem) of incidental sweetness is not limited to sweets, or even sugar. High-fructose corn syrup makes its way into everything from soft drinks to tomato sauces, supermarket yogurt and fast-food french fries, offering calories but not instant energy that most cells in the body can use. (Glucose, not fructose, is what your cells need.) So the energy tends to be stored as you know what. After trans fats, corn syrup is probably the most offensively fattening ingredient in processed foods. (*En passant,* I should say that most fruit juices, high in naturally occurring fructose, are very fattening for the same reason; the body can't easily use the sugar. So my advice is eat, don't drink, your fruit.)

But back to your morning cup of coffee. A teaspoon of sugar once or twice a day is a reasonable indulgence that won't make anyone fat, but lots of people are conditioned to add several to each cup, as well as to having several cups a day—not a good idea in any case. Once our taste—whether for sweetness, fat, salt—is recalibrated over time, an excess that used to taste good comes to taste awful.

Edward always took his coffee with a teaspoon or two. That's how he was raised. One day when he was about to put a heaping teaspoon of sugar into his cup, I asked him if he could drink his coffee without sugar. He looked at me and asked, "Would you eat french fries without ketchup?" (I said, "Yes, I do.") He had never even thought about it. Some days later, I suggested he cut the sugar in half and try it. He saw it as a challenge. He did, and enjoyed the coffee just the same. Within a few months, he had cut the half in half, and for the past ten or fifteen years he has taken his morning coffee (his only coffee of the day) with no sugar but plenty of pleasure. Deploying the 50 Per Cent Solution is an effective way to reduce these calories while helping you build up a greater sensitivity to sweetness. (Sugar substitutes, by contrast, while not fattening, only preserve our preternatural taste for the sweet—they are therefore an *un*-useful self-deception.) Eventually you will find the taste of added sugar cloying. You may even discover that you actually like the true flavour of coffee.

I have a theory about how we originally came to sweeten our coffee, which the French generally don't do. When I came to America, the coffee was simply awful: poorly made, often from inferior blends, over-roasted beans, stale grounds. It was burned in percolation and reburned in keeping it warm all day. (Freshly brewed coffee holds its peak flavour for about twenty minutes.) So the standard was a bitter pill, strong and caffeine-infused. You needed to add sugar to get it down. Nowadays—thanks to all sorts of beans; better roasting and preservation techniques; and grinders, pods, drip filter coffee makers, and pressure gadgets; and especially to Starbucks and other such chains—excellent coffee is an affordable luxury. Who would have thought that people would be willing to pay more for quality? I'm sure that idea sounded pretty wacky when first uttered in the "elevator".

BUFFETED BY ABUNDANCE

If you have to travel on business, not even the 50 Per Cent Solution will help you before the sprawling, unlimited servings of any decent hotel's breakfast buffet. Let me confess: I love it. But I avoid it. I believe in a good breakfast. Without one, you're bound to snack or overeat at lunch.

I've found two safe ways of dealing with the buffet behemoth. First, I make breakfast or brunch at a buffet a special occasion, not a regular occurrence, even when the breakfast comes free. I order room service. It's the same food, and I can eat only what they deliver, which is what I want in the first place.

When I do indulge, I indulge fully but compensate at lunch and perhaps even dinner. (It is all part of thinking about and adjusting food intake over a two- or three-day period. While we should try to balance on a daily basis, that's much harder to do 365 times a year.) I still protect myself from getting carried away by not piling my plate, and instead I make a series of trips around the buffet, sitting down between each "course". My advice: make a first pass without a plate. Fly one reconnaissance mission to see what really looks good, then work out in your head what you're going to have. When I do this, I don't load up in one shot but fly three sorties—say, one for yogurt and fresh berries, another perhaps for oatmeal or for scrambled eggs (or I should say egg, as I usually ask for one egg, never three). After that, I'm usually no longer hungry. But if I do fly a third sortie to "try" the croissant (you never know) or some speciality dish, that's okay. Being perfectly aware of what I'm doing, I just enjoy the buffet and skip the guilt. As a grown-up, I am sure to balance the intake account later that day or the next. Compensations. Not a catastrophe.

On no account would even the most accomplished French woman dream of facing two buffets in one day! Not only is it too disorienting, but those colossal lunch and dinner steam-table affairs just don't have the allure of breakfast. Simply not worth the confrontation. But if you indulge—and we are all invited to functions with buffet meals—remember the three-sortie-rule strategy. Final advice: use only small starter plates, and treat what's on offer as tapas.

LA GYM

The modern hotel suggests another useful parable. A young woman in my office recently said that when she travels for business, "the diet goes out the window". (As with so many familiar expressions, this betrays the sad, unreflective way that "the diet" has become a permanent fixture of life.) But then she said something unexpected: "I always compensate, as you suggest in your book—the hotels have such great fitness centres." She went on to describe how a good hotel often has better machines and classes than her own gym, and so she can't resist the double temptation: eat too much; overdo the exercise, "just to try" every elliptical and Gravitron. There is a fallacy here from the French woman's point of view: exercise is not a compensation for eating; eating is what we do to fuel an active body. Yes, we should all be more active, but "hitting the gym" to offset your calories is backward thinking. It can have the reverse effect of making you a gym addict as well as an overeater.

Gyms are fine if you like that sort of thing (they are somewhat social and give people pleasure and activity), but what the body needs by way of exercise is not all that elaborate. You need to get your heart rate up several times a week for about thirty minutes (a French woman's brisk half-hour walk every day will do this just fine). And particularly after age forty, we should all do some resistance training. Light free weights can be used almost anywhere. Your body, too, can be its own resistance machine: basic push-ups, sit-ups, and lunges are excellent and pretty comprehensive. So is my overall favourite exercise for body and mind, yoga. If you move in order to eat, rather than eat in order to move, you are in effect running yourself into the ground. The French woman's lifestyle is an active one, but it requires that you learn to adjust your intake to support a normal and healthy level of exertion.

This is the meaning of equilibrium, the point at which one can feel *bien dans sa peau.* I may have forgotten to tell you that in the management of their equilibrium French women are especially good at automatically regulating their metabolism. They are most definitely not all naturally endowed with perfectly calibrated ones. With their frequent walks and trips up and down stairs, French women give several boosts to their metabolic rates in the course of each day. Even those many drinks of water require the metabolism to perk up (they don't just make you feel full). So instead of gruelling intervals of burning off massive numbers of calories several times a week, French women consume fewer calories and routinely rev the engine higher without even slipping into spandex. In the race of the tortoise and the hare, the French woman is definitely the tortoise.

CONNAIS-TOI TOI-MÊME; OR, BE YOUR OWN BRAND

All women are not created equal, of course. Women are different—unique indeed—coming in all shapes and sizes, and being *bien dans sa peau* is an individual determination and more important than being skinny. Being overweight to the point that it is a short- or long-term danger to your health is not something I condone, of course, but I forget to say often enough that if you are comfortable being *un peu ronde* (a tad overweight) and you are content, so be it. I believe in living and eating more joyfully.

Today, there is some truth to the glib assertion that age fifty is the new forty. (I'm somewhat more dubious about the Beverly Hills nip/tuck-based claim that *sixty* is the new forty.) There's no denying that women are extending their careers, even their biological clocks, past the point that would have seemed possible even a decade ago. Enjoying the full benefits of these opportunities requires that we pace ourselves, not overdoing our food and drink, our work, or our exercise. But sometimes being fifty is being fifty. I was recently reminded of that last New Year's Eve when I ate and drank as I did when I was thirty-five. I lived to regret it the next day. No matter if in my head I feel like I did ten or twenty years ago, I have to listen to my body sometimes. And I cannot indulge the way I once did without paying a price. A thirty-five-year-old probably feels the same about her twenty-year-old self. Certainly it is okay to indulge or overindulge once in a while, knowing that you are doing so. I didn't. I was not living in my current real world or being *bien dans ma peau.*

Cultivating a positive emotional outlook is vital, too: studies of centenarians find them overwhelmingly to be lifelong optimists, in many cases despite having faced crushing adversity. Indeed, cultivation of outlook, as of taste and proportion—of all aspects of the self, really—is the key to *l'art de vivre* (the art of living). French women don't get fat because they know the secret of pleasure. But the secret *to* pleasure is cultivation: a life of ongoing exploration, experimentation, practised enjoyment, and—most important—self-discovery.

None of us is born appreciating the finer things as fully and satisfyingly as we might. How are we, then, to make our way to the good life? The prescription hasn't changed much in twenty-five hundred years, though French women have kept the faith better than most. *Connais-toi toi-même*—Know Thyself, as the Delphic oracle advised.

The key is also being true to your unique outward self (in addition to your inward, emotional self), developing your own style, a look and manner that feels comfortable and right to you and that you are happy to present to the world. You are your own brand. What's your brand's DNA, and how is it expressed? Clothes? Jewellery? Make-up? Hair? Voice? Laugh? Touch? All of the above, and more. I have a good friend who always wears hats—autumn, winter, summer, spring. Another woman I know has a collection of lizard brooches and always wears one. As for me: scarves, necklaces, sunglasses—I couldn't be me without them . . . and not being twenty, I no longer dress like a twenty-year-old. (If you do and you are not, you are certainly making a brand statement.) So too is someone who wears lots of make-up or large costume jewellery (or large precious jewellery, for that matter) or carrot-coloured hair (which you will see in Paris). Some work, some don't. You have to decide for yourself. For instance, I don't wear jeans. They're just not my style.

A FRENCH WOMAN FOR ALL SEASONS; OR, *À LA RECHERCHE DU TEMPS PERDU*

No satisfaction is more elemental, more vital to well-being, than the pleasure we seek in what we eat. In *French Women Don't Get Fat*, I provided a thumbnail understanding of the importance of seasonality to the French woman's lifestyle. But as I may have forgotten to tell you, seasonality is far more than knowing what's in season and appreciating nature's best from month to month, important as that is. Seasonality is a manner of being that is responsive to all conditions and stimulations of our environment throughout the year. Learn it, and you will enjoy peak experience. The well-diverted senses have no need of the consolations of excess and inferior experience. Learn and even time will be on your side: a full experience never feels hurried. Eating with pleasure is about pacing yourself during the meal. Losing weight is a matter of finding your equilibrium of intake and exertion week by week. But the plan for life involves us in the perpetual cycle of adjustment that is the seasons of the year. The art of living is pacing yourself in the long run.

How do you keep track of time? Do you measure it out in coffee spoons like Eliot's hapless J. Alfred Prufrock? Is a season to you eight or fifteen new episodes of some reality TV show? For French women, the most elemental cultivation of pleasure traditionally comes from living as mindfully as possible of the annual progression of the natural cycle.

Now, it's true that the four seasons French women observe are not the same all over the world. Much of mankind lives in the tropical zone, where the seasons are reduced to a rainy and a dry time. Even in our temperate zone the seasons can be a variable experience: in most places, winter is the most barren and lifeless; in others, it is relatively mild and summer is the time of greatest hardship. I point this out in recognition of the fact that the seasons as I represent them, and as I experience them living in the U.S.A. and France, are not the seasons of every woman's reality—even though people with weight problems are overwhelmingly concentrated in the temperate zone, which comprises most of the developed world. The secret is to master the variations that the year presents where you live, and to live in each interval to the full.

There are things in the recitation of my year that I hope you will recognize and wish to adopt, and certainly lots of delicious recipes you can follow practically anywhere. The menus are suggestions, as suitable for losing weight (following the other advice in *French Women Don't Get Fat*) as for maintaining equilibrium. But the larger point is to give you a way of thinking about the way you live, first and foremost in relation to the passage of time. There are seasons of the earth, but also, as Keats pointed out, seasons of the mind, and these exist wherever you may be. Observe them, tune in to them:

not only will your satisfactions multiply but they will become fuller, too.

As I've suggested, so many of our woes are rooted in our modern imperative to beat the clock, a fight we feel we've lost before we even begin. As a result, time has no meaning, only cost. The most repeated complaint I heard in connection with *French Women Don't Get Fat* was "Who has the time [to buy and cook food]?" ("I can't find leeks" was a distant second.) What you should come to understand, however, is that time is not something we are given; it is something we make. We all have more to do than can possibly get done in a day. Even French families have been forced to choose which meals they will have *en famille;* the time-honoured ritual can no longer be observed with the traditional regularity. The world is no longer set up to furnish such occasions; we make them for ourselves. We must: life would lose all satisfaction without the time we set aside—the days and hours and even the odd moment—that we reserve to enjoy it. This is not selfishness; it is just living, an opportunity too precious to waste.

See whether it doesn't make sense to you as the year progresses.

2

AU PRINTEMPS: SPRING INTO LIFE

When does your year begin? My husband is an academic, and all his life, September has marked the start of the year. So, since our marriage, the end of summer has inevitably marked the start of something for me, too. And some of us never lose the foreboding that accompanies the start of a new school term. French kids are no different, fending off despair at the approach of *la rentrée*—literally, the re-entry, as if summer were a trip to the moon.

The corporate world's fiscal years also don't always match the calendar year. For decades my year, at least professionally, has been defined as an annual budget. *C'est normal*: making order from the chaos of our time is quite human as long as we remember that each order we invent serves a particular master.

For thousands of years before electrical power, nature ruled overtly. The days were defined by the appearance and disappearance of the sun, the year by changes in the height of its arc at midday. Springtime, when the days start gaining on the nights, was always the natural start of the year, which explains why in French it's called *printemps,* the first time, and in Italian, *primavera.* Today spring is still seen as a time of regeneration, when we wipe the cold sleep from our eyes and awaken to the elaborate interplay of new sensory stimuli: light, fragrances, tastes, sounds. To live according to the season is to be alert to this awakening, not to sleep through it. We can't help responding to the sunlight on our face, but there is infinitely more for the senses to register. Cultivating attention to the full spectrum of sensations affords French women a wealth of slimming experience, of compensations and distractions. Day by day, there is so much to take in, so much potential pleasure, that they become less vulnerable to mindless eating and its consequence, getting fat. That works out pretty well as the forgiving layers of winter are being peeled off.

With the arrival of spring produce in the market comes the prospect of many gastronomic pleasures. But for me, the most precious heralds of spring are flowers. I count the days until the crocuses will pop up their little heads and cherry blossom will appear seemingly overnight, its petals scattering almost at once to cover the ground like a snowfall. When I observe the dance of the tulips and daffodils, something stirs within me.

I may sound like a Romantic poet, but you should understand: I grew up with flowers, some cultivated in our garden, others found in the fields and woods surrounding my grandmother's house in Alsace. Next to cooking, flowers were my mother's great passion; she couldn't live without them. Neither can I, whatever the season. Like meals, they were part of our daily rituals. I loved learning their names, picking them, and helping *Mamie* create her gorgeous, unfussy bouquets. Early on, I was taught the loving care they demand once taken from the garden and placed in a vase. As a little girl I learned to cut the stem diagonally and change the water every other day. And in a big house with flowers in every room, this was no small chore. But to handle them, to smell them as they opened until the bloom was off them, intensified the experience of having them around. It still does.

As fortune would have it, I married someone who enjoys flowers as much as my mother did. On Saturday mornings in springtime, our sensory nourishment includes going to the market to bring home some of these tokens of the first season. Flowers don't have to be expensive, and you don't need tons: as in all things, less can be more. One or two simple stems of sweet peas in a small vase can provide great pleasure, adding a dash of colour and a delicately sweet scent to a room.

Flowers, *Mamie* told me, are very much like us, none more so than the tulip. Tulips smile at you, talk to you, let you know when they need water, have too much light; and before they die, they are at their most serenely beautiful, stems flagging as if reaching out for a final embrace, the folding petals expressing in their contortions every imaginable emotion. Just look at them. The shapes are fascinating: the small, round petals and the pointed ones; the so-called long-stemmed French tulips and my favourite, the parrot tulip. As for colours, tulips, like roses, come in an astonishing variety, and I can remember every one in our garden. The first spring tulip announced to me what was coming. Tulips still lift my spirits when I see them in a vase, though never more than when I see them rising from the earth in springtime.

By then, I am delirious with spring fever. I find myself buying armfuls of flowers, drinking in scents and colours. The vernal mania extends even to selecting more brightly coloured linens for the bed and table, putting away the austere monochromes or crisp whites I love in winter. Fortunately, I have long been in the habit of doing my spring cleaning in late winter (actually very therapeutic exertion on a grey Saturday afternoon). By springtime, I know where everything is to be found in the cupboards, and I won't find myself doing chores when all I want is to be outside.

In spring, there is no excuse for not making the most of a French woman's most powerful equilibrium manager: walking. Even when it's raining, I love being out and about. And when the weather is clear, the possibilities multiply, and it's time to take out the bike. This past spring, many people who could have sworn they lived in car towns took to their bikes as the price of petrol soared. (It's a matter not of what's possible but of what's imaginable.)

Cycling has well-known health benefits: it's a low-impact, mild aerobic exercise that strengthens your heart and lungs; tones the large (read: fat-burning) muscle groups; keeps joints, tendons, and ligaments flexible; builds stamina; and is generally fun, reducing stress and boosting your mood. But in colder climes—France included—it's just not a safe or comfortable year-round activity, at least not for me. I cross off winter, which makes my first ride in spring something to look forward to.

French and other European women are much more likely to use bicycles to get around than are Americans, who see cycling more as recreation and sport. Remember, the French invented the Tour de France yet still have not forgotten the practical uses of the bike. For my mother's generation (and those like the 122-year-old Jeanne Louise Calment), riding was something women did every day. When you think of it, most commutes today are under five miles, less than thirty minutes by bike. Cycling is something Edward and I can do together just for fun, but anyone who can do it for more practical reasons should.

We rarely cycle in New York or Paris any more, except a bit at weekends, when there's less traffic. But when we were younger, we would pedal regularly through the side streets of Greenwich Village and on the bike path along the Hudson River when heading up- or downtown. Even more regularly, we'd cart the bikes to the country. Nowadays, most of our cycling is done in Provence, where the view, the feel of rolling hills, and the olfactory splendours give us the potent sensation of being beyond workaday cares, outside of ourselves. In fact, I feel that way any time I am *en vélo* (on my bike). It requires just enough attention to concentrate the mind pleasantly, and I have never lost the child's thrill at propelling myself faster than my legs could carry me—quite a different pleasure from motoring.

This past winter, Edward surprised me with a new silver-and-black bike from Peugeot, legendary maker of bicycles (not just cars) for more than a century. He selected and purchased the bicycle secretly, then gave me a picture of it in New York on Valentine's Day, with a nice bicycle poem as well; the real thing was delivered to our home in Provence and was there to greet me when I arrived. Though the official start of spring was a few days off, I just could not resist taking the Peugeot for an inaugural spin. There was still a chill in the air, but in the sun I didn't mind at all. I went all the way to the market.

Au marché, where French women observe the arrival of springtime most seriously: nothing is more meaningful than our choice of what to consume as the grip of winter yields.

For centuries French women felt springtime's anticipation even more keenly than they do now. Since the Middle Ages, the predominantly Catholic population observed a Lenten fast. Mardi Gras (Fat Tuesday) was less the bacchanal staged in New Orleans or Rio and more what it was conceived to be: the last day that meat and other rich foods, including eggs and dairy, could be enjoyed before the forty-day period of abstinence between Ash Wednesday and Easter. Those would-be French women who have baulked at the rigours of my Magical Leek Soup weekend (which I prescribed in *French Women Don't Get Fat*) might do well to consider the virtues of old French ways. During Lent, not only did one forgo the richest foods, but those young enough to endure it took only one daily meal, at the end of the workday. (Charlemagne, by imperial prerogative, took his at 2 p.m.; it's good to be the king!) While I, a latter-day French woman of Huguenot extraction, would hardly prescribe a regimen so severely penitential, it does suggest to me a reason why traditionally French women don't get fat. Like a prolonged version of the Magical Leek weekend, the Lenten fast would reset the body's dials, making it more alert to the tastes it can enjoy and, eventually, more appreciative of those that for a time it had to forgo. Come the *fêtes de Pâques* (Easter), everything enjoyed in celebration was consumed more mindfully. Meanwhile, probably not a few excess winter pounds had been shed. (The psychology of this cultural and spiritual discipline is very different from the tedium of dieting, a decidedly modern perversion by which we try to subtract the meals we've already eaten.) After the fast, every food of springtime, from the fresh vegetables to the spring lamb, must have tasted like the first. The body accustomed to less finds that indeed less is more. In fact, a body conditioned to enjoy less will naturally tend to find excess unpleasant.

The market is my own lesson in patience as spring approaches. The time of pears and apples is all too slowly winding down; I'm getting a bit bored with citrus fruit and bananas. And although global agribusiness can today summon forth the fruits of the other hemisphere, which is enjoying its summer in the middle of our winter, it's somehow not the same as receiving what comes into its own locally, in sync with everything else that is changing around me. I find myself longing to switch gears with my menus and start planning the first brunch outdoors.

The march of seasonal produce that begins in spring, while not quite the equal of summer's bounty, is more than enough to whet my appetite for the feast of freshness to come. The first peas in their pods. The first bunch of crisp spinach. Honestly, fresh local produce is nothing like what the transnational conglomerates bring to your supermarket hub. The local version registers true colours and oozes with subtle flavours. It is produced by people who will look you in the eye when they sell it to you. And it is picked and sold when ripe! Now, we don't live in Eden, and not everything can be as we would have it. But whatever else you eat, if you make it your business to find some such fresh local produce every week, the rewards of its flavours will make the simplest dish satisfying in a modest portion.

I do recognize that this is easier said than done. A couple of hundred years ago, when virtually everyone was a farmer or lived near one, it was easy to acquire these seasonal blessings. Times change, but together with all the improvements to our lives we have inherited a global obesity epidemic. (It seems a cruel truth that people are growing fatter everywhere they aren't starving.)

However much I manage to enjoy nature's bounty, I cannot ignore the impoverishment relative to my childhood, when my father, a white-collar worker and an avid gardener in his spare time, surrounded us with extensive fruit and vegetable plantings. Come spring, before every meal we would gather ripe fruit and vegetables. After dinner it was a family ritual to walk to the garden and admire nature's work. Not that I remember needing one, but this evening stroll was an antistress pill par excellence and never failed to put me in a proper frame of mind for a good night's sleep. The twenty-first-century paradise we have tried to create can't hold a candle to such satisfaction, but if nature is no longer at our door, we must go looking for it.

PETITS POIS À POINT

We grew peas in our garden, and so they were a spring treat by which I was spoiled rotten. I would graze on them raw straight from the pod as my father picked them, not an hour before they would be served at table. Steamed or boiled and served with a little butter, they regularly furnished "colour" on our dinner plates. Peas, like sweetcorn, are vegetables that cry out to be bought at farm shops and eaten fresh. When picked, peas (and corn) are rich with natural sugars, but these immediately begin turning to starch. A perfectly ripe just-picked pea is a special sensation. All others might as well be dancing with diced carrots in a can.

BROWN RICE WITH PEAS

Serves 4

INGREDIENTS

200g brown rice
1 tablespoon olive oil
15g unsalted butter
2 tablespoons finely chopped shallots
Zest of ½ lemon
500g fresh peas, shelled
Salt and freshly ground pepper
3 tablespoons finely chopped parsley

1. Cook the rice according to packet directions.
2. Warm the oil in a frying pan over medium heat. Add the butter, shallots, and lemon zest, and sauté for 5 minutes.
3. Add the peas, and cook until tender, adding a little water if the shallots start to brown before the peas are tender.
4. Add the cooked rice, season with salt and pepper to taste, and stir to combine. Remove from the heat, and add the parsley.

SPRING PEAS WITH BUTTON ONIONS

Serves 4

1. Warm the oil in a saucepan over low heat. Add the onions, peas, and herbes de Provence. Cook over low heat for 20 minutes, stirring occasionally.
2. Season with salt and pepper to taste, and serve immediately.

INGREDIENTS

1 tablespoon olive oil

90g button (pickling) onions

300g fresh peas, shelled

1 tablespoon herbes de Provence

Salt and freshly ground pepper

ASPARAGUS

One can find asparagus all year long, but whether from local farmers in New York City's Union Square Greenmarket or Paris's Raspail market or restaurants with seasonal market menus, there's nothing that tastes like spring asparagus. Somewhere, not far from you, the real thing is to be had, ready to compensate for the effort, with flavour that is to the supermarket variety as fresh whipped cream is to Cool Whip.

I've loved asparagus since childhood. It's no surprise: the agreeable rituals and foods we discover as kids remain reference points throughout life (mothers and fathers, take note). In those days, only white asparagus was available in Alsace. Grown out of sunlight (limiting photosynthesis) and more delicately flavoured than the green variety, the white stalks were a Sunday lunch treat. My mother would make a mayonnaise from scratch and blanch the asparagus at the last moment, serving them as a starter. We each had four to six stalks to dunk in the mayonnaise with our fingers, sucking and chewing till we reached the inedible fibrous end. At the end of the course we'd dunk our fingers in the *rince-doigts,* a little bowl of water with a slice of lemon (to cut the grease) floating in it. It's the subject of many jokes (mostly apocryphal, no doubt) about confused guests uncertain whether to drink from the bowl. But when your fingers are sticky with asparagus and mayonnaise, it is not hard to figure out what the *rince-doigts* is for.

I discovered green asparagus when I came to New York, and my first experience was actually not a happy one, although colour had nothing to do with it. Wanting to show off our West Village digs, we invited Edward's sister and her husband to lunch one Saturday in spring. At the market, I had fetched some bunches (always make sure they are not droopy or browning and that the flowering ends are shut tight). I had decided to make a one-course brunch, *asparagus quiche sans dough* (asparagus quiche without the pastry) whose delicious simplicity American friends had enjoyed. Eggs and asparagus go splendidly together (in fact, a simple poached egg makes a nice *fausse* hollandaise, when whipping up a mayonnaise seems too ambitious for the boiled-asparagus starter), and some fried bacon cubes provide extra tang and color. But when the large white ceramic dish came out of the oven and we sat down to eat, I saw an uncomfortable look on my sister-in-law's face. She was the first person I'd ever met who hated asparagus. I made her an omelette as Edward, sheepish at not having remembered, poured more wine.

Food aversions and allergies seem much more common in

America than in France, where in many years of entertaining I've suffered relatively few such faux pas. You do get the occasional youngster allergic to (or perhaps just grossed out by) seafood. Still, *à chacun son goût,* and since we are preaching a gospel of tastes, it's only right to honour those of our friends. So if you are serving an all-or-nothing dish, especially using a potential allergen, pay heed. (Believe it or not, a French friend of mine is allergic to garlic! Anything is possible.)

Now that I'm fortunate enough to spend a few days in Paris and Provence each spring, I can live on asparagus for a week. (Variety is key to the French woman's gastronomy, but the obsessive enjoyment of a particular food briefly in season is no sin, provided the food is not full of fat or processed sugar. The good news is that almost all vegetables are fair game for occasional monomania.) Fresh green asparagus can be as delicious as the white variety (though the latter still seems more sophisticated when served in the U.S.A.). I simply boil or steam them, adding a piece of salted butter (the famous Guérande is itself a luxury) and a touch of freshly ground pepper to the cooked, drained spears, then serve them with some protein, which becomes secondary as I feast on the asparagus. One blessing of seasonal vegetables is that they allow you to be satisfied with smaller amounts of protein—high-energy, low-fibre food that, regardless of Atkins and South Beach advice, can make you fat if taken too liberally without the perverse restriction of carbohydrates. In fact, try to eat your protein first to slow digestion and promote satiety; if you come to think of it as the "side" and the vegetables as the main dish, you will be cluing into a very common trick by which French women stay slim.

WHITE ASPARAGUS WITH MAYONNAISE, *MAMIE*'S VERSION

Serves 4

INGREDIENTS

1 egg yolk, at room temperature

1 teaspoon Dijon mustard

1 to 2 teaspoons sherry vinegar

150 to 250ml extra virgin olive oil

Fine sea salt

Freshly ground white pepper

16 to 24 white asparagus stalks, peeled and blanched

Fresh parsley

1. In a warmed bowl (fill it with boiling water and let stand for a few minutes), whisk together the egg yolk, mustard, and vinegar. Slowly, by droplets, whisk in the oil until at least half has gone in and the mixture has the thickness of double cream. Continue whisking in the oil, now in a thin but steady stream, until all of it is incorporated. Season with salt and pepper to taste.

2. Serve the asparagus warm on a plate. Garnish with sprigs of parsley and add 1 to 2 tablespoons of mayonnaise per person. This is finger food: dunk each spear in some mayo and enjoy until you get to the end of the stalk, which is tough and may still have some inedible fibres. Use a *rince-doigts* to clean your fingers.

N. B. MANY OF US ARE INTIMIDATED BY THE PROSPECT OF MAKING MAYONNAISE, BECAUSE WE KNOW THAT IF THE OIL ISN'T ADDED SLOWLY ENOUGH, THE MIXTURE MAY CURDLE. TO CORRECT SUCH A SNAFU, JUST PUT ANOTHER EGG YOLK IN A BOWL , ADD THE FAILED MAYO, AND CONTINUE ADDING THE REST OF THE OIL. WHISK WELL. VOILÀ.

N.B. IT IS ADVISABLE NOT TO SERVE DISHES INCORPORATING UNCOOKED EGGS TO PREGNANT WOMEN, SMALL CHILDREN, THE ELDERLY, AND PEOPLE WITH IMMUNE SYSTEM DEFICIENCIES.

ASPARAGUS AND CASHEW OMELETTE

Serves 4

1. Roast the cashews for a few minutes in a dry frying pan over medium heat to release the flavour. In a bowl, beat the eggs with the nuts, water, cheese, and parsley. Season with salt and pepper to taste.
2. Warm the pan over medium heat. Add the oil and butter. When the butter melts, pour in the egg mixture and cook, letting it sit until it is softly set but still moist. Add the asparagus tips and cook 4 to 5 minutes longer. Serve immediately.

INGREDIENTS

60g unsalted raw cashews, chopped

6 eggs

2 tablespoons water

120g grated cheese (Swiss or Parmesan)

1 tablespoon coarsely chopped parsley

Salt and freshly ground pepper

1 teaspoon olive oil

15g unsalted butter

250g boiled asparagus tips (green or white)

ASPARAGUS WITH HONEY SAUCE

Serves 4

INGREDIENTS

½ teaspoon salt

500g fresh asparagus, ends trimmed

4 tablespoons Meaux or other wholegrain mustard

2 tablespoons honey

1 tablespoon finely chopped shallot

Pinch of fresh thyme

1. Fill a saucepan large enough to hold the asparagus with water. Add the salt and bring the water to a boil. Add the asparagus and cook with the lid on until barely tender, about 3 minutes. Drain.
2. Combine the mustard, honey, shallot, and thyme, and mix well. Pour over the asparagus, and serve.

N. B. MEAUX MUSTARD IS MADE FROM CRUSHED MUSTARD SEEDS RATHER THAN FROM SEEDS GROUND TO A POWDER, AND IT IS GENERALLY MILD. I PREFER MEAUX FOR ITS COLOUR, TEXTURE AND TASTE. IN CONTRAST, DIJON IS LIGHT IN COLOUR AND FAIRLY STRONG IN FLAVOUR.

FETTUCCINE WITH SCALLOPS AND ASPARAGUS

Serves 4

1. Bring 2 litres salted water to a rolling boil in a large saucepan. Cook the pasta according to the packet directions. Add the asparagus to the pan during the last minute of cooking. Drain the pasta and asparagus, and set aside.
2. Warm a large frying pan over medium heat, and add 1 tablespoon of the oil. Add the scallops, and cook 3 minutes. Turn the scallops, and cook 3 minutes more, or until seared. Remove the scallops from the pan, and set aside.
3. In the same pan over low heat, combine the lemon zest and juice and the remaining oil. Add the pasta, asparagus, and scallops, and toss well. Season with salt and pepper to taste. Garnish with basil. Serve immediately.

INGREDIENTS

275g fettuccine

Salt and freshly ground pepper

16 asparagus stalks, trimmed and sliced diagonally into 5cm pieces

2 tablespoons olive oil

350g scallops, rinsed and dried on paper towels

Zest and juice of 1 lemon

2 tablespoons chopped basil

Pasta, like other carbs, has in the past year or two been rehabilitated. At the same time, food manufacturers (the oxymoron says it all) have rushed to clear the shelves of their low-carb science projects. But that doesn't mean it's totally safe to go back in the water. Individuals who haven't forsworn pasta (and no one should) are still well advised to use their heads. It is, as the nutritionists say, a relatively high glycaemic food. (I have scant use for glycaemic indexing, much less the GI Diet, whose name alone probably puts me off: a friend had to correct my impression that the initials stand for the Gastro-Intestinal Diet.) Suffice it to say, pasta does elevate the insulin level but *can* produce cravings for more and more. Loving it so much, I'm prone to overdo without proper care. Especially in a post-low-carb world, it's important not to lapse into carb abuse.

When I was growing up, we had pasta a few times a month. Since children naturally love it, my mother saw it as a way to make us eat our vegetables. Being a working woman, she developed a few one-dish meals for hectic days (eating in courses is optimal, but at a pinch you can achieve a balanced variety of satisfying foods in one dish). We would get carbohydrates (though no bread was on the table when pasta was served), a leftover piece of chicken or tuna or calf's liver was chopped in to take care of our protein needs, and the all-important vegetables were let in the back door. In terms of flavour they were the true stars of the dish, though all we knew was that we were eating *pasta*.

Still, I don't think it was until I started travelling to Italy with my husband that I truly fell in love with pasta. One summer, while Edward was working on a photo exhibition at Casa Guidi, the Browning home in Florence, we lived in a small hotel along the Arno, in a big room with a view from the terrace. And what a view it was: just above roof level the whole city centre spread before our eyes, with the majestic Duomo full-frame and the surrounding hills beyond. *"O bella libertà, O bella!"* as Elizabeth Barrett Browning wrote. Since I wasn't there to work, I was left in charge of meals and entertainment. I quickly discovered that all the small local food shops had marvellous pasta dishes that I could buy just before Edward "came home" for lunch. Every day we had a different pasta, but remembering my mother's example, I'd make sure we also had some greens (for extra vitamins and fibre) and some salami or other protein (to promote satiety). To this day, I can't recall any more elementally perfect meals than those Florentine affairs. Sitting on our little shaded terrace at midday, when everyone in Italy went home for lunch, we enjoyed the most quietly romantic idyll, outside time and worldly cares: warm breezes, good, simple food, a glass of Chianti, and some fruit before settling down for a siesta. Could there be any purer bliss?

Remarkably, we ate pasta every day (sometimes twice a day!), but always in the portion the Italians enjoy, about 120 grams. You can easily implement portion control with pasta at home if you weigh it first; no one boils another pot just to eat more pasta, and by the time the water was boiling, you wouldn't be hungry anyway. I advise saving a bit of the cooking water to add later to moisten the pasta and dilute overly rich sauces.

After a month of this we had not gained any weight at all.

Sure, we were young, and we walked a lot. But all around us were Italians of every age who were eating likewise and generally not overweight. (If only it were still true today, some two or more decades later, but Italy, like France, is headed away from, not towards, the benefits of gastronomic tradition and moderation.) Why didn't the Italians of our youth seem to be fat? Simple: it was all a matter of proportion. Like us, they were having pasta with their other food, not other food with their pasta. The key was to eat not just pasta with some bland *marinara* and pre-grated Parmesan. These were well-considered, balanced meals, almost sufficient unto themselves, to which pasta had been *added* as a kind of matrix for other things, comprising a wide variety of nutrients and flavours. Eating a relatively small portion of such a "thoughtful" pasta was filling enough to stave off afternoon hunger pangs and snacking: our stomachs, having been taken good care of, were usually content to skip the afternoon *gelato* treat. When we did have an ice cream, we certainly relished it, but never on account of feeling unsatisfied by lunch.

My mother's trick of mixing vegetables with starch is one French women still deploy, especially as a vegetable delivery system for children. Brillat-Savarin said, *"Le nombre des saveurs est infini"* (there is an infinite number of flavours). So it is with vegetables and pasta: there is no limit to the ways they can be blended. The vegetables bring the fibre (soluble for slowly released energy, insoluble for bulk and satiety), and the pasta brings a quicker complex-carb energy fix; together they are the perfect time-release package. Ask any endurance athlete.

Recently Edward and I went to dinner at a good local Italian restaurant in the seventh arrondissement near the Eiffel

Tower. It is owned and run by two sisters from Bergamo, helped by an elderly Chinese waiter. The clientele was strictly French, and the place was so packed it was turning away people without reservations—not so common at French restaurants without Michelin stars. Two local couples who had reserved came in with their children, four in all, between the ages of six and twelve, I'd say. The kids had a pasta course, then left. "Call me on my mobile as soon as you get home," the father, still enjoying his starter, said to the eldest. Although the kids' dine-and-dash wasn't my idea of a meal properly enjoyed *en famille,* I couldn't help noting that the pasta had proved itself once again as a fail-safe way to feed the young. And I heard myself, perhaps the kid in me, say, "You know, Edward"—actually, in France I call him Édouard—"I could eat pasta every day." I really could, but I don't. I was enjoying a first course of spaghetti with langoustines. Edward had spaghetti carbonara. We tried each other's dish, and both were excellent. Fortunately, my inner French woman and not my inner child still calls the shots—usually. I content myself with pasta once every week or so.

SPAGHETTI WITH FIDDLEHEAD FERNS AND PROSCIUTTO

Serves 4

Fiddlehead ferns are a spring delicacy in some parts of the world. The ostrich fern and a few other varieties are edible and in spring send out shoots that are tightly curled at their ends before the leaves unfurl. They look like the scroll of a lute or fiddle. But don't blink or you'll miss them: the season is short, and they are highly perishable. At New York's Union

Square Greenmarket, where I first encountered them, I also learned that they were something of a New England delicacy, since pre-Colonial times a staple in the local Native American diet. They are also eaten traditionally in Asia, Australia, and New Zealand. They are decidedly not French, however, and have the look of something that defies you to divine a way to prepare them. Fortunately, the farmer with his basket of fiddleheads at Union Square was forthcoming and saved me the trial and error. Once I mastered them—very simple to do, actually—it took only a short French woman's leap to try them with pasta. Now they are something we look forward to, if ever so briefly, in spring.

INGREDIENTS

500g spaghetti

Fiddlehead Ferns (see next recipe)

60g prosciutto or pancetta, cut into small pieces

4 tablespoons grated Parmesan

2 tablespoons chopped parsley

Salt and freshly ground pepper

1. Cook the spaghetti according to packet directions. Drain and set aside, reserving 125ml of the cooking water.
2. Add the reserved water to the frying pan with the cooked fiddleheads, and mix well. Add the prosciutto, and cook 2 minutes more while stirring.
3. Toss the pasta with the fiddlehead sauce, transfer to a serving bowl, sprinkle with Parmesan and parsley, season with salt and pepper to taste, and serve immediately.

N. B. IF YOU CAN'T FIND FIDDLEHEAD FERNS, SPROUTING BROCCOLI IS AN ALTERNATIVE.

FIDDLEHEAD FERNS

Serves 4

1. Clean the fiddleheads thoroughly by washing them several times in cold water to get rid of the brown coat some of them have. Steam them for 6 minutes.
2. Warm the oil in a frying pan over medium-high heat. Add the garlic, fiddleheads, and lemon juice. Season with salt and pepper to taste, and sauté, stirring, for 5 to 10 minutes until the fiddleheads absorb the flavours of the garlic and lemon. Be careful not to overcook. Serve as an accompaniment to meat dishes or as part of the preceding pasta dish.

INGREDIENTS

300g fiddlehead ferns

2 tablespoons olive oil

2 cloves garlic, finely chopped

1 tablespoon lemon juice

Salt and freshly ground pepper

N. B. IF YOU CAN'T FIND FIDDLEHEAD FERNS, SPROUTING BROCCOLI IS AN ALTERNATIVE.

PAPPARDELLE WITH SPRING VEGETABLES

Serves 4

Whenever I make this, I am reminded of pasta primavera (spring pasta), a dish that became all the rage in America in the 1980s and remains to this day something of a classic. The genesis (at least the name) can be traced to Sirio and Egi Maccioni, owners of the legendary Le Cirque restaurant in New York. The story goes like this: In the late 1970s Sirio and Egi and some friends, including Pierre Franey and Craig Claiborne, then both food writers at the New York Times, *found themselves in Canada in a house with not much to eat (that's a story in itself). Luckily, Egi and Pierre, true culinary magicians, were wonders at concocting meals from practically nothing. They found pasta and a can of peas and some fresh vegetables and . . . well, the rest is history. It's actually not such an unusual story. As with so many now standard dishes, necessity was the mother of invention. The only difference is that Sirio—running what was then one of the most famous restaurants in the world, a cafeteria for ladies who lunch as well as titans of industry and government—had a bit more influence than the proprietor of the average eatery. Though Tuscan by birth, he was famed for his impeccable temple of French haute cuisine, and so it was nothing less than* scandale *when he decided to add his impromptu farmhouse pasta to its menu. His French chef refused to make it. (I believe he may have humoured Sirio by producing various versions that turned out to be completely* dégueulasses*—ridiculously horrible.) But Sirio eventually gets what he wants, and being a great showman, he came up with the idea of preparing the dish tableside. So take* zat, *you French chef. The pasta primavera was never on the menu, though it was occasionally announced as a special and always available on demand. If you are a tastemaker like Sirio and you feature something* *new, the speed of the knockoffs, as in the fashion business, could make your head spin. Eventually pasta primavera reached not only the West Coast but the Old World as well, remaining a standard in both hemispheres, though there is no classic recipe, except pasta and spring vegetables. Unbeknown to him, Sirio was adventurously channelling the adaptive spirit of French women without borders. Sirio's original was made with spaghetti, a cream sauce, and chopped tomatoes; my variation is but an homage.*

1. Blanch the asparagus in salted water until just tender, about 5 minutes. Blanch the peas separately for about 1 minute.
2. In a heavy saucepan, gently sauté the shallots in the oil over medium-low heat until they begin to turn golden. Add the peas and asparagus, and cook for a few minutes.
3. Cook the pappardelle according to packet directions, drain, and toss in the saucepan with the vegetables. Add the pine nuts, Parmesan, and parsley, and season with salt and pepper to taste. Serve immediately.

INGREDIENTS

500g green asparagus (ends trimmed), sliced in half crosswise

300g fresh peas, shelled

2 tablespoons finely chopped shallots

60ml extra virgin olive oil

350g pappardelle pasta

25g toasted pine nuts

60g freshly grated Parmesan

1 tablespoon roughly chopped parsley

Coarse sea salt and freshly ground pepper

Leeks: the star vegetable of *French Women Don't Get Fat,* whose publication actually caused many a local run on them—no joke. You would think the French owned the rights to the leek, which enjoys almost noble rank in France. *Le poireau* is both the vegetable and what they call the green-and-white ribbon of the Ordre national du mérite agricole, the national honour for distinction in food, wine, or agriculture. But the leek is also the staple and historical symbol of the Welsh (see Prince Charles's escutcheon) and makes a memorable appearance in *Henry V* (act 5, scene 1), when King Harry's faithful Fluellen defends his Welsh pride using the vegetable as a cudgel and delivers himself of the ungrammatical truism "Ay, leeks is good". A few more words are due this most distinguished bulb, with its slightly sweet, oniony, even nutty taste, its wealth of nutrients, and its mildly diuretic effect (a secret I have been doing my best to expose).

In France we consume leeks most of the year, except from late summer to early autumn. In winter they are huge, and we avoid the fattest ones as they are often too fibrous. In spring and summer they tend to be thin and tender and are followed by the *poireaux baguettes,* a very skinny variety. Come spring, ah, the farmers' markets abound with them—lately the baby leeks called ramps have been the season's first celebrity sightings.

The local leek shortages in America that followed the introduction of my Magical Leek Soup were truly *incroyables,* especially when one commentator predicted speculation on the commodities exchange. But when several health magazines published the recipe with a photo of whole leeks cooking in a pot, I knew there was still work to be done in bringing the leek Stateside. When cooking with this mild and refined form of garlic, you should cut away and discard most of the green: the white bulb and the white part of the stalks are the edible part! With that off my chest, let me add that a world of possibilities is open to you with leeks, the Magical Leek Soup from *French Women Don't Get Fat* being only the most Spartan alternative (though still a good one for recapturing your equilibrium from time to time, as we all need to).

MAGICAL LEEK SOUP (BROTH)

Serves 1 for the weekend

INGREDIENTS

1kg leeks

1. Clean the leeks and rinse well to get rid of sand and soil. Cut off the ends of the dark green parts, leaving all the white parts plus a suggestion of pale green. (Reserve the extra greens for soup stock.)
2. Cut the leeks into 2cm slices, put them into a large saucepan and cover with water. Bring to a boil, and simmer, uncovered, for 20 to 30 minutes. Pour off the liquid and reserve. Place the leeks in a bowl.

N.B. THIS IS A DETOX WEEKEND, NOT TO BE OVERDONE. DON'T BE TEMPTED TO REPEAT IT TOO OFTEN. I RECOMMEND ONCE EVERY THREE MONTHS.

IF YOU ARE USED TO A HIGH-CALORIE INTAKE EACH DAY, YOU MAY OBVIOUSLY FEEL HUNGRY AND TIRED. SO NO JOGGING OR STRENUOUS ACTIVITIES. RESTING, READING, AND RELISHING IS WHAT THIS WEEKEND IS ABOUT.

FOR THOSE WHO CAN'T LIVE ON LEEK SOUP FOR THE WHOLE WEEKEND, ONE DAY EVERY TWO MONTHS IS GOOD, ALTHOUGH IT WON'T HAVE QUITE THE SAME EFFECT. A TYPICAL FRENCH WOMAN WILL DO THE LEEK WEEKEND TWO TO FOUR TIMES A YEAR.

. . . . . .

The juice is to be drunk (reheated or at room temperature to taste) every 2 to 3 hours, 250ml at a time.

For meals, or whenever hungry, have some of the leeks themselves, 100–125g at a time. Drizzle with a few drops of extra virgin olive oil and lemon juice. Season sparingly with salt and pepper. Sprinkle with chopped parsley if you wish.

This will be your nourishment for both days, until Sunday dinner, when you can have a small piece of meat or fish (120–180g—don't lose those scales yet!), with 2 vegetables, steamed with a bit of butter or olive oil, and a piece of fruit. Leeks are so versatile, I guarantee you'll find your own uses once you get to know them. Meanwhile, a few more of my favourite recipes follow.

OYSTERS ON STEAMED LEEKS

Serves 4

1. Preheat the oven to gas mark 2/150°C.
2. Clean the leeks (see p. 63). Slice them thinly. Steam for 4 minutes and set aside.
3. Scrub the oyster shells and discard any that remain open. Spread closed oysters on a baking sheet over a layer of salt (to hold them in place). Put into the preheated oven for a few minutes, until the oysters open. Remove the meat from the shells, and reserve and strain the liquor. Preheat the grill.
4. Nestle the steamed leeks into half of the shells, top with oysters, then cover with the remaining half shells and set aside.
5. Prepare the sauce by cooking the oyster liquor with the wine until reduced by half. Remove from the heat, add the egg yolks, then whisk in the butter to obtain an unctuous consistency. Season with salt and pepper to taste.
6. Put the closed oysters under the grill for 30 seconds. Remove the top shells, and top each full bottom shell with a tablespoon of sauce. Serve immediately with a warm baguette and the rest of the bottle of wine.

INGREDIENTS

225g leeks, white parts only
24 oysters
125ml white wine
2 egg yolks
100g unsalted butter
Salt and freshly ground pepper

LEEK AND SPINACH "QUICHE"

Serves 4

INGREDIENTS

1 head savoy cabbage

2 leeks, white parts only, sliced finely

2 medium onions, peeled and diced

1 tablespoon olive oil

150g spinach, washed and chopped

Salt and freshly ground pepper

2 large eggs

250ml cream (more may be needed)

120g grated Gruyère cheese

Pinch of nutmeg

1. Preheat the oven to gas mark 4/180°C.
2. Discard the outer leaves of the cabbage, and blanch the inner leaves until tender, about 10 minutes (the water need not be salted). Put the cooked leaves on paper towels to cool and dry out, then line a non-stick baking dish or flan tin with the leaves.
3. Clean the leeks (see p. 63). Sauté the leeks and onions in the oil over medium heat until tender. Add the spinach. Season with salt and pepper to taste. Continue to cook until the spinach has begun to wilt, then drain the vegetables in a colander.
4. Blend the eggs, cream, cheese and nutmeg. Season with salt and pepper, and fold the mixture into the drained vegetables. Carefully pour it into the cabbage-lined dish.
5. Bake in the preheated oven for 25 to 30 minutes, or until the quiche is firm to the touch. Allow it to rest for 10 minutes before serving.

LEEKS FETTUCCINE

Serves 4

1. Cook the fettuccine in salted water according to packet directions.
2. Meanwhile, warm the oil in a frying pan. Sauté the (cleaned, sliced) leeks over medium-high heat until translucent.
3. When the pasta is ready, toss it with the leeks, add the cheese, and season with salt and pepper to taste. Serve immediately with the prosciutto as a garnish.

INGREDIENTS

350g fettuccine

6 tablespoons olive oil

500g leeks, white parts only, sliced into 2cm pieces

120g Parmesan cheese, freshly grated

Salt and freshly ground pepper

8 thin slices of prosciutto

PRAWN AND LEEK "MIMOSA"

Serves 4

INGREDIENTS

8 leeks

2 eggs

1 shallot, peeled and chopped

1 teaspoon Meaux or other wholegrain mustard

2 tablespoons red wine vinegar

Pinch of curry powder

Salt and freshly ground pepper

3 tablespoons olive oil

250g cooked prawns, peeled and deveined

1. Clean the leeks (see p. 63). Trim them, keeping about 5cm of the green part in addition to the whites, and boil them in salted water for 6 to 10 minutes, until they are cooked but still firm. Drain, and set aside.
2. Cook the eggs for 8 minutes in boiling water, then peel, chop, and set aside.
3. Place the shallot in a bowl with the mustard, vinegar, curry powder, and salt and pepper to taste. Whisk everything together, then whisk in the oil to make the sauce.
4. Place the prawns in the centre of a serving dish, surrounded by the leeks. Pour the sauce over all, then sprinkle with the chopped eggs.

N.B. THIS DISH IS BEST WHEN SERVED WITH LEEKS THAT ARE LUKEWARM. ANOTHER VERSION CALLS FOR CRABMEAT INSTEAD OF PRAWNS, AND IN PROVENCE WE DO THIS RECIPE WITH MARINATED ANCHOVIES. ALL THREE INGREDIENTS MARRY REALLY WELL WITH LEEKS. THE CRABMEAT OFFERS THE MORE ELEGANT DISH, THE ANCHOVIES THE STRONGER AND MORE RUSTIC.

SEA SCALLOPS AND LEEKS IN CHAMPAGNE SAUCE

Serves 4

1. Melt the butter in a large pan. Add the shallot, and cook over medium heat for 5 minutes. Clean and slice the leeks (see p. 63). Add the leeks and Champagne, season with salt and pepper to taste, and let "sweat" 10 to 15 minutes, until the leeks are tender.
2. In a separate pan, warm the oil over medium-high heat. Reduce heat to medium, and sear the scallops 1 minute on each side. Be sure not to overcook the scallops (if you do they'll taste like rubber). Season with salt to taste.
3. Spread the leeks on a serving dish, and top with the scallops. Drizzle with the Champagne sauce, sprinkle with parsley, and serve immediately.

INGREDIENTS

15g unsalted butter

1 tablespoon finely chopped shallot

4 leeks, white parts only, thinly sliced

150ml Brut Champagne

Salt and freshly ground pepper

1 tablespoon olive oil

16 sea scallops, rinsed and dried on paper towels

1 tablespoon chopped parsley

N.B. SERVE THE REMAINING CHAMPAGNE (OR DRY WHITE WINE) AS AN ACCOMPANYING BEVERAGE. ANOTHER OPTION IS TO REPLACE THE PARSLEY WITH SALMON ROE OR–IF YOU WANT TO SPLURGE FOR A SPECIAL OCCASION–CAVIAR, ABOUT 1/2 TEASPOON ON EACH SCALLOP.

LEEKS MOZZARELLA

Serves 4

INGREDIENTS

1kg leeks, white parts only

40g fresh basil leaves

225g mozzarella

1 to 2 tablespoons olive oil

1 teaspoon wine or sherry vinegar

Salt (preferably freshly ground—sea salt works magic) and freshly ground pepper

1. Preheat the grill.
2. Boil the leeks in salted water 6 to 10 minutes, until cooked but still firm, then drain.
3. Put the leeks into a baking dish, and cover with a layer of basil leaves. Cut the mozzarella into 5mm slices, and place over the basil layer. Put the dish under the preheated grill, and watch carefully. In 3 to 5 minutes the cheese should start to melt and brown; at this point, remove the dish.
4. Mix together the oil and vinegar and drizzle over the mozzarella. Season with salt and pepper to taste. Serve immediately with a slice of country or wholemeal bread.

SARDINES WITH CARROTS AND LEEKS

Serves 4

There can scarcely be a health-conscious eater out there who hasn't heard about the benefits of omega-3 fatty acids in fish such as salmon, mackerel, and sardines. Though I'm no doctor, many have asked me about the health benefits of these versus all the dangers one is also told lurk in fish. Here I'm guided by the French woman's principle of everything in moderation: have it once a week. Still, salmon can be pricey, especially if it's wild, which is really the only kind worth eating: some studies indicate that farmed salmon can have eight times the concentrations of environmental toxins as the wild, and only a fraction of the good fats. Yet, as I don't expect the seas to get any cleaner, I fear for what may happen to wild salmon in a generation. For this reason I'm very keen on sardines as a much more affordable alternative. I enjoy the flavour; they're just as rich in omega-3s as wild salmon; and since they're small, they're further down the food chain, with that much less opportunity to harbour toxins in the creatures they eat. In this dish the accompaniment is simply carrots and leeks, two vegetables found in my fridge most of the year, either cooked or waiting to be. Leftovers are great served on a piece of country bread covered with a slice of Swiss or Cheddar cheese and grilled until the cheese melts.

INGREDIENTS

3 tablespoons olive oil

180g carrots, peeled and thinly sliced

Salt and freshly ground pepper

275g leeks, white parts only, thinly sliced

2 tablespoons finely chopped shallots

15g unsalted butter

12 medium sardines (about 700g)

1 tablespoon finely chopped fresh oregano

Juice of 1 lemon

1. Preheat the oven to gas mark 4/180°C.
2. Warm 2 tablespoons of the oil in a large frying pan. Add the carrots, and cook over medium heat for 5 minutes. Add 80ml water, season with salt and pepper to taste, and stir in the leeks and shallots. Cover and cook for 5 to 7 minutes, stirring occasionally, until the vegetables are tender. Add the butter, and cook a minute or two more.
3. Put the sardines in one layer into a shallow (23×13cm) baking dish. Drizzle the remaining oil over them, season, and sprinkle with oregano. Bake 5 to 7 minutes on each side. Drizzle with the lemon juice, and serve with the carrots and leeks.

MACKEREL WITH CARROTS AND LEEKS

Serves 4

Mackerel, another salmon alternative, offers fine taste and excellent value. It reminds me of fresh tuna twenty years ago, when it was relatively cheap because few wanted it—before the sashimi-sushi craze, when it became "toro" and the price went through the roof, leaving only lesser cuts for those of us not wielding a sushi knife. A mackerel mania may not be far off, so get with it while the getting is still good. The best fishing begins in late spring, and the season runs into autumn. (Ditto for sardines.) A lovely Spanish lady who works at a Union Square Greenmarket fish booth gave me the following very simple preparation for this delicious, underappreciated fish.

1. Make a marinade by combining 2 tablespoons of the oil with the rosemary, shallots, and lemon juice. Pour over the mackerel, and marinate 10 to 20 minutes.
2. Warm the remaining oil in a large frying pan, and cook the mackerel over medium heat, about 3 minutes on each side.
3. Season with salt and pepper to taste (be careful not to oversalt, as mackerel is already salty), and serve with the carrot-leek mixture.

INGREDIENTS

3 tablespoons olive oil

4 tablespoons finely chopped fresh rosemary

2 tablespoons finely chopped shallots

Juice of 1 lemon

700g mackerel fillets

Salt and freshly ground pepper

Carrot-leek mixture from previous recipe

SALMON WITH FENNEL *EN PAPILLOTE*

Serves 4

INGREDIENTS

75g fresh ginger, peeled and cut into thin sticks

Zest and juice of 1 lemon

4 tablespoons olive oil, plus extra for brushing

Salt and freshly ground pepper

2 fennel bulbs, cleaned and sliced thinly

4 salmon steaks, 120g to 150g each

1. Preheat the oven to gas mark 6/200°C.
2. Place the ginger, lemon zest and juice, oil, and salt and pepper to taste in a bowl, and mix well.
3. Cut 8 pieces of parchment paper (or aluminum foil) into squares large enough to cover each salmon steak and leave a 5cm border all around. Lightly brush 4 squares with oil. Put some fennel and a salmon steak in the centre of each oiled square and drizzle with the ginger-lemon mixture.
4. Place the remaining parchment squares on top of the salmon, and fold up the edges to form parcels. Simply double folding each of the four sides is enough to seal each parcel.
5. Put the *papillotes* on a baking sheet, and bake in the preheated oven for 12 to 15 minutes. Set each *papillote* on a plate, and serve.

ROAST CHICKEN WITH CHICORY

Serves 4

1. Preheat the oven to gas mark 6/200°C.
2. Season the chicken well inside and out with salt and pepper. Put the lemon rind in the cavity. Drizzle the chicken with the oil, and put it into a roasting tin. Place the tin in the preheated oven. Turn twice over the next 30 minutes. Reduce the temperature to gas mark 4/180°C, then cook for 20 minutes more. Add the onion and shallots to the tin, cook for 10 minutes, then add the wine. Reduce the temperature to gas mark 2/150°C, and cook for 15 minutes more (a total cooking time of 1 hour and 15 minutes).
3. While the chicken cooks, halve the chicory lengthwise, brush with 2 tablespoons of the melted butter, and place on the grill. Once they are slightly browned, turn to brown the other side. Remove the chicory halves to an ovenproof dish, season, and add the lemon juice. Place the chicory in the oven for 5 minutes, until the cores are tender.

[continued]

INGREDIENTS

1×1.5kg chicken

Salt and freshly ground pepper

Rind and juice of 1 lemon

1 tablespoon olive oil

1 red onion, peeled and sliced

2 tablespoons finely chopped shallots

250ml red wine

6 heads chicory

60g unsalted butter, melted

2 tablespoons red wine vinegar

4. Remove the chicken from the oven, and reserve its juices (you should have about 250ml). Carve the chicken, and arrange on a serving plate with the chicory.

5. Add the cooking juice from the chicory to that of the chicken, and strain into a small bowl. Add the vinegar, stir in the remaining butter, and pour over the chicken. Serve immediately.

DANDELION SALAD

Serves 4

One of the more startling cultural divides between, for example, Americans or the British and the French (and Italians, for that matter) remains their respective views on the dandelion. Many people regard the plants mostly as a pest; they want only to kill them. The French, however, prefer to eat them. I can recall dandelion traumas in Weston, Massachusetts, where, readers may remember, I first got fat as an exchange student; and years later in Dix Hills, New York, where Edward grew up. Both communities have well-manicured lawns and gardens. The sight of a dandelion on a lawn is met like the eruption of a pimple on a teenage girl's nose: bring on the chemical warfare, consult the experts, kill, kill, kill before it spreads. Dandelions may do nothing for the beauty of Kentucky bluegrass, but their greens are tasty things. Fortunately, there are signs that the gourmands are gaining on the lawn doctors. More and more it is possible for a little French girl in New York, or anyone else, to buy a bag of wild dandelions (or pick some along roadsides or unkempt lawns!). What a treat you have in store, whether enjoying them raw in a salad or sautéed with a bit of olive oil and lemon, as they are served in Greece.

INGREDIENTS

1 teaspoon finely chopped shallot

1 teaspoon Meaux or other wholegrain mustard

1 tablespoon red wine vinegar

1 anchovy fillet, finely chopped

Salt and freshly ground pepper

3 tablespoons olive oil

1 bunch dandelion greens (about 275g), rinsed and dried

30g piece of Parmesan cheese

1. Whisk together the shallot, mustard, vinegar, and anchovy. Season with salt and pepper to taste, and whisk in the oil in a slow stream.

2. Toss the dandelion greens with the dressing, and top with Parmesan shavings (you can shave the cheese with a vegetable peeler).

SALMON-AND-SPINACH SALAD

Serves 4

Where fresh wild salmon is not available, canned sockeye salmon is a suitable alternative to farmed—the French are far from believing everything in a tin is wicked.

1. Mix together the shallot, salt, and sherry vinegar. Pour onto the salmon, and let marinate for at least 1 hour, preferably 3.
2. Drain off the marinade, and cut the salmon into very thin slices. (This step can be done in advance.)
3. For the dressing, mix the mustard and pepper in a bowl with the red wine vinegar. Add the oil, whisking well.
4. Pour the dressing over the spinach in a large bowl, tossing gently. Place the salmon slices all around. Serve with buttered wholemeal toast.

INGREDIENTS

1 shallot, finely chopped

Pinch of sea salt

125ml sherry vinegar

400g uncooked salmon fillets (or smoked salmon or canned salmon)

1 teaspoon Meaux or other wholegrain mustard

Freshly ground pepper

2 tablespoons red wine vinegar

60ml olive oil

400g spinach, washed and dried

GREEN BEANS WITH TOMATOES

Serves 4

INGREDIENTS

2 tablespoons olive oil

4 anchovies, finely chopped

2 shallots, peeled and finely chopped

2 medium-sized tomatoes, coarsely sliced

Salt and freshly ground pepper

1 tablespoon finely chopped fresh basil

500g thin string beans, steamed for 8 minutes

1. Warm the oil in a frying pan over medium heat. Add the anchovies and shallots, and cook for 2 minutes. Add the tomatoes, and cook a few minutes more. Season with salt and pepper to taste, then add the basil.
2. Put the steamed beans into a serving dish, and top with the tomato-anchovy mixture. Serve immediately.

STEAMED COURGETTES WITH BASIL

Serves 4

1. Steam the courgettes for 6 minutes.
2. Combine the lemon juice and oil. Season with salt and pepper and whisk well.
3. Place the steamed courgettes in a serving dish, and top with the dressing and Parmesan shavings (you can shave the cheese with a vegetable peeler). Sprinkle with the basil, and serve immediately.

INGREDIENTS

4 medium-sized courgettes, cut into 2cm slices

Juice of 1 lemon

2 tablespoons olive oil

Salt and freshly ground pepper

120g piece of Parmesan cheese

2 tablespoons finely chopped fresh basil

SAUTÉED MUSHROOMS

Serves 4

INGREDIENTS

675g mixed mushrooms (1 to 3 varieties)

2 tablespoons olive oil

Juice of ½ lemon

15g unsalted butter

Salt and freshly ground pepper

2 tablespoons chopped parsley

30g grated Comté or Gruyère cheese

1. Wipe the mushrooms with paper towels (or clean pastry brush), and slice coarsely.
2. Warm the oil in a frying pan, add the lemon juice and mushrooms, and cook for a few minutes. Add the butter, and cook a few minutes more, until the liquid has evaporated. Season with salt and pepper to taste, and add the parsley.
3. Add the cheese, and cook a minute or so more, just until the cheese starts to melt. Mix gently, and serve immediately.

SPINACH WITH SULTANAS AND PINE NUTS

Serves 4

1. Wash the spinach and trim, if necessary.
2. Warm the oil in a large frying pan. Sauté the sultanas and pine nuts until golden, 1 to 2 minutes. Remove from the pan, and set aside.
3. Add the spinach to the pan. Season with salt and pepper to taste, cover, and cook over medium heat for 3 to 5 minutes or until the spinach is wilted. Add the sultanas and pine nuts, and toss constantly while cooking for 1 more minute. Serve immediately.

INGREDIENTS

1kg spinach

2 tablespoons olive oil

2 tablespoons sultanas

25g pine nuts

Salt and freshly ground pepper

In Europe, the Middle East, and North Africa, lambs have been sacrificed in connection with Christian, Jewish, and Muslim customs as long as those customs have existed (which suggests that people were offering up lambs in the cradle of civilization long before). I remember driving in Morocco—where lamb is the most commonly consumed red meat—during the feast commemorating the sacrifice of Isaac (known in Morocco as Eid el-Kebir) and seeing in village after village lambs hung by their feet with their necks sliced and blood dripping, in the ritually prescribed manner. In France, as elsewhere in Europe, spring lamb is associated with Easter, where it is a traditional dish, but it is now available year-round, not only because of demand-driven breeding but because of the complementary seasons of New Zealand and Australia, the world's largest exporters.

Since spring lambs are slaughtered at three to five months, they don't have the strong muttony flavour that sometimes puts off those unused to lamb. But the flavour, as well as the texture, can vary enormously. America produces lamb as good as can be found anywhere, though small local producers are the ones most likely to have taken the care to optimize the feed and hence the taste. Occasionally a fancy New York butcher has disappointed me, but the lamb man at the farmers' market can't afford to make mistakes.

CURRIED LAMB WITH AUBERGINE

Serves 4

1. With a fork, beat together half the yogurt, half the lemon juice and 1 tablespoon of the curry powder. Pour over the lamb, and let marinate 2 to 3 hours in the refrigerator.
2. Steam the aubergine for 4 minutes, and set aside. Warm the oil over medium heat, and lightly brown the shallots. Add the cinnamon stick, star anise, and remaining curry powder and cook for 1 minute. Stir in the aubergine and tomatoes. Season with salt and pepper to taste, and cook over low heat for 15 minutes.
3. Turn the grill on, and cook the lamb with its marinade for 10 minutes, turning the meat a couple of times.
4. Combine the remaining yogurt and lemon juice with the aubergine mixture, and cook for 5 minutes over medium-low heat. Add the coriander. Serve the lamb (2 slices each) and aubergine.

INGREDIENTS

250g yogurt

Juice of 2 lemons

2 tablespoons curry powder

500g lamb shoulder, deboned and sliced

1 large aubergine, washed and diced

2 tablespoons olive oil

4 tablespoons finely chopped shallots

1 cinnamon stick

1 star anise

2 tomatoes, diced

Salt and freshly ground pepper

4 tablespoons chopped fresh coriander

RACK OF LAMB PERSILLADE

Serves 4 to 6

Easter Sunday was always my family's first taste of spring lamb, and Mamie *would always pick the simplest recipe (maybe that's why it was our favourite). Our next "lamb" of the day was actually a re-reading of Saint-Exupéry's "lamb" chapter, in which the Little Prince asks,* "Dessine moi un mouton" *(draw me a sheep).*

INGREDIENTS

3 tablespoons olive oil

3 cloves garlic, peeled and finely chopped

2 tablespoons finely chopped shallots

35g fresh breadcrumbs

3 tablespoons finely chopped parsley

Salt and freshly ground pepper

2 racks of lamb (4 ribs each)

1. Preheat the oven to gas mark 8/230°C.
2. Warm the oil in a frying pan over medium-high heat. Add the garlic and shallots; stir for 10 seconds, add the breadcrumbs and parsley, and stir for a minute more. Season with salt and pepper to taste, and set aside.
3. Season the lamb with salt and pepper, and arrange the racks in a baking tin. Pat the crumb mixture onto the meat sides and the fat of the lamb. Cook until a meat thermometer inserted into the thickest part of the meat registers 55°C (for medium rare). Let the lamb stand for 5 minutes before carving. Cut the racks between bones into individual chops, 2 per person. Serve with fresh peas.

Spring is full of harbingers, but none is more evocative of summer than the first great strawberries at market. As a child I liked to think that my father had planted the rows and rows of them in our garden with special affection, knowing them to be my favourite fruit. (I would have had him plant strawberry fields forever, if the song had then existed.) The ground around the plants was covered with straw so that each precious berry, after soaking up the vast amount of sunshine needed to ripen it, had its own cradle in which to fall, and therefore would need little or no washing. Papa grew two or three varieties with different ripening times to make the season last as long as possible. Those small- to medium-sized berries were moist and sweet and seductive. Alongside them, some of the big, red, photogenic supermarket hybrids have as much claim to the name *strawberry* as today's steroid-enhanced athletes have to the mantle of Babe Ruth. Not surprisingly, "ersatz" strawberries have the same sort of non-descript taste and texture one finds in supermarket tomatoes: just enough to be discernible as the thing it's called, but ultimately only a taunt. They are over-refrigerated and served very cold—death to the flavour of most fruits.

Strawberries are versatile, so I try to observe the principle of *faire simple* (keep it simple), which should always be remembered when preparing them. Shortbread can be delicious, but why overwhelm the taste of really good fruit? My favourite way to serve strawberries is sliced in a pretty dish with a tablespoon of mascarpone, crème fraîche, plain yogurt, fresh ricotta, whipped cream, or vanilla ice cream. A bit of freshly ground pepper can really pull the fruit and dairy flavours together, and today one can play with the huge variety of peppercorns.

For more elaborate desserts, I mostly avoid preparations such as meringues that are heavy on sugar. As a rule, one should enjoy natural sweetness, and with good strawberries that's what you'll get. In Italy, great strawberries are served with just a squeeze of lemon, or sometimes a dash of fine aged balsamic vinegar. On the other hand, a nice *tarte sablée* (shortbread pastry) covered with strawberries and a thin glaze of strawberry coulis is a platonically perfect confection—but I think of that more as a special treat than as the end of a meal. Desserts should be only as sweet as they need to be to cleanse the palate following the last savoury course.

The sweetness of good strawberries can be channelled to help other fruits. I like to add some strawberries a few minutes before I'm done making my rather acidic rhubarb compote. This I serve with yogurt or fresh ricotta, or with *fromage blanc,* a common marriage in French bistros during strawberry season.

For a further variation *aux fraises,* this on the sweeter side, try mixing a few fresh sliced strawberries with raspberries and serving them with a *panna cotta* or a custard: it's a nice contrast of textures, and though you're adding a bit of sweetness, you're still nowhere near the sugar surge of a strawberry shortbread.

RHUBARB-STRAWBERRY COMPOTE

Serves 4

Another simple, traditional recipe from childhood that has become the stuff of exquisite moments. The aroma of fresh fruit, so subtle and yet so intense, returns me to that bower where it seemed the strawberries would never end.

INGREDIENTS

70g sugar

¼ teaspoon cinnamon

1 tablespoon lemon juice

500g rhubarb, trimmed and cut into 1cm pieces

80g strawberries, washed, drained, hulled, and sliced

1. Combine the sugar and cinnamon. Put the lemon juice into a saucepan with 60ml of water and a third of the rhubarb, then sprinkle with the sugar-cinnamon mixture. Continue layering until all the rhubarb and the sugar-cinnamon mixture are used up. Cover and cook gently over low heat until barely tender, 10 to 20 minutes.
2. Add the strawberries, and cook a few more minutes. Refrigerate until serving.

N.B. THE COMPOTE CAN ALSO BE EATEN AT ROOM TEMPERATURE AND IS A LOVELY ACCOMPANIMENT TO YOGURT (ABOUT 1 TABLESPOON PER 125G YOGURT).

STRAWBERRY SOUP WITH MASCARPONE

Serves 4

INGREDIENTS

500g strawberries
2 tablespoons lemon juice
2 tablespoons sugar
250g mascarpone (or ricotta cheese)
Fresh mint

1. Wash the strawberries. Gently pat dry, and hull all but 4 (reserve for decoration).
2. Mix the hulled strawberries, lemon juice, and sugar, and crush the strawberries slightly with a fork to release some juice.
3. In a separate bowl, beat the mascarpone with a whisk.
4. Pour the strawberry soup into martini glasses, and top with a dollop of the mascarpone. Decorate each glass with a strawberry and a sprig of mint.

SPRINGING OUT OF THE CLOSET

Beyond cuisine, half the fun of the French woman's seasonal adjustment is the spring reorientation to life outdoors. And with that comes the seasonal adjustment of wardrobe, from heavy to light, from woollens to cottons, from darker to more vibrant colours. Some may take the view that colour is "in" or it's "out" this year or that, but for me what nature is showing in a given season is far more influential than any designer's collection. With the freedom to unbundle oneself that warmer weather brings, spring is a great time to experiment as long as you *faîtes simple* with your look overall. I favour starting with clean lines and solid, often neutral separates—classic T-shirts, polos, woven shirtings—of a quality that doesn't announce itself too loudly. A flattering, neat look can be had inexpensively by choosing clothes that fit, rather than constrain or billow. Trim, not tight, trousers, at a waist height dictated by your shape, not MTV.

Upon this neutral base I work the timeless custom of variation on a theme, namely, an arrangement of what have become my own signature accessories: necklace, sunglasses, and above all, scarves. French women and scarves go together in people's minds. French women generally effect their ever-changing self-styling with the cunning choice of accessories, most famously the scarf. Two of my most reliable ways to tie one in spring are the super simple classic kerchief and the more daring jacket scarf.

Classic Kerchief

This tie requires a square scarf and results in a V spread across your back with the knot hanging somewhere under your chin. A large scarf will flow over your shoulders; a small one creates the perfect spring look with a light, trimly cut crew-neck sweater. You can also wear the scarf under the sweater for more of an ascot effect.

For a bit more glamour, in the evening, say, tie the scarf loosely and pull it down and around both shoulders to serve as a shawl. This is especially effective over low-cut dresses. Here's how:

1. Take the square scarf and fold it diagonally to form a triangle. Holding each end of the long length of the

triangle, keep folding over the remaining point of the triangle until you have a band about five centimetres wide.

2. Still holding the long ends, drape the scarf around your neck and tie a square knot in front with a few inches of scarf flowering below the knot—that is, pull one of the long ends around the other, forming a loop through which to pass the first end. Tighten *comme tu veux.*

Mireille's Jacket Scarf

This requires a large, especially long rectangular scarf. I sometimes sew bands of silk onto the ends to add length and facilitate the knot.

1. Drape the scarf over your shoulders with one side hanging much longer than the other. For an average-sized woman that means one end should come just below your waist and the other just above your knees.
2. Crisscross the ends and wrap the longer end completely around your body until it meets the shorter end just above your hip. Tie with a simple knot.

The marvellous thing about this look is its versatility: it never comes out exactly the same twice. And depending on the scarf, it works as well for an outdoor café as for an outdoor cocktail with café society.

Ah, spring is here—but end it must, like all good things. I started this interlude with a bit of gushing about flowers as my dearest tokens of spring. Among those who don't suffer hay fever, I'm sure I would find not a few who feel the same about nature's Technicolor cinema. Hardened indeed is the heart unmoved by the succession of crocuses, then daffodils, then tulips. The blooms on the almond trees of Provence in March. April's sacrament of the cherry blossom in the American Northeast and Japan. And the dogwood in New York leading into May. What we sometimes forget to appreciate, on the other hand, is the satisfaction of their passing. If cherry blossom lasted for months, it would fast become a banality. Its mystery, its command of our attention, is exactly in proportion to its fleeting presence, what the Elizabethan poets obsessively referred to as *mutabilitie*, a Norman word (and still a French one). It was for this reason, I suppose, that van Gogh painted the irises in Provence rather than a still life of its more enduring lavender, however lovely that is.

A feature of our globalized marketplace is the constant availability of plant life out of its time; for a price, we can have the rarest orchids in our midst whenever. But this seems to me quite beside the point of flowers, if they may be said to have a point beyond their mere existence. What we appreciate, we appreciate in the fullness of time, though we can agreeably fool ourselves by protracting this a bit.

"*Le menu que je préfère* (My favorite menu) / *c'est la chair de votre cou* (is the flesh of your neck)," sings Georges Brassens in *"J'ai rendez-vous avec vous"* ("I Have a Date with You"). Now that's a French menu. All about pleasure. Alas, the menus in this book, pure and simple, are not erotic. There's a place for that in healthy, balanced living, but I leave it to you to find it.

It goes without saying (or at least it should) that every day, every season, every menu for living should begin with the essence of life: a glass of water. If your tap water is unpalatable, as many are, get a water filter or find a bottled one you like and cultivate a taste that banishes those dubious drinks sweetened artificially or naturally. When starting her day, a French woman would no more neglect to have her glass of water than to dab a little perfume or *eau de toilette* on her neck.

Beyond water, bear in mind it is essential to have three meals. Your morning bread should be toasted (more digestible, and, in France, yesterday's bread never goes to waste when there is always breakfast tomorrow). A sliver of butter is pure pleasure and much better for you than pseudo-fat substitutes like margarine, which should be tossed in the trash together with most cooking oils.

My three-meal-a-day menus provide a mix of proteins, carbohydrates, and fat, according to a rough ratio of 50–60/40–30/10 per cent respectively. Remember you can be flexible—including a bit more here, paring back a bit there—but make sure that over the course of the week you find the balance. And enjoy! Eating is sensory, so eat with all five senses, and appreciate little experiences (of small portions and three bites) which produce through association and memory a gamut of emotions. Focus on the pleasurable ones and get rid of the destructive ones.

As they are subject to individual adjustments, my menu templates are equally suitable for maintaining a healthy weight and losing a few pounds or kilos following the principles of *French Women Don't Get Fat*, especially chapter 3 on short-term recasting. You'll need to tailor the menus somewhat to your own lifestyle.

The portions here are for little beings, like me, so if you are taller than average and proportionally heavier though not necessarily overweight, increase your portions a bit. (Experiment with the 50 Per Cent Solution to see what satisfies you without causing weight gain.) And if that's not enough, incorporate a snack, yogurt being my first choice. (French woman are the European champions, consuming on average over 20 kilos of yogurt per year . . . on the way to not getting fat.)

As your sense of proportion evolves, feel free to make substitutions. I present a range of what I like, but you should suit yourself. If you prefer red wine with fish, go for it. If you don't like wine, you are missing one of the greatest foods on earth, but so be it. When I suggest non-calorific beverages I mean water or herbal tea (including green tea) or coffee. Try to limit other tea or coffee to no more than two cups a day, as the caffeine can make you hungry, especially on certain days of the month. It also dehydrates you, and the water in highly caffeinated beverages does *not* meet the requirement of drinking lots of plain water.

If you don't care for dried apricots, have cranberries or whatever you like. Remember you can eat any good food in moderation . . . in three bites (so to speak). Small portions and variety are what matters. Learn to reduce at your pace by eating slowly and chewing well.

With soups especially, don't feel you have to follow the recipes to the letter. The same soup never tastes the same twice anyway. So don't panic if you are missing an ingredient: replace it with what you have on hand or prefer. (That goes for all dishes: you may, for instance, find that you prefer almonds over cashews with your spring asparagus. Nothing wrong with that.) I often throw in whatever I have in the fridge or find at the market. Be creative, bearing in mind the pleasures of mixing colours, though sometimes a delicious green soup needs no adornment.

For salads, I firmly believe the best dressing is a top-quality olive oil and vinegar (1 tablespoon vinegar for 3 tablespoons olive oil, an amount for 60g salad leaves). If you need "spice" in your salad, add a bit of mustard to the dressing, and, of course, always plenty of fresh herbs. There is no such thing as a good bottled salad dressing.

Finally a few simple rules of thumb for easy portion approximation:

- For bread or chocolate, 15g (those little scales are so useful).
- For cereal, 60g, with 125ml milk. You can double the quantities if you've found your equilibrium.
- For rice, 70g cooked; potatoes, 80g; pasta, 80g cooked (as a side dish; 150g as a main dish).
- For fruit, usually one piece or 80g is a portion. However, a whole banana, pear, grapefruit, or mango counts as two portions.

MONDAY

Breakfast

60g muesli
125ml skimmed milk
80g strawberries
1 slice multigrain bread, toasted and buttered
Coffee or tea

Lunch

60g spinach salad with mushrooms
Olive oil-vinegar dressing
60g cheese of your choice
1 small roll
150g blueberries
Non-calorific beverage

Dinner

Calf's Liver with Greens (page 272)
80g sautéed potatoes
125g yogurt
2 clementines
1 glass red wine

TUESDAY

Breakfast

2 prunes
125g yogurt with 1 tablespoon oats or muesli and a drizzle of honey
1 tablespoon soya nuts
Coffee or tea

Lunch

Salade composée with hard-boiled egg, tuna, and green beans
Mustard-oil-vinegar dressing
1 slice wholemeal bread
1 pear
1 square chocolate
Non-calorific beverage

Dinner

Salmon with Sorrel (page 274)
½ serving Tagliatelle with Lemon (www.mireilleguiliano.com)
2 slices baguette
Coffee *Petits Pots* (page 352)
1 glass red or white wine

WEDNESDAY

Breakfast

60g bran flakes
125ml skimmed milk
½ banana
1 slice rye bread, buttered
Coffee or tea

Lunch

Chicken breast with asparagus
125g yogurt
1 mango
Non-calorific beverage

Dinner

Roast Chicken with Chicory (page 75)
Steamed Courgettes with Basil (page 81)
Strawberry Soup with Mascarpone (page 90)
1 glass red or white wine

THURSDAY

Breakfast

125ml freshly squeezed orange juice or 1 orange
1 soft-boiled egg
1 slice wholemeal bread, toasted and buttered
Coffee or tea

Lunch

Roast beef sandwich
Grated carrots with lemon-juice dressing
1 apple
Non-calorific beverage

Dinner

Spaghetti with Fiddlehead Ferns and Prosciutto (page 57–8)
Green salad
150g strawberries with a scoop of vanilla ice cream
1 glass red wine

FRIDAY

Breakfast

1 slice ham
125g yogurt
½ English muffin, toasted and buttered
1 kiwi fruit
Coffee or tea

Lunch

Broccoli salad
Saumon à l'Unilatéral (www.mireilleguiliano.com)
Drizzle of olive oil on salmon and broccoli
1 slice brown bread
150g fruit salad
Non-calorific beverage

Dinner

Mackerel with Carrots and Leeks (page 73)
80g boiled potatoes
Fruit tart
1 glass red wine

SATURDAY

Breakfast

60g cheese
65g oatmeal with blueberries
80ml skimmed milk
1 small brioche or slice of sourdough bread, toasted and buttered
Coffee or tea

Lunch

Leeks Mozzarella (page 70)
1 slice wholemeal bread
1 tangerine
Non-calorific beverage

Dinner

Steak
100g Mashed Potatoes *Mamie*'s Version (page 164)
Green Beans with Tomatoes (page 80)
Chocolate flan
1 glass red wine

SUNDAY

Breakfast

125ml freshly squeezed
orange juice or 1 orange
Asparagus and Cashew
Omelette (page 51)
1 slice rye bread,
toasted and buttered
Coffee or tea

Lunch

400g steamed vegetables
Olive oil-vinegar dressing
1 slice wholemeal bread,
buttered
125g yogurt
125ml Rhubarb-Strawberry
Compote (page 89)
Non-calorific beverage

Dinner

Curried Lamb with
Aubergine (page 85)
80g pasta
Mixed green salad
120g strawberries with
mascarpone
1 glass red wine

3

EN ÉTÉ: SUMMERTIME SMILES

And the livin' is easy. The French may have their much-ridiculed or envied six weeks of holidays—still but a fantasy for me, working in America, as for most of the world—but this is not to say that French women content themselves in summer with collapsing into a hammock and watching the cotton grow high. (Actually, we don't grow any.) In fact, most, myself included, seem to wake up a bit earlier and go to bed a bit later, taking full advantage of those precious few months of extra daylight. As long as I mind my equilibrium, I am full of energy, and it's never so easy to do as in summer.

Whether in New York, Paris, Provence, or elsewhere, the longest days are the most enlivening, the only limitation being heat, which can become oppressive—even in Provence. There are places where the broiling, humid outdoors of summer is simply unbearable; in such places, summer can seem a kind of winter, an interval of harshness from which to take refuge. (It's no coincidence that summer and winter are the seasons that are also verbs. No one goes somewhere else "to autumn".) I do not dispute the discomfort of people in these places, but to some degree, it is another way we have become victims of modern conveniences and modern expectations. Even in places where summer seems quite pleasant, people spend too much of it in an air-conditioned bubble as the standard for comfort has changed. As for those places that verge on the tropical in summer, there is no debating the matter. In Houston, for instance, a fascinating and vibrant town despite having won in 2005 the dubious distinction of the fattest city in America (supplanted in 2006 by Chicago—likewise a place of sometimes unbearable extremes of temperature), winter is mild while summer is harsh, with people scurrying from car to shops to car to house, if not fleeing to Colorado. (Some of the most elaborate "swankiendas" even have air-conditioned backyards.)

It's sad to imagine summer as an event to be escaped, but in more and more places it has become that. It occurs to me that we used to make less evasive accommodations to nature, such as screened-in verandas, fans, and plenty of lemonade; in the course of an agreeably slower but still active way of life, we would tolerate a bit of sweat (not the social abomination Madison Avenue makes it seem). I don't think it's coincidence that the fattening of America—and Britain—has tracked with the spread of climate control and television. We cannot go back to the way things were, but the goal should still be to seek out the season as one can, and not only during holidays. Summer is the interval of peak experience, a state of being and a state of mind, and properly speaking, not a time we should be getting fat.

For me summer registers with evenings and weekends spent outdoors whenever conditions permit. Outdoor food markets crop up in summer like mushrooms after a storm. The variety of seasonal produce—fresh berries, vegetables whose brilliant colour announces the nutrients packed within (nature's food labelling), fresh and fragrant herbs, and gorgeous flowers—is truly an embarrassment of riches. I find walking among the market stalls a superb way to relax, a fine occasion to see or meet friends, talk to farmers, and drink in the blue sky and the sun—protected, of course, with SPF 15, sunglasses, and a hat. French women are very careful about the sun, especially where their faces are concerned, for nothing adds years to the face, and hands too, like too many youthful days spent unprotected in solar radiance. Saying this, I must note that enjoyment of the sun seems to bring out a tendency towards unhealthy extremism. Devoted readers of health and beauty magazines, ever on the lookout for new products with astronomical SPFs, seem obsessed with going anywhere *but* towards the light. Others take the arrival of summer sun as the occasion to roast like *poulets* on a spit, heedless of common sense, let alone medical fact. Raising the bar for what constitutes a healthy glow, they compel their more vampirish sisters to slather on the tanner-in-a-tube, which leaves virtually all complexions some shade of cantaloupe. We need a little *bon sens* here: the sun is essential for our synthesis of vitamin D, without which our bones would turn to coral. So we should make sure to get some sun but limit our exposure (a burn can occur in ten minutes without protection), take extra pains to protect face and hands, and neither a sun worshipper nor a vampire be.

Summer dress is light dress, often light colours, mostly cotton. But don't forget what is obvious in hotter climes with less forgiving sun: on the hottest days more cover can keep you cooler than less, to say nothing of protecting unnoticed body parts from sun damage and far worse. In a French city you'll see few locals over the age of twelve wearing shorts, and decent "cover" is the norm (except perhaps in Saint-Tropez). I lose the heels in favour of lower sandals or espadrilles—a classic style that never disappears from the maritime regions of France and all along the Mediterranean. With regular cycling and swimming, two of my favourite activities, I wind up washing my hair too often for a cut that requires a lot of styling. Summer is a good time to *faire simple* with your hair, although you shouldn't ignore the necessity of special care. Hot climates, whether dry or humid, do wreak havoc on both hair and skin. As in winter, the need to moisturize is great. For the hair a thick shea butter conditioner is advisable several times a week, depending on how naturally dry your hair might be. Before moisturizing, however, I rinse my hair with cold water to which I've added a teaspoon of vinegar or the juice of a lemon, as my mother taught me to do: this will make it shinier than expensive products will. I also like to rinse my body in the shower with cold water; it's good for the circulation. These are cold-water beauty routines that are actually a good year-round habit, but if you didn't grow up in northern France, you might find it easier to start them in summer. The same might be said for my morning ritual of putting an ice cube or two in a facecloth to avoid breaking capillaries and gently stroking my face, especially around the eyes. I do this right after I've had my day's first glass of water; the day's first one is vital, also regardless of season.

So, creams, sun protection, and moisturizers for hair and body are part of the seasonal toolbox. But in summer, make-up too takes a holiday. Go light, without foundation for the chic, un-made-up look of Parisians. Put on some sunscreen, and let your skin breathe. A mask is a good idea. My mother had two wonderful ones for summer: strawberry (mash a few strawberries and mix with ½ teaspoon of Vaseline moisturizer. Apply to your whole face; after fifteen minutes, rinse off) and cucumber (mix a few cucumber slices with 2 teaspoons of yogurt and apply to your face and eyes. Cover with a wet cloth; after fifteen minutes, rinse off). As for fragrances, I vary them by season, too, in spring and summer preferring *eau de toilette* to perfume, light florals and refreshing citrusy scents, nothing too complex or heady.

High-maintenance looks take time away from what ought to be the most routinely active season of the year, when the urge to be outside keeps us on the go and even in America work does slow down a bit. If we do not seize the day, if we become summer hibernators, we will be working against the season's natural mechanism for preserving our weight equilibrium. Here it is *en bref:* summer gives us a bounty of super-satisfying flavours, which, if consciously savoured, steer us clear of "offenders". The heat of summer is not conducive to overeating, as the body craves food rich in readily digestible energy and much-needed water and electrolytes. It feels great to be out and about, so routine exertion is easy, especially if we make a point of doing our walking early in the morning and evening. The urge to participate in summer fun also creates occasions for sport, however undignified. Don't be proud—go with it. I'm hardly a great swimmer but, whenever possible, I avail myself of one of the most joint-friendly and meditative of activities. There is much to do because it's fun. Thus not getting fat becomes a fringe benefit rather than an end in itself.

On Saturdays in summer when I was a child, my mother would serve us a cold lunch on the shaded terrace overlooking the garden. The day would have started and ended, as it still does, with a tall glass of water. She took pains to be sure that we were never dehydrated; there would be a full jug, frequently refilled, all day long. Mother would bring a baguette, a couple of cheeses, some salami or ham, while I, with a visiting friend or two, would go to the garden to pick a few tomatoes, some radishes, and some fresh lettuce (we would rinse our pickings at the garden tap, never setting foot in the house). That labour was rewarded later with free, exclusive access to the berry bushes; after eating our sandwiches, slowly of course, there was a digestive pause, and then we were each handed a little bowl with which to forage. It's as if my mother knew we would otherwise just crouch there putting berries into our mouths without a thought for the others waiting at the table. We did, however, manage to make it back with bowlfuls for them, too. Afterwards, we'd just sit and talk lazily till mid-afternoon. Even with the doors and windows arranged for a cross breeze, it was simply too hot at midday to sit indoors, much less to exert oneself outside.

Evenings were when we played, and on the longest days it would be light out until ten.

We were left to our own devices in the big garden. Mid-afternoon, one of our neighbours, Madame Regnaud, would often come with a new children's book she was reading to her grandchildren, and she would read us a story or two in the shade of the terrace; with our eyes shut, we could hear nothing but her voice over the happy chatter of the birds. *Mamie* would reappear around *le 4 heures* for the afternoon refreshment, not a *goûter* (snack) but glasses of lemonade she had made fresh, mindful of our need for water, especially in summer. It was neither tart nor especially sweet. Looking back, what strikes me most is not how much this scene resembles one from the nineteenth century but how remote it seems from the twenty-first. In fact, the pace of lifestyle change has picked up dramatically within only the past few decades. Unfortunately, we seem to have taken little care to compensate for the things subtracted. Most children today would choose the air-conditioned family room, with the latest version of PlayStation by the light of the plasma, over sitting around outside in summer's heat. Needless to say, it's a different sort of conditioning in terms of comfort and pleasure. As for me, I'm quite grateful that to this day, given a choice, on a Saturday afternoon in summer I can be found outside in a shady refuge amid flowers, a book in hand, a glass of lemony water or cooled herbal tea of mint or basil nearby.

Of course, we're not kids any more and can't all spend the whole summer as we might like. Many of us with jobs indoors spend most of the day in the air-conditioned bubble I mentioned. On workdays, the heat seems particularly uncomfortable because it can defeat our efforts at neat professional presentation. And we must devise accommodations for passing from the sultry street into the cold storage that most offices and shops and restaurants—all public places, really—become in summer. And this is the case now even in some parts of Europe, which was slower to accept air-conditioned living.

Summer being the traditional time for *les vacances,* when I was younger it also meant going away somewhere, whether for a few weeks to my grandmother's house in rural Alsace, a summer job in Austria, or relief work in Yugoslavia. Whatever the itinerary, the point was to be closer to the season, not to escape it. I came to the custom of a beach holiday fairly late, first on the Riviera (not as glamorous for French people as it sounds to others), then as an exchange student on Nantucket with my adoptive American family. The latter was a much more exotic experience, in terms of both landscape (*sandy* beaches, not the norm in France) and social anthropology. There is a point to travel that is very much like the point of seasonality: it helps our mental organization of time, breaking it up, and makes our overall experience seem fuller. As nature designed us, our senses perk up in any unfamiliar setting, trying to take everything in, feeding information directly to our so-called reptilian cortex, a vestige of a time before we had mastered our surroundings and needed to be watchful for dangers and potential meals. For this reason, Chianti at home doesn't taste the way it tastes in Tuscany. Lavender bundles even at the Paris markets don't smell like the air in Provence. The play of the light in Miami is one glory, the play of the light in the Alps another. A change of scene is good for us because it gives all our senses a new world of stimuli to react to.

But not everyone seems as clued in to the importance of this phenomenon to overall health. While the serenity of the beach makes it a holiday destination I love—nothing is more meditative than the sea, and a walk along the edge of the surf is the most pleasant of exertions—I have met many women of all ages who think of it as an occasion to lose consciousness. "I just want to veg" is an expression I've heard countless times from hardworking people explaining their beach holidays from mindfulness. True, modern living gives us too much to think about, and the world is changing faster than we can make sense of it. The antidote, however, may not be to stop thinking but to think of something else. Being lulled into oblivion by tropical drinks and drowsy heat may not furnish nearly as much rest or renewal as we can be tempted to imagine. It's just a respite. Occasionally, *ça suffit* (it's enough). In general, though, you may find, as I do, that time away is better spent immersing oneself in something different—a landscape, a culture, even a different language, and *bien sûr* a different cuisine. You don't need to trek through the Atlas Mountains or bobsled to the Arctic—certainly too extreme for me. But a sense of place and time—of journey—is vital for me. My years feel fuller for having been marked by incredible moments in unimposing places: an out-of-the way little restaurant in southern Sicily, a small temple near Kyoto, an inn with an aspiring chef in the Massif Central. In such circumstances, gluttony never seems to occur to you. There you simply feel free.

As I say, it doesn't have to be exotic, just consistently

stimulating. For the past fifteen years, since we first started to rent a house in Provence and especially now that we own one, summer has increasingly been centred on one place. But it's a place of such intensities that for us it remains an undiscovered country: the heat, the crickets, the lavender, the bountiful markets, the mesmeric sunsets—a world full of stimulation. Provence is, in a way, my summer state of mind, the dream of perfect abundance and peace that abides with me year-round. It's not hard getting friends to visit us, although some wonder why I do it so regularly, since taking good care of people can be hard work. Actually, I find it stimulating to help other people relax. My only demand is that when they cross the threshold they surrender all handheld devices—at least telephonic ones. Some city friends really have a hard time and truly don't know how to relax. But once the mind is engaged, once we call their attention to this little wonder and that small miracle, the spirit follows.

Summer weekend meals at home, whether in town or country, whether *à deux* or with friends, are as simple as it gets with us. The fresher the produce, the less you need to do to it. So much of cooking was invented to make something edible out of something unpalatable as found in nature, especially at those times of year when nature offers the least. This necessity has no bearing in summer, when there is plenty to eat raw, and even more that requires only the lightest culinary touch. Besides, who wants to fuss in the heat?

Very little is gastronomically out of bounds, especially if it can go on the barbecue. The scope of food that can be cooked on the barbecue has been deliciously expanded by inventive chefs in recent years. We love barbecued vegetables as starters;

fish, meat, and chicken are a dream; and barbecued peaches for dessert are simply heaven. (We haven't yet devised a barbecue version of baked Alaska, but Edward is working on it.) Picnics are another great way to *faire simple:* some cheese and smoked sausage and ham plus some wine and bread can seem a feast in a field or under a tree, especially after you've walked around and let the surroundings do a number on your senses. And last, though they come first for French women, soups—the indispensable staple for all seasons—have a special part to play in summer. They're the easiest way to release the fleeting intensities of seasonal produce, a light and digestible but extremely satisfying and versatile meal. (If you work at it, you can almost manage never to make the same soup twice.) Most important, they help keep us hydrated in the months when we quite naturally sweat. A hot soup, like hot tea, can cool you off, but a cold soup sometimes seems more palatable; though the range of possibilities may be smaller, when a cold soup is good, it's great.

Many people are surprised by how easily soup can be made, without the bother of an endlessly simmering pot, provided that you have set aside half a day during those long winter months to make some fresh stock, which can be frozen, then thawed as needed. When serving chicken to guests, I often throw the carcass into a stockpot with *mirepoix* (diced root vegetables and bacon) while Edward serves the dessert; they're finishing one meal, I'm starting the next. (If that soothing activity is too much for you, take heart: simple and delicious soup can be made using water, with no stock at all. Or you can buy good chicken stock.) Many vegetables you regularly cook—roasting, grilling, boiling them, whatever suits the particular type—can then be puréed in a mill with a bit of stock or water. This mixture is an excellent base upon which to start inventing with your favourite spices and herbs, perhaps finishing with a dollop of yogurt, a piece of soft cheese, or a powdering of the grated hard stuff. The starch in the puréed vegetables gives the soup body, making unnecessary the cream or eggs of a *bisque* (creamy shellfish soup) or a *velouté* (rich white sauce) as well as the attendant fuss.

QUICK, COLD CUCUMBER SOUP

Serves 4

My Provençal friends call this soup Gazpacho à la Mireille, although it lacks the acidity of its Spanish namesake—something of an acquired taste (as we both are). I love to serve it for lunch on hot, dry summer days. Sometimes I purée it before chilling. The cucumber is, like the leek, a mild diuretic, rich in potassium and low in sodium; both help flush out the toxins. The prawns provide protein; with a slice of baguette or brown bread and some fresh fruit for dessert, the dish makes for a deliciously well-rounded summer lunch in the shade, listening to the crickets, or your children's chatter.

1. Cut the cucumbers in half lengthwise, scoop out the seeds with a teaspoon, and cut into 2cm pieces. Sprinkle with salt, and let stand 10 minutes. Drain and pat dry.
2. Mix the cucumber with the milk. Add the yogurt, lemon juice, and chopped mint, and season with salt and pepper to taste. Serve sprinkled with the prawns and garnished with mint leaves.

INGREDIENTS

2×20cm cucumbers (about 500g), peeled
Salt and freshly ground pepper
250ml cold milk (regular or skimmed)
250g yogurt
Juice of 1 lemon
4 tablespoons finely chopped mint leaves
60g cooked small prawns, peeled and deveined
1 tablespoon mint leaves for garnish

GREEN SOUP

Serves 4

My friend Jacqueline is nuts about greens and is always coming up with new recipes. Here's her latest, which I love.

INGREDIENTS

2 tablespoons olive oil

2 leeks, white parts only, thinly sliced

300g thin string beans, cut into 5cm pieces

200g small broccoli florets

2 medium courgettes, sliced

1.2 litres vegetable stock (or water)

Salt and freshly ground pepper

600ml milk (regular or skimmed)

4 tablespoons finely chopped parsley

1. Warm the oil in a heavy-based, flameproof casserole over medium heat, and cook the leeks for a few minutes. Add the green beans and cook for 5 minutes, stirring occasionally. Add the broccoli, courgettes, and vegetable stock. Bring to a boil, then reduce the heat and simmer for 20 to 25 minutes. When the vegetables are tender, put through a vegetable mill.

2. Return the milled vegetables to the pot. Season with salt and pepper to taste, add the milk, and cook, stirring, over medium heat for 10 minutes more. Sprinkle with parsley, and serve.

BEETROOT SOUP

Serves 4

For taste and texture, nothing beats beets in a salad or soup. I make this soup in advance and serve it right out of the refrigerator. I ask my guests if they want theirs the traditional Russian way (hot with a swirl of sour cream) or the French way (cold, as here).

1. Combine the beetroot and yogurt, and stir well. Add the shallots, garlic and cumin. Season with salt and pepper to taste, and mix well. Refrigerate for at least 2 hours.
2. Serve in chilled soup bowls after correcting seasoning and sprinkling with the dill.

INGREDIENTS

500g fresh beetroot, cooked and cubed

250g yogurt

2 tablespoons finely chopped shallots

1 teaspoon finely chopped garlic

Pinch of cumin

Salt and freshly ground pepper

2 tablespoons chopped dill

COLD FENNEL SOUP

Serves 4

My friend Christine is a fennel freak (not to be confused with fenugreek), and I daresay I am, too. All summer long, I eat it raw or cooked, by itself or in combination, as in this soup. In Indian restaurants, you'll often find the seeds in a little bowl as you are leaving—like parsley, they are nature's great breath freshener. Christine makes the soup using small, young, tender fennel bulbs. Being in Provence, she adds the local brousse *cheese, but I have made it in New York using fresh ricotta with comparable results.*

INGREDIENTS

1.2 litres vegetable stock (or water)

500g fennel bulbs, cleaned and chopped

125ml ricotta cheese

1 tablespoon olive oil

2 tablespoons lemon juice

Salt and freshly ground pepper

4 tablespoons finely chopped parsley

Pinch of paprika

1. In a large saucepan, bring the stock to a boil. Add the fennel pieces, and simmer for 20 minutes. Put the fennel and stock through a blender or vegetable mill, using a blade with small holes. Let cool, and refrigerate for 2 hours.

2. Add the ricotta, oil, and lemon juice to the chilled soup. Mix well, and season with salt and pepper to taste. Serve in soup dishes, garnishing with the parsley and paprika.

SUMMER-VEGETABLE SOUP WITH CHEESE

Serves 4

Those females in my family, with their tireless imaginations, would find no end of ways to slip in an extra food group, turning a soup into a more nutritionally balanced meal. Why make a béchamel when protein is so easy to add in the form of a little cheese? With good bread and some fruit, how could you want for more?

1. Warm the oil in a large heavy-based, flameproof casserole over medium heat, and sauté the onion and shallots until translucent. Add the potatoes, carrots, sweet pepper, and 1.5 litres water. Bring to a boil, then lower the heat and simmer for 15 to 20 minutes.
2. Sprinkle with the feta, and add the lemon juice. Season with salt and pepper to taste, and serve.

INGREDIENTS

2 tablespoons olive oil

1 onion, peeled and finely chopped

2 shallots, peeled and finely chopped

500g potatoes, peeled and cubed

500g carrots, peeled and sliced

1 sweet pepper (green, yellow, or red), seeds removed, sliced into 5cm strips

180g feta cheese

1 tablespoon lemon juice

Salt and freshly ground pepper

COLD CARROT SOUP

Serves 4

INGREDIENTS

675g carrots, peeled

1 medium-sized potato, peeled

320ml cold milk (regular or skimmed)

3 tablespoons finely chopped basil

Salt and freshly ground pepper

1. In a large saucepan, bring 750ml salted water to a simmer, and cook the carrots and potatoes until tender, about 20 minutes. Cool, and put through a vegetable mill. Refrigerate for at least 2 hours.
2. Add the milk and basil, mix well, season with salt and pepper to taste, and serve very cold.

MELON SOUP

Serves 4

As refreshing as it gets, and a delicious tease for those with a sweet tooth.

1. In a large saucepan, bring 1 litre water to a boil, then add the ground almonds. Bring back to a boil over low heat, then turn off the heat, cover, and leave 15 minutes to infuse. Filter through a fine sieve.
2. In a large bowl, beat the egg yolks with the sour cream. Add the warm infusion a little at a time, stirring all the while. Allow the mixture to cool. Season wth salt and pepper to taste.
3. Cut the melon in half and remove the seeds. Cut the flesh into small dice, and add to the soup. Serve with a garnish of dill and almond slivers.

INGREDIENTS

90g almonds, finely ground

2 egg yolks

2 tablespoons sour cream

Salt and freshly ground pepper

1 melon

2 tablespoons chopped dill

45g almond slivers, toasted

VICHYSSOISE (COLD LEEK & POTATO SOUP)

Serves 4

INGREDIENTS

30g unsalted butter

4 leeks, white parts only, finely chopped

1 onion, minced

225g potatoes, peeled and diced

1 litre chicken stock

Salt and freshly ground pepper

60ml sour cream

Dill for garnish

1. Melt the butter in a large, heavy-based, flameproof casserole over medium heat. Add the leeks and onion, and cook for 10 minutes over medium-low heat. Add the potatoes, then the stock, and bring to a boil. Lower the heat, and simmer for 35 minutes, partly covered.
2. Put through a vegetable mill (and then, if you want a very thin soup, press through a sieve). Return the liquid to the casserole, and season with salt and pepper to taste. Bring back to a boil, and whisk in the sour cream.
3. When the soup has cooled, refrigerate for at least 6 hours. Serve cold, preferably in coffee cups, and sprinkled with chopped dill.

N.B. A VERSION MADE BY AN ITALIAN FRIEND IN PROVENCE REPLACES LEEKS WITH COURGETTES (REDUCE COOKING TIME BY 10 MINUTES) AND USES MASCARPONE INSTEAD OF SOUR CREAM AND BASIL INSTEAD OF DILL. *ASSOLUTAMENTE DELICIOSA.*

French women and virtually all foodies rave about tomatoes in season. If you've heard nothing else about the magic of seasonality, you have almost surely heard (dozens of times) that the difference between a fresh tomato in season and a supermarket tomato in winter (or summer, for that matter) is night and day. A specimen of the real thing can seem like a meal; the common counterfeit defames even a BLT.

If daffodils and strawberries tell me it's spring, nothing says summer like the scent of a ripe tomato. Why do we wax lyrical over this most common vegetable, which everyone learns and then forgets is a fruit? (Important distinction, since you might *par hasard* put one in the refrigerator, and nobody would do that with a ripe fruit, would they? Of course not.) The thing about the tomato, my favourite fruit that isn't a strawberry, is that it actually *is* rather like a strawberry: of all fruits, these two have been optimally designed to capture the energy of the sun and turn it into some of the best eats on earth.

Now, do a tomato wrong—pick it unripe, ship it north, set it to brood on a supermarket shelf—and you'll get exactly what you deserve: a potato with a little extra lycopene. Actually, I'm being grossly unfair to the potato, but tubers will have their moment in winter. For now, however, it's summer, and in summer you should permit tomatoes to do their thing: let the sunshine in. The best tomatoes (and basil, for that matter) I ever tasted were in Puglia, Italy. French women brook no chauvinism where produce is concerned: best is best. Maybe it was the local combination of heat and dryness, but the intensity of the flavours was unequalled, and the Italians know a good thing when they taste it; on the autostrada near the tomato canning plant in Avellino I've seen caravans of trucks in summer laden with tomatoes on their way to becoming sauce. (By the way, a good tomato sauce in a can or jar is worth ten rotten tomatoes on the shelf: come winter, it's the best way to keep this sacrament of summer in your life and profit from its matchless concentration of nutrients. And, oh, the taste!)

An old friend of mine has tomatoes every day for breakfast during the season, which is basically the summer months, wherever he is. I suspect that, being an older gent, he's not only hooked on the taste but wants the lycopene, a known prostate-cancer inhibitor. A cousin who's never had a prostate, however, also likes tomatoes for her breakfast. She used to make her own *confiture de tomates,* a jam of seedless tomatoes (though she would keep the skin, which makes it more like marmalade), puréeing them with a pinch of sugar and adding a vanilla pod before transferring it to a sterile jar. At breakfast, she has her slice of bread with the confit smeared on it, hold the butter. Tell me it's not a fruit!

In New York, I could not survive summer without New Jersey beefsteak tomatoes, a large variety with a distinctive flavour. Brought to market fresh from the farm, they are delicious sliced and served with slivers of mozzarella, a light dressing, and fresh basil—what the Italians call an *insalata Caprese,* though it's enjoyed many places far from Capri. I apply the same recipe in Provence, where the day's main meal is lunch (as often as not followed by an afternoon dodge-the-heat siesta, then, towards sunset, an outing for some illicit raspberry picking from the communal bushes along the road). Late dinner, served outdoors, often consists of no more than a tomato salad with some nice country bread to mop up the juice and dressing, fresh goat's cheese, and various fresh fruits for dessert. Sounds like not much? Trust me, no one leaves the table unsatisfied.

A real treat for us tomato heads is an entire meal based on them. To this day the only chef I have found who can truly pull it off is Christian Étienne in Avignon. I have sent friends to him who liked it so much, they had to go back the same week. The versatility of tomatoes is such that you can contemplate even a multi-course meal centred on them without a chance of boredom. And no American ever sees a tomato dessert coming!

MIREILLE'S SIMPLE TOMATO SALAD

Serves 4

INGREDIENTS

6 medium tomatoes
1½ teaspoons coarse salt
4 tablespoons olive oil
Freshly ground pepper
4 tablespoons basil cut into chiffonade (coarsely shredded)

1. Slice the tomatoes 5mm thick, and spread equally over 4 flat dishes. Sprinkle with the salt, and let stand for 20 minutes. (This is the trick that extracts flavour.) Then remove the excess water with paper towels.
2. Drizzle each dish of tomatoes with 1 tablespoon of the oil, and season with pepper to taste. Sprinkle with the basil, and serve with country bread to dunk into that delicious juice and clean the plate.

OPTIONAL: SOME PEOPLE LIKE TO ADD A DROP OR TWO OF VINEGAR OR SOME FINELY SLICED ONIONS.

SWEET-AND-SOUR FRUIT-AND-VEGETABLE SALAD

Serves 4

1. Steam the beans for 8 minutes, and set aside.
2. Steam the sweetcorn for 3 minutes; cool, then slice the kernels off the cob with a sharp knife.
3. Sprinkle the avocado slices with the lemon juice.
4. For the dressing, put the mustard, salt and pepper to taste, and vinegar into a bowl, and stir well. Add both oils, and whisk well.
5. Put the lettuce, and all the fruits and vegetables into a serving bowl, pour the dressing over, and toss gently.

INGREDIENTS

225g fresh thin string beans

2 cobs sweetcorn, husks and threads removed

1 avocado, peeled and cut into thin slices

Juice of 1 lemon

1 teaspoon Meaux or other wholegrain mustard

Salt and freshly ground pepper

2 tablespoons red wine vinegar

3 tablespoons olive oil

3 tablespoons sunflower oil

1 head lettuce, torn into leaves, rinsed, and dried

1 grapefruit, peeled, sliced, and pith removed

275g fresh pineapple, cubed

ORECCHIETTE WITH TUNA AND COURGETTES

Serves 4

INGREDIENTS

350g orecchiette pasta

Salt and freshly ground pepper

2 medium courgettes, thinly sliced

15g unsalted butter *or* 1 tablespoon olive oil

2 cloves garlic

500g cherry tomatoes, halved

180g canned tuna in olive oil

4 tablespoons olive oil

2 tablespoons chopped basil

1. Bring 2 litres salted water to a rolling boil in a large saucepan. Cook the orecchiette according to packet directions.

2. Place the courgettes in a large serving bowl. Drain the pasta over the bowl, and let the courgettes stand in the hot cooking water for 2 minutes to soften. Drain, and return the courgettes to bowl.

3. Melt the butter or heat the oil in a large frying pan. Sauté the garlic and tomatoes over medium heat until softened. Remove from heat. Add the tuna. Toss with the pasta and courgettes, and drizzle the oil over it all. Season with salt and pepper to taste, and sprinkle with the basil. Serve immediately.

RED MULLET WITH SPINACH *EN PAPILLOTE*

Serves 4

INGREDIENTS

2 teaspoons olive oil

500g spinach, washed and dried

4 tablespoons crème fraîche

8 red mullet fillets, about 60g each

4 teaspoons sliced shallots

8 slices of lime

Salt and freshly ground pepper

1. Preheat the oven to gas mark 2/150°C.
2. Cut 8 pieces of parchment paper (or aluminum foil) into squares large enough to cover each fish fillet and leave a 5cm border all around. Lightly brush 4 squares with oil.
3. In the centre of each oiled square, layer a quarter of the spinach, 1 tablespoon of crème fraîche, 2 fillets, 1 teaspoon of shallots, and 2 slices of lime. Season with salt and pepper to taste.
4. Place the remaining parchment squares on top of the fillets and fold up the edges to form parcels. Simply double-folding each of the four sides is enough to seal each parcel. Put the *papillotes* on a baking sheet, and bake in the preheated oven for 15 to 20 minutes.
5. Serve at once by setting each *papillote* on a plate.

N.B. YOU CAN USE SOLE OR SNAPPER INSTEAD OF RED MULLET.

BARBECUED DUCK WITH PEACHES

Serves 4

INGREDIENTS

1 teaspoon honey
Juice of ½ lemon
2 duck breasts (4 *magrets*)
½ teaspoon butter
4 yellow peaches or nectarines, stoned and cut into slices (8 per peach)
Salt and freshly ground pepper

1. Preheat the grill.
2. Mix the honey with 60ml water and the lemon juice in a saucepan, place over medium heat, and stir until dissolved. This will take a couple of minutes. Let cool for 5 minutes.
3. Pour half the honey mixture on the duck breasts.
4. Melt the butter in a frying pan over medium heat and add the peach slices. Pour the rest of the honey mixture over and cook for a few minutes until the peaches are tender but not mushy.
5. Grill the duck 3 minutes on each side. Let rest a few minutes, and slice on the diagonal. Remove duck to a serving plate and cover with the peaches and their juice. Season with salt and pepper to taste.

N.B. SERVE THIS DISH WITH COURGETTES OR THIN STRING BEANS TO ADD COLOUR.

CHICKEN WITH PASTIS

Serves 8

Pastis is the Provençal drink par excellence.

Let me be honest: I have never been able to drink pastis, the anise-based liqueur . . . too strong for me. Many of my women friends feel the same. I love the smell of it, but when I grew up, I saw too many village pétanque *players drinking lots of pastis, and the final picture was not so nice. It goes to your head pretty quickly, and the stuff being so refreshing (30 millilitres or so mixed with water and ice), it's easy to go for seconds . . . and thirds.*

Now, there is finally an alternative, and I must say I love it. It's pastis without the alcohol and without the sugar. On the other hand, to cook with pastis you must use the real thing, and it is delicious and available in wine shops.

In Provence, we cook rabbit with it, and my friend Georgette introduced me to this dish years ago. I've tried it with chicken for my New York friends and find the dish equally yummy. One more way to cook chicken.

INGREDIENTS

FOR THE MARINADE:

150ml pastis

80ml olive oil

Salt and freshly ground pepper

1. For the marinade: Mix the pastis and oil. Season with salt and pepper to taste.
2. Arrange the chicken pieces in one layer in a shallow dish. Drizzle with the marinade and cover the dish with clingfilm. Refrigerate for 2 hours (it's even better to do the day before and let marinate overnight).

[continued]

1×1.5kg chicken, cut into 8 pieces
3 tablespoons olive oil
2 onions, peeled and sliced
4 tomatoes, diced
4 cloves garlic, peeled and finely chopped
2 teaspoons fennel seeds
50g black olives, stoned and chopped
40g basil leaves, shredded
Salt and freshly ground pepper

3. In a heavy-based, flameproof casserole warm the oil over a medium heat. Add the onions and cook until softened, about 6 minutes. Add the tomatoes, garlic, and fennel seeds. Continue cooking for 15 minutes, stirring occasionally.

4. Add the chicken pieces and marinade to the casserole. Cover and simmer over medium-low heat for about 30 minutes. Add the olives and a third of the basil. Cover and continue cooking until the chicken is tender, about 30 minutes. Season with salt and pepper to taste and garnish with the rest of the basil. Serve immediately.

N.B. YOU CAN SERVE THIS WITH RICE OR NOODLES. A RED CÔTES DU RHÔNE GOES NICELY, TOO.

TRICOLOUR PEPPERS

Serves 4

The pepper is another New World plant that has taken root in a big way in the Old. Far more than with asparagus, colour counts for peppers' taste. The common green variety, really only a pepper picked unripe, is less subtle and less delicately flavoured. The reds and yellows, which appear later, have had more of a chance to soak up the sun, making their skin thinner and more tender and their flesh sweeter. These baubles dazzle the eye and palate alike. They can be enjoyed equally well raw in a salad or stewed or grilled to enhance their extraordinary sweetness. As with strawberries, small ugly specimens are better than airbrushed symmetrical giants.

I love the taste and the colour and the versatility of this yummy vegetable, but I must confess that I don't understand people who spend time roasting them to get rid of the skin. I love the skin, which has lots of nutrients I want to keep. Almost every Saturday I buy one or two of each colour at the market, and here is one way I consume them.

INGREDIENTS

6 sweet peppers (2 each of red, orange, yellow)

1. Cut the peppers in half through the stem. Discard the stems, membrane, and seeds. Cut into large strips.
2. Put the red peppers at the bottom, followed by the orange and yellow. Steam for 6 to 8 minutes. *Voilà*.

I serve them hot as a side dish with fish, white meat, or pasta dishes. All one needs to add is a drizzle of olive oil and a pinch of seasoning. I refrigerate the leftovers, then use them for lunch during the week, with a piece of leftover chicken, tuna, or salmon, or a few prawns, or for a salad lunch over some mixed greens and a hard-boiled egg or chunks of feta cheese. Then all I need to add is a mustard-vinegar-oil dressing and always lots of chopped parsley. And, of course, the simplest thing is to serve them at room temperature on a *tartine* (a thick slice of country or rye bread) with a few grains of salt, a drizzle of olive oil, and parsley.

. . . . . .

WATERCRESS COULIS

Serves 4

1. Rinse the watercress well, and steam for 5 minutes.
2. Toss with the crème fraîche (or equivalent). Toss with the egg yolks and nutmeg, and season with salt and pepper to taste. Serve immediately.

INGREDIENTS

2 bunches watercress

4 tablespoons crème fraîche, sour cream, or yogurt

2 egg yolks

¼ teaspoon freshly grated nutmeg

Salt and freshly ground pepper

N.B. IT IS ADVISABLE NOT TO SERVE DISHES INCORPORATING UNCOOKED EGGS TO PREGNANT WOMEN, SMALL CHILDREN, THE ELDERLY, AND PEOPLE WITH IMMUNE-SYSTEM DEFICIENCIES.

AUBERGINE TAPENADE

Serves 4

INGREDIENTS

Salt and freshly ground pepper
2 medium aubergines, unpeeled, cut into 2cm slices
4 tablespoons olive oil
1 red onion, peeled and thinly sliced
500g chopped tomatoes
125ml red wine vinegar
2 tablespoons capers
8 green olives, stoned
8 black olives, stoned

1. Salt the aubergine slices, and let stand for 20 minutes. Rinse with cold water, and pat dry. (This process makes the aubergine more tender and less bitter.)
2. Warm the oil in a large frying pan over medium heat. Cook the aubergine and onion until brown and lightly crisp. Remove from the pan.
3. Add the tomatoes and vinegar to the pan, and cook for a few minutes over medium heat. Add the capers and olives, and season with salt and pepper to taste. Toss with the aubergine-onion mixture, and serve immediately.

VEGETABLES WITH YOGURT DRESSING

Serves 6

1. Put the mustard and vinegar into a bowl, and mix well. Whisk in the oil, then add the yogurt and chives. Season with salt and pepper to taste. Whisk well.
2. Pour the dressing over the remaining ingredients, and toss gently. Serve with pitta bread.

INGREDIENTS

2 teaspoons Meaux or other wholegrain mustard

2 tablespoons red wine vinegar

6 tablespoons walnut or hazelnut oil

125g yogurt

2 tablespoons chopped chives

Salt and freshly ground pepper

6 medium new potatoes, peeled and sliced, and cooked in boiling water for 10 minutes

1 large cucumber, peeled and cubed

2 tomatoes, cut into 8 pieces

4 stalks celery, cut into 1cm pieces

80g raisins

Barbecue, as I've said, is our secret weapon in summer. Few French people will admit it, but they envy the American—and Australian—knack for the grill, with its *Quest for Fire* immediacy to food. In the past few decades I've seen many of my compatriots return from visits to America toting barbecue paraphernalia.

Barbecue is not only perfect for entertaining. It also fits in with the trend among many French to desacralize gastronomy, keeping what is pure and elemental while forgoing the stuffiness of service and dining ritual—women still bring their lapdogs to restaurants, but men don't often wear ties. Some formalities will persist, as they should: close though the French may get to a BBQ shack, you will never find an eatery serving the finest quality steak on paper plates. And ketchup on fries? *Jamais.* But in most other respects, the French have shown themselves eager adaptors of this excellent American ritual. At Houston's renowned Goode Company Barbeque, I observed a sign inviting patrons to bring their own meat in for barbecuing—there, deep in the heart of Texas, an invitation to planned and thoughtful eating that could warm even a French woman's heart. Nowadays in France—all over Europe, really—you can buy any model barbecue you want, including gas grills like the one we've enjoyed in New York for sixteen years!

I fell in love with barbecue the first time Edward grilled me a steak. A friend had given us an extraordinary bottle of red wine, and so Edward decided to splurge on a porterhouse. As the grill heated he sprinkled the meat with just a few small pieces of garlic here and there and poured on the juice of a lemon, then grilled it with some portobello mushrooms. Seasoning took place at the table. Of such simple things are memories made.

The French being the French, and perpetually innovating in their obsessions with food, quality, and pleasure, they have taken a turn back to the future, rediscovering a nineteenth-century Spanish invention that does the grill one better, at least healthwise. *La plancha,* a magically conductive steel griddle, allows one to cook very fast without much fat, and because it is a flat, unbroken surface, there is less risk of charring the food. Purists will complain that this defeats the purpose of barbecue, but doctors agree that charred food in quantity is carcinogenic—don't we have enough of that in our food chain already?

Though it wants for the glow of coals, the *plancha* offers the great virtue of cooking, as chefs say, *à la minute*—basically, just before you're sitting down to eat. At the same time it preserves the textures and flavours of fresh produce. And not least, it can be used both indoors and out. The Spanish have used the *plancha* for years to make tapas, their very extemporaneous and varied food of small servings, which, naturally, the French adore. Variety is no problem, because you can cook most things in a matter of minutes once the *plancha* is really hot.

Maybe it was my American nostalgia. Or maybe it was the odd pleasure of dislocation, as Woody Allen expresses it: "When I'm in Paris I want to be in New York, and when I am in New York I wish I were in Paris." But one year Edward and I were in Spain around Thanksgiving, and I longed for turkey.

A friend in Barcelona indulged me with a delightful Spanish interpretation of turkey escalopes with Marsala and sage. Just two hours before our expatriate version of the feast that would have taken all day to prepare *à l'américaine,* she had put a small slice of the incomparable Iberico ham on each turkey slice and overlaid that with a sliver of mozzarella and some fresh sage leaves. She then rolled up the escalopes and secured each with toothpicks before transferring them to a deep dish; over it all she poured some Marsala wine (sherry works well, too), olive oil, and a dash of salt and pepper. After basting the escalopes a few times, she popped them into the fridge until it was time to cook them: eight to ten minutes on the preheated *plancha.* In the last two minutes, she added the lovely accompaniment of apple slices. We enjoyed it with a wonderful Rioja, but I have served the meal at home very happily with a good Zinfandel. Anyone who has suffered the blandness of the comical misnomer that is Butterball should give this delicious Thanksgiving *à la catalan* a try. It may not supplant the traditional roast turkey with all the trimmings in autumn. But in summer, you'll be thankful for an easy little taste of tradition while the leaves are still on the trees. The only thing missing will be the apples. Apples can be found in summer, as everything can, but they aren't meant to be. And with so many alternatives, we shouldn't miss them too much.

TUTTI FRUTTI

The summer offers such an orgy of fruits that I luxuriate in them *au naturel.* Not that *I'm* in the altogether; they are. I eat them as freshly picked as possible, at room temperature, usually as plain as nature gave them to us. (Okay, occasionally I put a dollop of vanilla ice cream on the berries or peaches.) Strawberries, blueberries, blackberries, varieties of cherries, white peaches, yellow peaches, plums large and small, apricots, figs, and all sorts of melons: most of the fruits you can name are summer fruits, and in summer they are so plentiful that even the big supermarkets sometimes have something good to offer. Typically, though, they over-chill produce, and it sits past its prime. Fortunately, where there are fresh vegetables, there are also fresh fruits. And if you can't be bothered to seek them both out, you are depriving yourself of one of the most essential ways French women fill their summers with eating pleasure without getting fat. (You're also missing the convenience of a perfect dessert that needs virtually no preparation.)

True, French women have it a little easier than most, with a gastronomic culture built around the market and a government that subsidizes the quality, not the quantity, of its agriculture. But that's the way the people have always had it, and that's the way they want it. In America, as elsewhere, supply chases demand. A relative indifference to premium summer produce is precisely what limits its availability. But if you plant it, they will come. Farmers' markets are the future, at least concerning those foodstuffs in which freshness counts. If there isn't a market very near you now, chances are there will be soon. Meanwhile, vote with your feet and find the nearest one. Don't miss out. With a balanced consumption of fruit and a cultivated taste for its splendours, summer can be a season-long holiday from the risk of getting fat. And we all deserve that kind of a break, don't we?

Even in an ideal world, not all the fruits of summer are destined to be eaten fresh, and the perfectly ripe cannot always be found. Sometimes we must make do with what we can find, even in farmers' markets. Apricots are one of my very favourite fruits, but as motivated as I am, I'm still hard pressed to find great ones, save right off the tree. More often than not, most of what's for sale tends to be woolly and lacking in that true apricot flavour, knowledge of which more often comes from jams than from encounters with ripe apricots. Cooked preparations concentrate the flavours and the natural sugars. Those of you who have experienced a fresh, juicy apricot can vouch for the rarity of same at any distance from where the best grow—in Turkey or California, for example. In my part of Provence they cultivate an *acidulée* variety available for only a few weeks. That doesn't give one much time. We savour what we can. At home, my mother would preserve them, to produce wonderful tarts in the winter. (Sour cherries and rhubarb are other favourites of the women in my family, who tend to like their sweetness cut with a bit of tartness.)

BAKED APRICOTS

Serves 4

INGREDIENTS

16 apricots, halved and stoned

1 teaspoon vanilla essence

180ml dry Vermouth

5 tablespoons honey

1. Preheat the oven to gas mark 4/180°C.
2. Lay the apricots, skin-side up, in overlapping rows in an ovenproof dish. Mix the vanilla with the Vermouth, and pour over the apricots. Drizzle the honey over, and bake in the preheated oven for 20 minutes, until the apricots are tender.
3. Allow to cool, then chill. Serve with crème fraîche or whipped cream (on top of yogurt is another option).

GRILLED PEACHES WITH CINNAMON AND ROSEMARY

Serves 4

Peaches, like apricots, demand to be eaten when perfectly ripe, but because they bruise so easily, they are frequently picked when they feel like baseballs. Set aside, they will mature, but you can't expect the peachiness of a ripe picking. Keep an eye out for those—you'll know them by the scent. Lesser peaches can be grilled, however, with excellent results.

INGREDIENTS

4 peaches
1 tablespoon sugar
1/8 teaspoon cinnamon
2 tablespoons olive oil
4 sprigs rosemary, finely chopped

1. Preheat the grill.
2. Rinse the peaches, pat dry, cut in half, and remove the stones. Place the peach halves in a baking dish. Mix the sugar and cinnamon, stir in the oil, and brush the mixture over the peaches. Sprinkle with the rosemary. Marinate for 10 minutes, turning over and basting once.
3. Grill the marinated peaches for 2 to 3 minutes on each side, until they are tender but not soft. Serve immediately, alone or with a scoop of vanilla or cinnamon ice cream.

FIGS WITH RICOTTA

Serves 4

INGREDIENTS

4 tablespoons honey
4 strips orange peel
1 tablespoon orange zest
8 fresh figs
250g ricotta cheese

1. Mix 125ml water, honey, orange zest and strips in a large frying pan over medium heat, stirring until the honey has dissolved, about 2 minutes. Bring to a boil, and cook until the syrup has reduced and thickened, 5 minutes or so.
2. Remove from the heat. Add the figs to the pan, and gently coat with the syrup.
3. Spoon a quarter of the ricotta into each serving bowl, add two figs, and drizzle with syrup.

. . . . . .

The simplicity of French women's self-styling is never handier than in summer. I often recommend starting the season with a uniform in mind. A few pairs of flattering trousers, a skirt, and fine cotton T-shirts. Buy the nicest you can. It's better to have a few good pieces than two weeks' worth of shoddy clothes. The shirts—mercerized or knitted cotton of good quality gives you a base of simplicity without looking slovenly—should be easily washed and ironed. Simple is best, though a few buttons, a ribbed weave, or subtle piping announce that you are not sporting Fruit of the Loom. The trousers, if of a light tropical wool, can be hung in a steamy bathroom or pressed with a not-too-hot iron several times before you need to take them to the dry cleaner (dry cleaning wears out fibres and makes new clothes look worn, so do it sparingly). If the trousers are linen, their wrinkling is perfectly stylish. With their nice T-shirts and trousers or simple sheath dresses, French women create different looks with accessories.

The jewellery does not require a trip to Cartier. I have a string of chunky wooden beads I bought in the souk in Marrakesh, and they lend a very sophisticated touch to a T-shirt and trousers. This year white beads were all the rage and didn't need to be made of ivory to look elegant. (Who would be so cruel to Babar, anyway?) You could buy a modish ornament at a fancy boutique, but often a look-alike piece from some other emporium—or even a street vendor—will create the same effect for a lot less money. (Makes sense, since the more determinedly fashionable the look, the less likely you'll want to embrace it next season.) With jewellery, less is most definitely more. If you have a choker making a strong statement, you don't need elaborate earrings—*de trop*. To be in fashion as well as stylish (the latter being a more evolved and personal state of being, a mind-set as much as a look), limit yourself to an element or two—a colour, a shape of handbag—that signals you are not totally oblivious to the pages of *Vogue* and *Elle*. Remember: French women do not "buy the mannequin". Nor do they adhere militantly to the haute bourgeois ideal of always looking totally "done". They do one part uniform, one part fashion statement, and one part strictly idiosyncratic and personal. The specific choices are yours.

This way, you should navigate the street chicly in summer. But what of the air-conditioned bubble? Don't blow money on trendy glad rags if you haven't invested in a classic crew-neck cardigan in light cashmere if you can afford it. It is always elegant, can be draped over the shoulders or folded into a tote, and save you from hypothermia at your desk. A good cashmere cardigan, occasionally hand washed and combed for pilling, can last for years. Next summer you can start building your collection, adding a new sweater each year. (A little quality goes a long way—you needn't bankrupt yourself buying *en masse.*) Start with a neutral colour you can wear all the time.

Another means of deliverance from the artificial Arctic is the scarf, which perhaps sounds like the last thing one would need in summer. In fact, like a cunning string of beads, a neckerchief can dress up and lend individuality to a simple tee-and-skirt ensemble while taking the chill off, too. When not wrapped in one, French women keep the scarf handily tied to the handles of their handbags. This is part of the effortless look commonly called BCBG (*bon chic, bon genre*)—half style, half attitude, meant to channel the *bien dans sa peau* spirit if not taken to fussy extremes. I wear cotton, muslin, or chiffon scarves in summer, and I tend to wear them differently from the way I wear them in other seasons.

Belt Scarf

One of the easiest ways to bring a scarf along to lunch or a shopping excursion is to wear it as a belt, unfurling it across your shoulders if you feel cold. For this you will need an oblong scarf.

1. Fold and refold lengthwise until you have created a band about thirteen centimetres wide.
2. Wrap the scarf about your hips and tie with a square knot

or bow. The bow side of the belt will be crimped to about eight centimetres wide.

3. Slide the bow to one hip, and spread the band downward on the opposite hip to create an isosceles triangle with its point at the bow.

Hip Wrap

A chic way to carry a large, square scarf.

1. Fold it diagonally in half. Wrap it around your waist with the triangle pointing downward behind you.
2. Tie the two ends in the front with a square knot. Tug the two sides down over your hips.

Stole

The simplest way—and a very common one—to wear a scarf is to transform your belt scarf or hip wrap into a stole.

1. Take the unfolded scarf and simply drape it evenly over your shoulders. The ends should fall into the crooks of your elbows.
2. Still cold? Pull one end to lengthen it and toss this longer side over the opposite shoulder for a double layer of fabric.

Pool or Beach Scarf Skirt or Dress

Long gone are the days of bronzing myself on the Riviera with teenage abandon (back when we still believed the sun could do us nothing but good). Today I wrap myself a bit when wearing a swimsuit in the company of strangers—except in the water, of course. And while a whole retail sector has sprung up to furnish "cruisewear", I find a lightweight scarf can cover it, and me. I wear it as a skirt with a one-piece, as a dress with a two-piece. You'll need a large, square scarf for a skirt and an even larger one, square or rectangular, for a dress. With a scarf wrap you can always make a quick exit from the beach to lunch without going indoors to change.

For the skirt:

1. Fold the square in half diagonally.
2. Flip or fold the long length into a little belt or band, wrap around your waist, and tie over your hips or behind your back. Adjust for length. *Et voilà.*

For the dress:

1. Drape the open scarf across your back; pass an end under each arm, and tie a tight knot in front.
2. Fold the upper edge of the scarf inward to conceal the knot. Pull down on that part to give the neckline a slight V for an illusion of constructedness.

BRINGING SUMMER INDOORS

The indoor gardener can do herself a favour with potted herbs. Among them, terribly delicate basil almost never makes it to market with its leaves intact; a small potted plant set on a windowsill will repay the small effort of its cultivation with fragrant leaves. As for other types of indoor planting, they're almost beside the point, since summer is to be met on its own turf, strictly outside. You hardly need visit a botanical garden, though I love doing that, to see the seasonal handiwork. The trees may have lost their blossom, but the roses are out, and so are all the annuals—among my personal favourites, salvia, lantana, and cosmos.

The feast is not so moveable for the seasonal container gardener, as a lot of outdoor plants simply don't do well indoors. Geraniums, for example, thrive in our terrace pots and window boxes but are far from happy to come inside. The potted plants that can make the migration well enough are the delicate ones, such as miniature roses and even marigolds, which as always can be complemented with *plantes vertes* for bulk and contrast, although their lifespan inside is akin to those of cut flowers. If you are lucky enough to have watched your garden grow, fresh-cut flowers are your reward. In her flower shop my acquaintance Anaïs has a sign reading *"Qui plante son jardin plante son bonheur"*—she who plants her garden plants her happiness—and I couldn't put it better. For the rest of us there is the surrogate garden of the market or the florist.

But even with flowers in summer, abundance has its limitations. I certainly never saw impatiens while I was growing up in France or when I first came to America, but after 1990 they were ubiquitous. Fed by watering systems and adopted as "a look" by international hotel and resort chains, impatiens can be seen from Florida to the Middle East, from China to Europe, and even on our terrace before we'd had enough of them. They are hardy, impatient to bloom, and provide a nice blanket of colour, especially in shady areas; but they have simply become too commonplace. Even in the season of abundance, more than enough can spoil a good thing.

MONDAY

Breakfast

Blueberry Baby Smoothie (www.mireilleguiliano.com)
1 slice multigrain bread, toasted and buttered
30g slice ham
Coffee or tea

Lunch

Vichyssoise (page 120)
1 hard-boiled egg
1 slice watermelon
Non-calorific beverage

Dinner

Grilled chicken with thyme
Aubergine Tapenade (page 134)
1 cob sweetcorn
Green salad
Grilled Peaches with Cinnamon and Rosemary (page 142)
1 glass white, rosé, or red wine

TUESDAY

Breakfast

30g Jarlsberg cheese
60g muesli
125ml skimmed milk
80g strawberries
Coffee or tea

Lunch

Tomato-mozzarella salad
1 slice country or wholemeal bread
150g cherries
Non-calorific beverage

Dinner

Snapper with Almonds (www.mireilleguiliano.com)
80g asparagus with 1 teaspoon olive oil
80g new potatoes
Mireille's Simple Tomato Salad (page 124)
150g mixed fruit salad
1 glass rosé or red wine

WEDNESDAY

Breakfast

2 prunes
1 soft-boiled egg
30g slice of salami or ham
2 slices baguette, buttered
Coffee or tea

Lunch

Cold Beetroot and Yogurt Summer Soup (www.mireilleguiliano.com)
80g fish
125g yogurt
1 slice olive bread
1 nectarine
Non-calorific beverage

Dinner

Orecchiette with Tuna and Courgettes (page 126)
Green salad
1 slice melon
1 glass red wine

THURSDAY

Breakfast

1 slice prosciutto
60g bran cereal
125ml skimmed milk
80g raspberries
Coffee or tea

Lunch

Yogurt with cucumber
100g green vegetables
3 fresh apricots
Non-calorific beverage

Dinner

120g veal escalope
1 large grilled tomato
70g Brown Rice with Peas (page 46)
150g mixed berries
1 glass red or white wine

FRIDAY

Breakfast

125ml tomato juice
125g yogurt
150g mixed berries
1 slice wholemeal bread, toasted and buttered
Coffee or tea

Lunch

Ratatouille (www.mireilleguiliano.com)
1 slice wholemeal bread
30g goat's cheese
1 peach
1 square chocolate
Non-calorific beverage

Dinner

Halibut *en Papillote* (www.mireilleguiliano.com)
Watercress Coulis (page 133)
5g unsalted butter
30g blue cheese
3 crackers
2 plums
1 glass red or white wine

SATURDAY

Breakfast

125ml freshly squeezed orange juice or 1 orange
125g yogurt
1 slice sultana bread
Coffee or tea

Lunch

Melon Soup (page 119)
Mini cheese board (3 types, 30g each)
1 slice wholemeal bread
Green salad
150g strawberries
Non-calorific beverage

Dinner

Red Mullet with Spinach *en Papillote* (pag 127)
Tricolour Peppers (page 131)
Mixed salad leaves
1 slice blueberry tart
1 glass Champagne or sparkling wine or white wine

SUNDAY

Breakfast

80g mixed berries
125g yogurt
1 croissant
Coffee or tea

Lunch

Grilled Steak with Wine Sauce (page 181)
Grilled vegetables
Green salad
150g strawberries with scoop of vanilla ice cream
1 glass red wine

Dinner

1 bowl cold soup (such as Beetroot Soup, page 115, or Cold Fennel Soup, page 116)
1 slice country or wholemeal bread
Salad with olives and hard-boiled egg
2 yellow plums

4

EN AUTOMNE: FALL AHEAD

For many of us, no season's passing is mourned as summer's is. We often complain that summer's not what it used to be, more like the rest of our busy year. But even those who work right through the season (as most now do) can't deny the attitude of relative *laissez-faire*: the pace is slackened, the energy dampened a bit, by the routine absence of colleagues in any given week. People work with a weekend-to-weekend mentality.

We don't appreciate the relative ease until everyone snaps back to attention. The first Monday in September is Labor Day in the U.S.A., when everyone squeezes in one more weekend holiday, mental or otherwise. The Going Back to School sales season and drama end for us. The curtain goes up on a new academic year . . . the games begin. In my business, as in many, autumn is the big selling season. Once again people are watching, keeping score.

This can be a rude awakening. While basking in summer, we tend not to address the big strategic issues such as unfulfilled professional or emotional hopes. But a fresh start can be quite energizing, too. Taking up new challenges, dealing more purposefully with work and goals: it can all add up to real stimulation, with genuine spiritual and financial rewards. But also stress. There are only so many waking hours in a day. As we return to a multi-tasking full speed, we may be psyched overall, but we also tend to lose focus on ourselves and, in a broader sense, on our place in nature. With everyone expecting more from us, our equilibrium can get swamped. And sometimes we get fat. We are not alone in this: many other mammals start layering it on as the chill permeates the air—though admittedly they stop eating almost entirely in the months thereafter. (Compensations.) But what are we humans to do? *C'est la vie, non?*

It's true that nature and tradition have ordained autumn as the last stop on summer's free ride of on-demand bounty, of peak flavour with relatively few calories. But the season is glorious in its own way: "Thou hast thy music too", as Keats wrote, addressing autumn's inferiority complex compared with spring. I would not trade for anything the rustle of autumn leaves, much less the changing light and hues of the landscape, the first smell of a neighbour's fire. When I first arrived in Weston, Massachusetts, as an exchange student, it was autumn, and I had not yet grown round. Being in New England, home of the Pilgrims, I could not have felt a more intense sense of arriving in America. It was then that I first celebrated Thanksgiving, the American holiday *par excellence*. I still remember my first taste of cranberry dressing, my first tumble in a pile of leaves of American oak and maple. There was no better place to observe the change of colours, and I became hooked on that seasonal rite. Today it can breed some anxiety among the New Englanders overrun with us gawkers, and I have even noticed people stressing out over missing the peak weekend—such is the modern condition! At the time, though, foliage was a joyous discovery.

But nature never intended this time to be frittered away in chasing the leaves. In fact, our modern rite of back-to-school, back-to-work is perfectly consistent with nature's plan, although in a different guise. This has always been the time to reap—in fact, for most of history, to reap for your life! Not so long ago, there was no surviving the winter without an abundance of those fruits of the earth that could be laid in for the mostly lifeless months ahead. (In the wine business, too, a bad harvest is death, at least in retail terms.)

I suppose one positive effect of mass agribusiness is to have freed those of us in the developed world from the fear of starvation. Perpetual plenitude, however, comes at a price: an impaired sense of seasonal rhythm and of pacing ourselves. Unlike summer, autumn doesn't give us irresistible guidance regarding how to eat. Our exertions also tend to become more sedentary. Still, there are meaningful ways of registering the season in our minds and bodies. You don't have to thresh your own wheat, but you can do better than collecting a couple of decorative gourds.

If you prefer taking your colour cues from the landscape rather than from Paris, Milan, or New York, try to look beyond the leaf pile embedded in our cultural consciousness. Even where the colours never change, children in autumn are made to draw leaves. True, the leaves are the season's glory, and outdoor flowers don't beckon to us as they do in spring and summer. But many do last well past summer, and the season "set[s] budding more / And still more, later flowers for the bees" (Keats *encore*)—else there would be no honey to harvest. Our favourite late bloomer is the chrysanthemum. Mums have become widely available in plastic containers, which we place inside decorative pots, often accented with ivy or ornamental grass.

In autumn we really have to begin to carve out our personal time and relaxation or we run the risk of not having any. Some call this deprivation virtue, but I call it a recipe for overeating. It shouldn't take much rousing to go out for a good long walk in fall, especially in a park. In New York and Paris I love the energy on the streets when everyone is back from *les congés d'été*—the summer holidays. I enjoy meeting a friend or a relative (one I like) for brunch. We might then take a stroll through a new museum exhibition or (less edifying, perhaps) through SoHo's stores—each in its way a wonderful distraction for an autumn weekend. But make the plan and stick with it. Relentless self-application may seem ambitious, but it takes the edge off your A game. Successful people know how to let it alone.

Autumn is also a good time to reacquaint yourself with

moderate free weights, especially if you're over forty. A bit of extremely simple resistance training is a French woman's answer to the hours of working aerobic machines that some other women favour. The French writer Colette, with her proto-Pilates contraptions, was the first modern woman to work out. As I've said, short but focused intervals of exertion several times a week are all you need to be physically healthy. (The rest we do for our head.) A little goes a long way, so don't let extremism overtake you. In the end, those who know how to stay fit while enjoying life come out ahead, mentally and physically.

Overall, a key to managing the uptick of seasonal stress is to increase your physical exertion indoors. Let's face it, the shorter the days, the less time you'll spend outside, where there is no sofa or flat screen. I walk and cycle as much as I can. And take the stairs. But I also turn more regularly to yoga. I do more work around the house as well. Sometimes we must make do with a short interior journey, such as focusing on a simple task—the French woman's zen. The smallest oases of serenity placed throughout the day can make all the difference to your heart and mental health.

Speaking of short journeys, my grandmother devised the perfect outdoor one for early Sunday mornings in the autumn. We'd walk into the forest, where, under the canopy of trees not yet denuded, the light would dance all around us as we stood in the utter silence, drinking in all the wonderful odours of decay from the humid *sous-bois* (forest floor), a bit like tasting an old wine. (There is, incidentally, a specifically autumnal gastronomy connected with the business of decay. The noble rot on grapes gives some wines their excellence; a magnificent Stilton could be mistaken for another cheese left out too long. There's sometimes a fine line between perfection and ruin.)

In the wood, we would catch sight of the occasional deer that hadn't caught a whiff of us. Or we would collect mushrooms, guided by my grandmother's faultless eye for distinguishing what was delicious from what was lethal in this dappled other world just a few hundred metres from her garden. A far cry from the supermarket shrink-wrapped buttons that may not kill you, but the taste is about equal to the thrill of finding them. But even more salutary was being out there in perfect stillness, in another world.

Nature is full of marvellous microcosms we can enter, even if only mentally. Another of these was the world of my father's beehives.

THE BEEKEEPER'S DAUGHTER

Honey's dark gold reminds me of autumn. And inevitably it reminds me of first learning to gather the bees' bounty. While we can keep and eat honey all year round (see how I use it in various recipes throughout the seasons), we harvest it in late spring and finally in late autumn, when "the maturing sun" conspires with the season (Keats again)

> *to set budding more,*
> *And still more, later flowers for the bees,*
> *Until they think warm days will never cease,*
> *For Summer has o'er-brimm'd their clammy cells.*

Just what those insects were up to in those "clammy cells" to produce such a heavenly food was a mystery. As an eight-year-old I couldn't quite fathom that bees collect the nectar from flowers and transform it in their honey stomachs. The *apiculteur* (beekeeper) loved to explain this to me over and over, and I never tired of hearing the story. The bees were his third hobby, the other two being his garden and his pigeons.

Granted the beekeeper was only an amateur, but my father seemed to know everything about keeping the colony clean, the queen healthy, and her subjects working—all conditions vital to a good harvest. Somewhat to my mother's annoyance, he kept a few hives square in the middle of the flower gardens. In bee real estate, location really is everything. We watched with great fascination, though Father was not particularly good at finding age-appropriate terms to explain how the queen was the only sexually developed female in the hive, how she mates with all the stout male bees, receiving millions of anonymous sperm cells and laying up to three thousand eggs in one day. Hard to imagine how the birds and the bees (or the bees, at least) ever became delicate models of sex education. The queen is a father's nightmare. Anyway, the game was more show than tell, and we spent hours and hours following the bees as witness to their purposeful busyness.

A solemn if scary moment was when I'd be allowed to put on long gloves and a straw hat with a veil of netting to help my father tend the apiary. There was no more exciting event than the extraction of the honeycomb from the hive in early autumn. As a child I felt a certain poignancy in seeing the fruit of my little friends' ceaseless labours taken from them. But the bees seemed to trust my father, and they were not wrong. Of course he knew when the honey was ripe for harvest, and exactly how much to leave them so the colony could survive the cold months without flowers. He said they made more than enough for themselves, and so we were welcome to the rest.

Everyone loved the honey, but only my father and I loved the comb. It was, first of all, beautiful to look at, a gorgeous waxen lattice of painstaking construction, an insect Chartres cathedral. It was also the choice of honey connoisseurs. We cut it up and ate it like a house of gingerbread, finally forgetting the life-and-death struggle of the bees to make it. Sometimes I'd mix it with my favourite cheese, *petit Suisse,* although today I would substitute homemade yogurt. The rest of the harvest remained liquid honey, poured into jars, and consumed in countless ways during the year or given away as gifts.

In winter, when on occasion breakfast was a thick slice of bread with a thick slice of butter drizzled with honey, we would always feel thankful for our father's *rapprochement* with the bees, even without knowing what is known today: that honey, in particular darker varieties, is a significant source of antioxidants. It also had uses in ancient Egyptian and Vedic medicine and, until the development of antibiotics, was used to inhibit bacterial growth and heal wounds. It still makes a good facial toner. There is also a very simple reason French women keep honey in their diet: because it's so sweet (approximately one and a half times as sweet as white sugar), as well as divinely flavourful, you can use less—in my case, about half the amount of processed sugar. It's also more slowly digested, therefore less likely to cause the unpleasant effects of blood-glucose spikes. And with honey, you'll never want for variety:

there are about three hundred kinds. My preferences: acacia, clover, brambles, and lavender. You can taste the flowers of summer in the honey of autumn. Don't worry if it appears cloudy; it stays edible for years—bacteria may spoil other foods but not the taste of honey.

Sometimes I add a few drops of honey to the water I sip during long walks or other exercise. When cooking or baking, I substitute half the sugar in a recipe with honey. I drizzle it over thick plain yogurt, waffles, or pancakes. And my New York friends adore receiving honey from Provence. In fairness, I should point out that my Provence friends love to receive the fabulous maple syrup from my adoptive homeland. This New World sugar substitute, popularized in the colonies when sugar was heavily taxed, also boasts health benefits, including concentrations of essential minerals such as manganese, to say nothing of its own distinctive earthy flavours.

FOR THE LOVE OF A GOOD POTATO

Some stereotypes are true: Italians eat pasta, Asians eat rice, and the French eat potatoes. In fact, these were cultural staples long before stereotypes existed. But one stereotype à la Atkins that has done harm is that of the potato as bad or junk food, starchy throwaway calories. The potato is actually filled with nutrients, and if we would speak of calories, an average-sized potato has only a fourth of the calories found in an equal portion of rice or pasta. *Vive la pomme de terre!* Oh, and did I mention vitamins? The potato has practically all of them, with a particular richness in C and the B gamut. And it is the most versatile vegetable: it marries well with anything. It becomes an "offender" only when deep-fried or when commandeered as a sour-cream-and-Cheddar delivery system.

When I was growing up, we ate potatoes in some shape or form at lunch—as one of the two vegetable accompaniments to fish or meat—an average of five days a week. The variations prevented any sense of spud monotony. There was steamed, roasted, or oven baked; mashed potatoes, potato salad, or, yes, even *frites* (though in careful moderation as a Sunday lunch treat). Different preparations called for different varieties: for example, we would never use new potatoes in the mash—not enough starch—though they roasted deliciously with rosemary or thyme. And some were precious: the famous and incomparable Noirmoutier, available only three months of the year, was as delicate, sweet, and (alas) pricey as potatoes get. A little steaming is all they require. On the other end of the spectrum, the King Edward stands up well to baking, the Maris Piper can take the deep-fry. À propos of deep frying, a word of advice about so-called french fries: much of the problem is America's addiction to oil—the bad kind. If it's changed only every twenty thousand miles and it's a trans fat (as is true in most fast-food restaurants), even one fry is too many. If you have French fries at a good restaurant or make them yourself with a good fat, go ahead. Just remember that one Mont Blanc-sized serving you get in most dining establishments can feed the whole table.

POTATO GRATIN À LA NORMANDE

Serves 4

Normandy being apple and cheese country, lots of regional recipes include these two delicious staples. If you've never tasted a perfectly ripe Pont l'Évêque (named after the town where it comes from in Calvados), a soft cheese with a savoury smell and a pronounced tang, you should try it. This recipe comes from a friend, and I especially like it for marrying protein with fruit flavour—a nice autumn lunch, with a simple green salad.

1. Preheat the oven to gas mark 5/190°C.
2. Cook the potatoes in slightly salted boiling water for 8 minutes, then drain.
3. While the potatoes cook, warm a non-stick frying pan, and toast the walnuts for a minute or two over medium heat. When cool, crumble and reserve.
4. Melt the butter in a frying pan over medium heat, add the apples, and let brown for 3 to 4 minutes while stirring. Cut crust off the cheese, and slice cheese thinly.
5. Butter a rectangular baking dish, and cover it with a layer of potatoes, then a layer of apples, a layer of cheese, and a sprinkle of walnuts. Continue layering until all the ingredients have been used. Top with sour cream, season with salt and pepper to taste and bake for 30 minutes.

INGREDIENTS

500g potatoes (King Edward or Desirée), peeled and sliced thinly

Salt and freshly ground pepper

30g walnuts, chopped

30g unsalted butter

3 Granny Smith apples, peeled, cored, and cut into 8 pieces each

1×350–400g Pont l'Évêque cheese

200g sour cream or crème fraîche

MASHED POTATOES (*MAMIE*'S VERSION)

Serves 4

There is much dogma concerning great mashed potatoes. Some famous chefs regard it as essential to have almost equal parts potatoes and butter, but they would have been fired from my mother's kitchen: her customers expected butter when we ordered butter, and potatoes when we were served potatoes. In other words, don't overdo the added fat. But do consider texture: it's very important to put the cooked potatoes while hot through a real vegetable mill or a potato ricer (a blender will give you not a mash but a purée—by my taste buds, that's good only for wallpaper paste). Always add very hot milk first, then add the butter. For variety, you can replace the butter with olive oil (though it should be heated slightly and added at the end). You can also omit the milk by cooking the potatoes unpeeled and using the starchy water to wet the mash. Season with nutmeg, cumin, or curry powder, adding parsley, tarragon, dill, or basil. Another bit of dogma that I reject outright is the categorical benefit of a heavy dose of garlic. Much as I love to cook with garlic, which is wonderful for you, it overwhelms the potato flavours. Let the potato be a potato.

1. Put the potatoes into a saucepan, and cover them with cold water. Add 1 teaspoon salt. Bring to a boil, cover partially, and cook over medium-low heat until tender, about 20 minutes.
2. Drain the potatoes, and put through a vegetable mill or potato ricer. Add the milk and whisk in the butter, then season with salt and pepper to taste. Serve immediately.

INGREDIENTS

1kg potatoes (Maris Piper or King Edward), peeled and cut into 5cm pieces

Salt and freshly ground pepper

175ml scalded milk (milk that has been heated to the point where it is almost boiling; regular or skimmed)

40g unsalted butter

N.B. IF YOU NEED TO PREPARE MASHED POTATOES IN ADVANCE FOR A DINNER PARTY, YOU CAN PUT THEM INTO A GLASS BOWL COVERED WITH ALUMINIUM FOIL AND PLACE OVER A PAN OF SIMMERING WATER. THEY WILL KEEP AT LEAST THIRTY MINUTES WITHOUT DRYING OUT. *MAMIE* WOULD STORE LEFTOVERS IN THE FRIDGE AND TWO DAYS LATER MAKE PATTIES THAT SHE WOULD REHEAT IN A BIT OF OIL WITH SOME SAUTÉED SHALLOTS. SHE COOKED THE PATTIES UNTIL THEY WERE NICELY BROWN ON EACH SIDE AND SERVED THEM WITH A GOOD TABLESPOON OF FRESHLY CHOPPED PARSLEY—ANOTHER QUICK SIDE DISH.

COD WITH POTATO SALAD

Serves 4

INGREDIENTS

750g Charlotte potatoes, peeled and cut into 5cm pieces

Salt and freshly ground pepper

4 rashers bacon, cut into 5mm pieces

5 tablespoons olive oil

2 tablespoons sherry vinegar

1 teaspoon Meaux or other wholegrain mustard

2 tablespoons finely chopped shallots,

500g cod

1. Put the potatoes into a saucepan, and cover them with cold water. Add 1 teaspoon salt, bring to a boil, and cook until tender, about 20 minutes, then drain.
2. Sauté the bacon until crisp in a non-stick pan. Pat dry on a paper towel.
3. Prepare the salad dressing: mix the oil, vinegar, mustard, and shallots, and season lightly with salt and pepper.
4. Put the cod into a pan, cover with cold water, and bring to a boil. Cover the pan, turn off the heat, and leave the fish to poach for 6 minutes. Drain, crumble the fish coarsely, set aside on a warm plate, and cover with foil.
5. Put some potatoes on each dish, add some cod and bacon, drizzle with the dressing, and serve immediately.

POTATO-OLIVE RAGOÛT

Serves 4

Another fruit that marries brilliantly with potato is the olive, of which so many varieties are available, even in America. They travel well, being easy to preserve, and lose nothing in transit.

1. Warm the oil in a large non-stick pan over high heat. Add the potatoes and brown on all sides. Add the peppers, garlic, shallots, and lemon, and sauté for a few minutes. Add the olives, season with salt and pepper to taste, and cover. Cook over low heat until the vegetables are tender, about 10 minutes.
2. Add the coriander, mix well, and serve immediately.

INGREDIENTS

3 tablespoons olive oil

500g potatoes (Desirée, Majestic, small reds, or a mixture), peeled and cut like big, fat chips

1 orange or yellow pepper, seeded and cut into julienne (thin) strips

1 red pepper, seeded and cut into julienne (thin) strips

2 cloves garlic, peeled and finely chopped

2 shallots, peeled and finely chopped

2 lemons, washed and quartered

180g green olives, stoned

Salt and freshly ground pepper

4 tablespoons coarsely chopped coriander

ULTRA RAPIDE MASH

Serves 4

INGREDIENTS

750g Maris Piper potatoes
Freshly ground coarse salt and pepper
4 teaspoons olive oil

1. Cut the washed but unpeeled potatoes into 2.5cm chunks. Put into a medium saucepan with ½ teaspoon salt and enough water to cover. Bring to a boil, then lower the heat and simmer until tender, 10 to 15 minutes.

2. Drain the potatoes, and place them in 4 soup or cereal bowls. Mash roughly with a fork. To each bowl, add ground coarse salt and pepper to taste, and drizzle on 1 teaspoon of the oil.

CAULIFLOWER GRATIN

Serves 4

1. Preheat the oven to gas mark 5/190°C.
2. Remove the leaves from the cauliflower, cut out the central stem, and break into florets. Wash in cold water, then steam for about 6 minutes. Put the florets into a baking dish.
3. In a bowl, combine the eggs, milk, cumin, garlic, and shallots. Pour the mixture over the cauliflower, and sprinkle with breadcrumbs. Add the wine to the baking dish, and bake in the preheated oven for 15 minutes. Season with salt and pepper to taste, and serve.

INGREDIENTS

1kg cauliflower

4 eggs

180ml milk (regular or skimmed)

½ teaspoon ground cumin

2 cloves garlic, peeled and finely chopped

2 shallots, peeled and finely chopped

30g fresh breadcrumbs

125ml white wine

Salt and freshly ground pepper

SAUTÉED ENDIVE

Serves 4

INGREDIENTS

2 heads curly endive (about 1kg)

3 tablespoons olive oil

1 tablespoon finely chopped shallots

Salt and freshly ground pepper

1. Remove the tough outer leaves from the endive. Wash thoroughly, and pat dry. Slice the leaves coarsely.
2. Warm the oil in a frying pan over medium heat. Add the shallot, and cook until golden. Add the endive, and cook over medium heat for 15 minutes, stirring occasionally, until tender. Season with salt and pepper to taste, and serve immediately.

N.B. YOU CAN SUBSTITUTE RADICCHIO OR SPINACH FOR THE CURLY ENDIVE. IF USING SPINACH, COOK FOR JUST 3 TO 5 MINUTES.

As the variety of vegetables bursting with natural flavour tapers off after summer, soups can tend to get a bit more complicated and hearty: people don't mind something a little heavier, and more things need to be added whereas one glorious flavour had sufficed before. Still, my favourite soups are the simplest. And fortunately, the autumn markets are not completely depleted of delicious vegetables that don't need much help. There is a wealth of ripe peppers, and now the little chillies begin to appear, for those who like it hot. Parsnips can be made into a velvety base you'd swear was laden with cream. The soup that most says "fall" to me is squash, although the recipes work as well with either the last of the summer squash still coming in or the first of the winter squash just beginning to appear.

BUTTERSQUASH SOUP

Serves 4

INGREDIENTS

1 medium butternut squash, peeled and cut into large pieces

1 large yellow onion, peeled and coarsely chopped

225g red-skinned boiling potatoes (about 2 or 3), peeled and cut into 1cm cubes

60g unsalted butter

Salt and freshly ground pepper

1. Put the squash, onion, and potatoes into a large pan. Add 1.5 litres water. Bring to a boil, lower the heat, and cover. Simmer gently, stirring occasionally, for about 45 minutes.
2. Remove the vegetables with a slotted spoon, and purée in a food mill or food processor, using the cooking water to thin it out to the consistency desired. (If you're preparing soup ahead of time, use all the cooking water, since the soup will thicken as it stands.)
3. Just before serving, add the butter to the heated soup, and season with salt and pepper to taste. Cook 2 minutes more, and serve.

N.B. JUST BEFORE SERVING, YOU CAN ADD FRESH PARSLEY FOR COLOUR, OR 1/4 TEASPOON GRATED NUTMEG, OR BOTH. A SWIRL OF CRÈME FRAÎCHE OR SOUR CREAM WOULD BE NICE, TOO.

LENTIL SOUP

Serves 4

1. In a large pan, bring the vegetable stock to a simmer, and drop in the lentils.
2. Heat the oil in a frying pan, and add the onion, garlic, and celery. Cook until golden, 3 to 5 minutes. Add the parsley and tomatoes, and cook 8 to 10 minutes more.
3. After the lentils have been cooking for 35 to 40 minutes, add the onion mixture to pot and cover. Let simmer until the lentils are soft, 5 to 10 more minutes. Season with salt and pepper to taste, and serve immediately.

INGREDIENTS

2 litres vegetable stock

225g lentils

2 tablespoons olive oil

1 medium yellow onion, peeled and chopped

1 clove garlic, peeled and chopped

2 stalks celery, chopped

1 tablespoon chopped parsley

1×400g can chopped tomatoes

Salt and freshly ground pepper

FARFALLE WITH EDAMAME

Serves 4

Soya beans, a major harvest crop used for so many things, are something I discovered in America. Once the food of privation in Europe, today they are offered in Japanese restaurants as the appetizer edamame in their salted pods. You can also buy them shelled, fresh or frozen from specialist shops, or you could substitute garden peas. Edamame make a good accompaniment to red meat—even pasta, as I learned from a young Asian woman selling them at the market. Curious at always seeing me buy them, she asked one day, "What do you do with them?" She revealed her own favourite way to enjoy them, and it has become one of mine.

INGREDIENTS

350g farfalle pasta
Salt and freshly ground pepper
400g shelled edamame
Zest and juice of 1 lemon
2 tablespoons olive oil
80g grated Parmesan
2 tablespoons chopped parsley

1. Cook the farfalle in salted water according to packet directions and stirring occasionally. In the last 5 minutes of cooking, add the edamame to the pan. Drain, reserving 80ml of the pasta water.
2. Place the lemon zest and juice in a large pan over medium heat. Add the reserved pasta water, oil, and 60g of the cheese. Mix well. Add the edamame and farfalle to the lemon mixture, and toss well to coat. Serve immediately, sprinkled with parsley and the remaining cheese. Season with pepper to taste.

MACARONI WITH SPINACH AND PANCETTA

Serves 4

1. Cook the pasta in plenty of salted water, according to packet directions and stirring occasionally.
2. Meanwhile, warm the oil in a large pan over low heat. Add the pancetta, and cook for 10 minutes. Add the white wine and spinach. Season with salt and pepper to taste, cover, and continue cooking over medium heat for 5 more minutes, until the spinach is wilted.
3. When the pasta is cooked, drain and add it to the pan with the pancetta and spinach. Add the cheese, and continue cooking for 5 minutes over medium heat, stirring continuously to mix the cheese with the pasta. Add some freshly ground pepper, and serve immediately.

INGREDIENTS

350g macaroni, penne, or rigatoni

Salt and freshly ground pepper

1 tablespoon olive oil

80g pancetta, diced into small pieces

125ml dry white wine

500g spinach, washed

120g grated Parmesan, or mix of Parmesan and Pecorino

CHICKEN AND GREEN BEAN SALAD

Serves 6

Although string beans are commonly known as French beans, the French didn't use them much before the nineteenth century because they were so expensive. They always seem like a token of springtime enjoyed in autumn.

INGREDIENTS

Sprig of parsley
Sprig of tarragon
1 bay leaf
½ onion, peeled and chopped
Salt and freshly ground pepper
2 boneless, skinless chicken breasts
2 teaspoons Meaux or other wholegrain mustard
2 tablespoons red wine vinegar
6 tablespoons olive oil
3 tablespoons double cream
2 tablespoons finely chopped basil
500g thin string beans
350g mushrooms, wiped and thinly sliced
1 serving Tricolour Peppers (page 131)
1 tablespoon lemon juice
120g walnuts, coarsely chopped

1. Bring 500ml water to a boil in a large saucepan. Add the parsley, tarragon, bay leaf, onion, and salt. Drop the chicken into water, and poach for 12 minutes. Cool and cut the chicken into small pieces. (This step can be done in advance.)
2. For the dressing: Put the mustard and vinegar into a bowl, and mix well. Whisk in the oil, then add the cream and basil. Season with salt and pepper to taste.
3. Steam the beans for 8 minutes. Drain, and place in a bowl with the chicken, the dressing, and all the remaining ingredients, and toss gently.

SKATE WITH CAPERS

Serves 4

Skate is a wonderful fish; its thin, firm but feathered white meat tastes sweet with a surprisingly pleasant accent of ammonia. I had my first great skate dish in one of New York's top French restaurants some fifteen years ago and decided to look for it to cook at home. It's often available at the Union Square Greenmarket, and when I buy it, the next person in line inevitably asks, "How do you cook it?" My answer: "Pure and simple".

1. Pour 500ml water into a large, deep frying pan. Add the salt, peppercorns, and vinegar, and bring to a boil. Add the skate wings, and simmer for 8 minutes. (You may have to do two batches if your pan is not wide enough.) When poached, drain the fish, and set aside on a warm plate. Cover with foil while preparing the sauce.
2. Warm the oil in a small saucepan, add the butter, and stir over medium heat until the butter is melted. Add the tomatoes, lemon juice, and 2 tablespoons parsley. Cook a few minutes, until the tomatoes soften. Add the capers, and cook another minute.
3. Put a skate wing on each plate. Top with the tomato-caper mixture, and sprinkle with the remaining parsley. You may also want to drizzle on a touch more oil.

INGREDIENTS

1 tablespoon coarse salt

1 teaspoon crushed peppercorns

1 tablespoon red wine vinegar

4 skate wings (about 750g)

2 tablespoons olive oil

60g unsalted butter

2 medium tomatoes, cut into quarters

Juice of ½ lemon

4 tablespoons chopped parsley

40g drained capers

MUSSELS IN WHITE WINE

Serves 4

A perfect dish to serve friends for a casual dinner. All you need to remember is to clean the mussels in advance. The best way is to scrub them with a small brush, then soak them in cold water with a teaspoon of salt for a couple of hours. Discard any that do not close when tapped.

INGREDIENTS

2 tablespoons finely chopped shallots

30g unsalted butter

2 tablespoons finely chopped parsley

1 sprig thyme

250ml dry white wine

Salt and freshly ground pepper

2kg mussels, cleaned

1. In a large, heavy-based, flameproof casserole, sauté the shallots in half the butter for 1 to 2 minutes. Add 1 tablespoon of the parsley, the thyme, white wine, and pepper to taste, and bring to a boil. Add the mussels, cover, and cook, shaking the casserole once in a while, until the mussels open (it will take about 5 minutes). Discard any unopened mussels. Remove the remaining mussels to soup bowls.

2. Add the remaining butter to the pot. Stir until melted. Season with salt and pepper to taste. Pour the buttery juice over the mussels, and sprinkle with the remaining parsley. Serve with country or wholemeal bread to soak up any sauce, and have an empty bowl for collecting shells. Serve with the remainder of the wine you used for cooking the mussels.

TURKEY ESCALOPES WITH PESTO

Serves 4

Turkey is one of the leanest white meats, an excellent protein source, and it has become the base for my American version of veal escalope. My husband, who loves this dish, is always pleased when I announce a "green turkey night", signalling that with the turkey we will have a baked potato garnished with a dollop of pesto, as well as a portion of steamed broccoli. A turkey breast is much easier to cook than a whole bird, and simpler still if you have the butcher slice it into escalopes, as with a far more expensive breast of veal. I usually buy a fresh, organic turkey breast at Union Square Greenmarket, but they are easy to find. You can even order them on the Internet.

1. To make the pesto: Wash the basil, pat dry and place it in a mortar. Add the pine nuts, garlic, and a pinch of salt. Pound the ingredients with a circular motion of the pestle until you obtain a green paste. Put the paste into a bowl, and add oil gradually. Add the cheeses just before serving, and more oil if necessary. (You can also do this in the food processor.) The pesto can be made in advance and frozen in small cubes for use when needed.

[continued]

INGREDIENTS

FOR THE PESTO:

225g fresh basil

60g pine nuts

2 cloves garlic, peeled

Pinch of salt

180 to 250ml olive oil

1 tablespoon grated Parmesan cheese

1 tablespoon grated Pecorino cheese

FOR THE ESCALOPES:

1 tablespoon olive oil
8 turkey escalopes
8g unsalted butter
Juice of ½ lemon
Salt and freshly ground pepper

2. Warm the oil in a frying pan over medium-high heat, and cook the turkey for a few minutes on each side. Add the butter and lemon juice. Season with salt and pepper to taste. Add the pesto, and cook a few more minutes. If the sauce is on the dry side, add a few tablespoons of hot water. Mix well. Serve immediately.

N.B. MANY PEOPLE HAVE FAR TOO NARROW A NOTION OF PESTO. BASIL IS SUBLIME. I LOVE USING IT IN SUMMER WHEN IT FLOURISHES, AND I FREEZE PESTO MADE OF IT TO GET ME THROUGH THE REST OF THE YEAR. BUT DID YOU KNOW YOU CAN ALSO MAKE A ROSEMARY PESTO? A HAZELNUT PESTO? FRENCH WOMEN DON'T HAVE *IDÉES FIXES* ABOUT SUCH THINGS AND LOVE TO INVENT THEIR OWN VARIATIONS. SO FEEL FREE TO EXPERIMENT. AUTUMN IS THE LAST CHANCE TO GET FRESH HERBS AT THE MARKET, SO NOW IS THE TIME TO MAKE PESTO.

GRILLED STEAK WITH WINE SAUCE

Serves 4

There is not much more a good steak needs than a bit of seasoning and grilling. While I don't generally recommend tampering with perfection, as the chilly months come on, we eventually put the barbecue away. When we cook steak less primally, I love to use this wine sauce. It's perfectly natural that preparations become a little more elaborate as the season progresses. The richest ones are best had in winter. My friend and Alsatian compatriot Jean-Georges Vongerichten—a chef and restaurateur known for the brilliant flavours, not the richness of his creations—used to make this dish when he was apprenticed in La Napoule on the French Riviera at Louis Outhier's L'Oasis three-star restaurant of many nouvelle cuisine pilgrimages. I have adapted it slightly.

INGREDIENTS

275ml red wine, such as a Côtes du Rhône

2 cloves garlic, peeled and crushed

Salt and freshly ground pepper

15g unsalted butter

2×500g steaks

1. Reserve 1 tablespoon of the wine. Combine the remaining wine and the garlic in a small saucepan. Bring to a boil over high heat, and reduce until syrupy (it will take about 10 minutes). Strain out the garlic, and season generously with salt and pepper. Return to a low heat, and stir in the butter and the reserved (uncooked) red wine.

2. Grill the steaks without adding anything to them. When ready, let them rest for a few minutes on a plate, divide, then pour the sauce over. Drink the rest of the bottle of wine with the meal.

IF I COULD KEEP PEARS IN A BOTTLE

One of my most vivid memories of childhood is sitting on my grandmother's lap as she peeled pears and told me tales of her youth. Truth to tell, I also have a pretty vivid memory of licking the egg-and-cream batter from the bowl my Aunt Berthe had emptied (she was obligingly inefficient about getting it all out) for her Alsatian version of a tarte tatin, the classic upside-down apple pie. When the tart of apples or pears finally went into the oven, infusing the house with an incense of cinnamon and fruit, that was almost as good as the batter. It's said that nothing (except love of "mom") is as American as apple pie, yet for most the experience is only of the finished product, often a store-bought version. How many of us still enjoy waiting for it to come out of the oven, that same anticipation that was proverbially so unbearable for children that they would steal it from the windowsill before it could cool? I love to imagine that sort of thing still happens, though it seems to be fading into myth, given our present way of life and relation to food.

Living in an area rich in apple and pear trees, my family had seemingly no end of recipes using them, as well as pleasures of watching them grow. You could mark the weeks of the season as the tiny green fruit swelled, taking on the progressive colours of autumn until they were ready to be picked and stored in the *cagettes* (rectangular wooden crates) in the cool dark cellar. They would last all winter, losing only a bit of their crispness while growing sweeter.

Every year my father would perform his impressive trick of putting a pear into a narrow-neck bottle. The bottle would then be filled with the highly alcoholic eau-de-vie that the local distiller had made from our crates of pears. This was Father's preferred method for producing Poire Williams, the pear brandy for which Alsace is famous, its name taken from the Williams Bon-Chrétien variety. Preserved by the alcohol, the pear would last forever, so long as the bottle was refilled every year. My father gave these magical bottles as gifts to relatives or special friends. The bottles always stumped our clever city cousins. At big family reunions the pear brandy would come out after a four-hour meal so the men could enjoy the obligatory *digestif*: how had our father got the pear into the bottle? They would squirm a bit, but soon we would reveal how simple it was and how each spring I helped Dad attach the bottle over a budding pear on one of his prime trees. More often than not, the tiny pear would grow as naturally as the others, the bottle permitting plenty of air and sunshine to pass through.

Marvellous as pears are, apples were and are consumed in far greater quantity. I eat at least one apple a day for as long as they are in season, and it's hardly a matter of virtue, since there are so many varieties that I like: Golden Delicious, Granny Smith, Mutsu . . . Their high concentration of antioxidants (especially in the skin) is well known, but I'm convinced that apples help French women avoid getting fat as well. This claim was exploited by a dietician from Washington State, who proposed a three-apple-a-day diet a couple of years ago. As ever, I don't do or recommend diets, and any strict consumption of three things a day could get monotonous, but there is a nugget of wisdom there. Apples have plenty of fibre for relatively few calories: I can't imagine increasing your consumption of them without achieving a slimming effect, provided you didn't simply add apples to an already overloaded intake. The key to reaping this apple benefit is—big surprise—the pleasure principle: the apple must be full of taste and of an agreeable texture. If an apple has been freshly picked and shipped locally, there's a far better chance that it was picked ripe (not green, for the long haul) and that it won't have lost moisture, the key to crispness. Pears can lose a little water and get sugary; apples only get mealy. If you have an unripe apple, put it in a brown paper bag to be ripened by its naturally emitted ethylene (this also works well for bananas and pears). If you have a ripe one, the best thing to do is eat it. If you must keep it, however, seal it in a food container and refrigerate it. Heresy, I know, putting a fruit in the fridge, but the cold does arrest the ripening process, and the container keeps the apple from drying out. (The same goes for a ripe avocado.) So, while it's always best not to refrigerate fruit, the apple is a rare exception whose life can be extended slightly in the fridge. And if you do refrigerate one, remember to take it out early enough that it can get to room temperature, at which point its flavours will be at their peak, before you eat it. A good apple can be a most satisfying dessert, eaten sliced, with the skin on for the full array of nutrients, and with a knife and fork to make the experience fuller, though still simple and pure. Have you noticed that people tend to chomp on apples without even looking at them? No wonder we were kicked out of the Garden of Eden.

PEAR-APPLE COMPOTE WITH HONEY

Serves 4

INGREDIENTS

500g apples
300g pears
Juice of 1 lemon
2 tablespoons honey

1. Peel, core, and dice the apples and pears. Pour lemon juice over them and toss. Into a heavy pan pour 125ml water and the fruit mixture. Cover and cook over medium heat for 10 minutes, stirring occasionally to prevent the fruit from sticking or burning.
2. With a fork, crush the fruit coarsely while continuing to cook for another 3 to 5 minutes, or until the excess water evaporates. Remove from the heat, add the honey, and mix gently. Serve lukewarm or cold (if you store it in the refrigerator, take it out 30 minutes before serving).

N.B. PLAY WITH DIFFERENT VARIETIES OF APPLES, PEARS, AND HONEY TO RENEW THE TASTE OF THE COMPOTE. FOR A SPECIAL TREAT, ADD A SMALL SCOOP OF ICE CREAM.

JARLSBERG, APPLE, AND MUSHROOM SALAD

Serves 6

INGREDIENTS

500g mushrooms (brown caps go well with the cheese), wiped and thinly sliced

1 medium Golden Delicious apple, peeled, cored and cut into thin slices

3 tablespoons lemon juice

120g Jarlsberg cheese, cut into strips 2cm long and 3mm thick

1 large head lettuce, rinsed and dried, leaves torn

FOR THE DRESSING:

2 tablespoons red wine vinegar

2 tablespoons Meaux or other wholegrain mustard

8 tablespoons walnut oil

2 tablespoons chopped parsley

Pinch of curry powder

Salt and freshly ground pepper

1. Sprinkle the mushroom and apple slices with the lemon juice.
2. For the dressing: Mix all the dressing ingredients together, and season with salt and pepper to taste.
3. Add the mushroom-apple mixture and the cheese to the dressing. Toss gently with the lettuce. Serve immediately.

N.B. YOU CAN REPLACE LETTUCE WITH A VARIETY OF SALAD LEAVES, INCLUDING RADICCHIO AND CURLY ENDIVE.

SPICED APPLES

Serves 4

A nice autumnal accompaniment to white meat, and you can substitute pears if you like. With a little dollop of whipped cream or yogurt, these apples make a nice dessert, too.

INGREDIENTS

2 apples

1 orange

2 tablespoons honey (clover or acacia)

Freshly ground pepper

1. Peel and core the apples and cut each into 8 slices. Cut the unpeeled orange into thin slices. Layer half the orange slices in the bottom of a steamer, cover with a layer of apple slices, and end with a layer of orange slices.
2. Steam for 6 to 7 minutes, until the apples are tender and infused with orange perfume. Discard the oranges and serve the apples warm, drizzled with honey. Season with pepper to taste.

BAKED APPLE *AIXOISE*

Serves 4

Another Provençal "variation" from my cousin Andrée, the creator of the Provençal version of "Mimosa" Leek Soup in French Women Don't Get Fat. *She also loved the family's classic Alsatian recipe for baked apple.*

INGREDIENTS

4 Golden Delicious apples
1 lemon
4 rosemary sprigs
2 tablespoons olive oil
4 cloves
2 tablespoons lavender honey

1. Preheat the oven to gas mark 4/180°C.
2. Carefully remove part of each apple's core to form a cavity in the centre of the apple (but not a tunnel through it). Peel the lemon into strips and reserve the skin.
3. Into each apple put a strip of lemon skin, a sprig of rosemary, ½ tablespoon oil, 1 clove, and ½ tablespoon honey.
4. Put the apples into a baking dish and add 150ml water. Cook in the preheated oven for 45 minutes or until the apples start splitting. Serve warm.

PEARS WITH CHOCOLATE AND PEPPER

Serves 4

The pear is one of nature's most remarkable inventions; its versatility is second to none. What other fruit could wed so perfectly with chocolate one minute, blue cheese the next?

1. Bring 1 litre water, the orange zest, and sugar to a boil. Peel and core the pears, keeping them whole by cutting the core out from the bottom, and put them into the boiling syrup over low heat for 20 minutes. Place each pear on a dessert dish and let cool.
2. Bring the cream to boil, then pour over the chocolate in a bowl and stir to melt it. Whisk in the butter, piece by piece. Pour the sauce over the pears and season with pepper to taste. Serve immediately.

INGREDIENTS

Zest of 1 orange

150g sugar

4 Conference pears

150ml double cream

120g dark chocolate, coarsely chopped

15g unsalted butter, cut in small pieces

Freshly ground pepper

N.B. PEPPER IS SURPRISING WITH DESSERT. IT ENHANCES THE FLAVOUR OF FRESH FRUIT. IN MY FIRST BOOK, I INCLUDED A PINEAPPLE DESSERT. YOU CAN ALSO USE PEPPER WITH STRAWBERRIES.

PEARS ON BRIOCHE

Serves 4

INGREDIENTS

2 ripe pears

15g unsalted butter

4 slices brioche

2 tablespoons honey

2 tablespoons sliced almonds

1 dollop sour cream or crème fraîche

1. Preheat the grill.
2. Peel the pears and cut them into small cubes. Melt the butter in a saucepan and sauté the pear cubes for 2 to 3 minutes over medium-high heat.
3. In a baking dish, arrange the pear cubes on the brioche slices. Cover with the honey and almonds. Put the dish under the preheated grill for 2 minutes, watching carefully. Serve warm with a dollop of sour cream or crème fraîche.

PEAR AND GOAT CHEESE *PAPILLOTE* WITH YOGURT SAUCE

Serves 4

1. Preheat the oven to gas mark 4/180°C.
2. Peel the pears, cut them into quarters, and slice each quarter into thirds. Add the lemon juice.
3. Cut 8 pieces of parchment paper (or aluminum foil) into squares large enough to hold a quarter of the goat cheese and one pear's worth of slices and leave a 5cm border all around. Lightly brush 4 squares with oil. Arrange the pear slices in the centre of each oiled square and spread a quarter of the goat cheese over each pear. Crumble the blue cheese over the goat cheese and pear slices, drizzle with oil, sprinkle with the chervil, and season with salt and pepper to taste.
4. Place the remaining parchment squares on top of the others and fold up the edges to form parcels. Simply double folding each of the four sides is enough to seal each parcel. Put the *papillotes* on a baking sheet, and bake in the preheated oven for 12 to 15 minutes.

[continued]

INGREDIENTS

4 pears

Juice of 1 lemon

120g fresh goat cheese

60g blue cheese

2 tablespoons olive oil

1 tablespoon chopped chervil or tarragon

Salt and freshly ground pepper

FOR THE SAUCE:

1 pear

250g yogurt

Juice of 1 lemon

Salt and freshly ground pepper

5. For the sauce: Peel the pear, cut it into small pieces, and mix with the yogurt and lemon juice. Season with salt and pepper to taste. Set aside.

6. To serve the *papillotes*, open each parcel and slide the contents onto a dish while they are still warm. Serve with your choice of greens and the yogurt sauce on the side.

PEARS WITH GINGER AND CHOCOLATE MOUSSE

Serves 4

INGREDIENTS

4 Conference pears

2 lemons

70g sugar plus 30g sugar (separated)

1 teaspoon freshly grated ginger

150ml double cream

80ml rum

275g dark chocolate, coarsely chopped

1 egg yolk

4 egg whites

1. Peel the pears, keeping them whole, and remove the stems. Put the pears into a saucepan and cover with 500ml water. Add the zest of 1 lemon, juice of 2 lemons, 70g sugar, and the ginger. Cover and cook over low heat for 15 minutes. Remove the pears and cook the liquid down over medium-high heat until it is reduced to 125ml syrup (about 10 minutes). Let cool.
2. For the chocolate mousse, bring the double cream to a boil. Stir in the rum and cook for a few minutes. Remove from the heat. Add the chocolate pieces and egg yolk to the cream-rum mixture and combine.
3. Beat the egg whites until firm, adding the remaining 30g sugar bit by bit. Mix a third of the egg whites into the chocolate mixture (which should be lukewarm). Fold in the remaining egg whites.
4. Refrigerate the mousse for 2 hours. Serve it as an accompaniment to the gingered pears, drizzled with the reserved syrup.

AU CHOCOLAT

If there is any food I look to as compensation for the shortening of days, it is chocolate. Let me be clear: I don't start gobbling it down as soon as summer is over. But somehow chocolate seems less necessary in summer, besides tending to melt. In autumn, and even more so in winter, I depend on it. It must be recognized as potent stuff: potent in taste, potent in nutrients, potent in calories as well. But you don't have to abuse it to enjoy it. A little square savoured goes a long way.

My friend Ségolène recently told me that 17 million French people eat chocolate every day, and she is one of them. She takes it always in mid-afternoon, when she feels the need for a little pick-me-up, the operative principle being "little". Chocolate isn't strictly seasonal, so there isn't anything wrong with year-round moderate enjoyment. But as with any pleasure, the experience is heightened by sometimes doing without it. And a basic French woman's rule of weight management is to ask herself how much does she want what she is about to eat. It isn't until autumn, when the heat is off meteorologically and the heat is on professionally, that I find my thoughts turning irresistibly towards the dark brown richness of chocolate.

Chocolate is *"ma drogue"* with no negative side effect, and it always puts me in a delicious mood. Considering its effect on the neurotransmitter dopamine as well as its abundance of heart-smart flavonoids (a potent kind of antioxidant), I would advocate that chocolate be covered by health insurance, but that is admittedly a very French public policy perspective. Until that day, when presumably chocolate quality would be regulated as well, it is a good idea to bear in mind that the healthful part is the cocoa content, not the milk fats. For good health, eat the darkest chocolate you can. Taken sparingly and as needed, it is beneficial and should not be fattening.

Admittedly, most of us could use some guidance in dosing, as chocolate intake sometimes seems governed by the old fallacy: if a little is good, more must be better. At a book signing on the West Coast, I had just finished reading a passage from the Bread and Chocolate chapter of *French Women Don't Get Fat* when a gentleman approached the lectern to offer me a huge shopping bag I could barely lift filled with an amazing variety of top-quality chocolates. It was obviously a supply for a month even for a serious chocoholic, and little did he know that I was flying to Australia the next day. Yes, I had a fleeting vision of locking myself in my hotel room for a chocolate orgy that night—we all have wicked thoughts, now and again—but fortunately, I was able to gather my wits. I thanked him and told the audience of his beneficence, adding that I knew he wouldn't mind if I shared the gift with everyone at the signing. The applause was thunderous. I'll never forget the sight of this heavenly bounty laid out on the table next to the books, as the line of the devoted (undoubtedly more to chocolate than to me) filed past. Some pieces were bigger than others, the centres held different ganaches (cream fillings), and it was fascinating to observe each person pick out his or her morsel of choice. What except chocolate could bring out both our individuality and the pleasure of sharing?

I always knew the best chocolate moments are not *"en cachette"* (on the sly), but as a communal treat, with friends or family, especially at the end of a meal. Special occasions like a birthday or anniversary, or other joyous times, can be honoured with chocolate, though as I discovered, anywhere two or more people relish chocolate together can be a special occasion.

Even in autumn and winter many chocolate confections are better enjoyed on their own, but I sometimes do indulge in them for dessert, provided the meal has not been on the heavy side. I like chocolate desserts that combine hot and cold, like *profiteroles au chocolat:* the dark warm chocolate sauce and the cold vanilla ice cream colliding in luscious sweetness cut by the dough of the *pâte à choux.* More often I enjoy the way deep, dark chocolate marries with fruits—strawberries, raspberries, and cherries, but also pears and oranges, prunes, dried apricots, and dates—or with nuts, including pecans, pistachios, and my supreme favourite, chestnuts. My mother's *Ardèchois au chocolat et marrons* is a living memory in taste, image, and spirit.

When I invite people for dinner at home, I usually make two desserts, and one has to be chocolate. At the beginning of my married life, we often had dinner for six in our Greenwich Village apartment. One time we had invited some of Edward's college friends whom I barely knew, and, as usual, the last course included chocolate, in this case a "flourless" (some cornflour but no regular flour) chocolate cake with a bit of whipped cream. I served a small piece to each of our guests and offered no seconds at the end of a rather long and elaborate dinner. As the last couple was leaving later in the evening, I noticed Edward's friend John eyeing (actually, more nearly devouring with his eyes) the remaining half of the chocolate cake, which was resting on the kitchen counter. We were leaving for Europe the following night, so I offered to let him and his wife take it home for the weekend. The next morning, John phoned to thank us for dinner and especially for the incredible chocolate cake, which he had eaten on the way home (an hour's drive outside the city)—he couldn't remember eating anything so good. What could I say? I felt a bit of guilt, having led him into temptation. Next time I would remember that friends don't let friends who aren't French women drive with half a chocolate cake.

DARK AND EASY CHOCOLATE CAKE

Serves 8

I always prefer this cake the next day. It's a perfect, rich dessert for cool weather. There is no need to refrigerate—just cover loosely with greaseproof paper and keep it in a cool place. If refrigerated, make sure to take it out at least 2 hours before serving.

INGREDIENTS

225g dark chocolate, broken into pieces

225g unsalted butter, at room temperature, plus extra for greasing mould

4 large eggs

200g sugar

60ml Grand Marnier or orange-flavoured liqueur

6 tablespoons cornflour

1. Preheat the oven to gas mark 4/180°C. Brush a 1-litre ring mould or a 23cm springform cake tin with butter.
2. Melt the chocolate in a heatproof bowl set above a simmering pan of water. Remove and let cool. While the chocolate is cooling, cream the butter in a large mixing bowl.
3. Pour the cooled, melted chocolate into the mixing bowl with the butter and beat for 2 minutes. The mixture should be thick. Set aside.
4. In a separate, large bowl, beat the eggs. Start adding the sugar, beating at high speed, until the eggs are thick and very pale yellow (6 to 8 minutes). Both the egg-sugar and chocolate-butter mixtures should have a similar consistency.
5. Beat the chocolate-butter mixture into the egg-sugar mixture and stir in the Grand

Marnier. Beat another minute to mix. Sift the cornflour into the batter and gently fold in.

6. Pour the batter into the prepared mould. Level off the top and cover with buttered greaseproof paper. Put the mould into a baking dish and fill the dish with near-boiling water, almost up to the top of the mould. Put the baking dish with mould into the oven for 45 to 50 minutes. Let cool. Turn upside down on a serving plate, but wait 30 minutes to remove the mould.

7. Serve with unsweetened whipped cream.

. . . . . .

We are all adults, and therefore we are ultimately responsible for our respective indulgences. We have to learn restraint so we know how to face a shopping bag full of great chocolate or half a chocolate cake. As ever, the key to eating a proper amount is really enjoying what you do eat: gluttony is a desperate bid to satisfy our head, not our stomach. You know you are really eating for pleasure when you surprise yourself by having less than you expected.

And sometimes by just saying no. A few years ago, I was invited to a holiday-theme lunch at a famous food magazine with the top brass. When coffee was served (and it's only after a special lunch that I would have a second coffee during the day after my breakfast one), out came the chocolate truffles. They looked divine, and I decided to savour one with coffee. Conversation was animated, and before I knew it the plate was circulating a second time with some people already eating their third truffle. But one small bite of the first one was enough to tell me these truffles were not very good, let alone first-rate. I discreetly left the rest on my saucer. An observer might have imagined I was exercising astonishing self-control, but it was really quite easy to pass on something that offered little or no pleasure. With the holidays approaching, I knew I would be eating truly irresistible chocolate before long. I didn't mind waiting.

We do get a little careless at this time of year, because so many "goodies" are put before us, even if many of them are not so good. It also seems that the remoteness of bikini season gives many of us licence to let ourselves go and take cover under less revealing clothes. But that only sets you up to face losing weight in springtime. Sure, it happens, but there is no need to regard autumn/winter weight gain as inevitable. If you tend your equilibrium, eating for pleasure mindful of taste and choice, you can enjoy the season without fear of getting fat. Anyway, clothes should not be a way of concealing ourselves but of flattering ourselves.

As many women will admit, there is no better time of year for wearing clothes. Not that they would otherwise be topless: it's merely that in autumn we can wear things without feeling like we're overbundled or a sweaty mess. Springtime, too, is this way in theory, but in many places one goes straight into summer dress. The spring coat, so common until the sixties and still favoured by the ultra-chic, has alas become an anachronism for most. People today seem to revel in going out wearing as little as they can. When I see kids at New England schools and universities wearing shorts at the first sign of the winter thaw, I imagine a sort of pagan invocation of warmth. I mind that much less than those unseasonably skimpy styles that just won't go away. Let's draw a veil over those, or at least a scarf.

Long Necklace Scarf

You'll need a rectangular scarf long enough so that each end reaches down to your belt when it hangs around your neck.

1. Fold the scarf in half once or twice depending on its width.
2. With the scarf around your neck, take one length and loop it into a simple knot that hangs just above your first rib.
3. Pull the other end through the loop and then tighten the loop knot, adjusting the two lengths so they are even and the knot is well positioned.

Side-knotted Oblong Scarf

This knot and style have become very fashionable. A short scarf works best over a sweater and a longer version over a jacket or coat.

1. Fold an oblong scarf in half lengthwise and then double by bringing both of the long ends together (like a rope).
2. Place it around your neck and pull the folded loop end across to one side of your body and pass the other end of the scarf through the loop.
3. Pull down on the hanging end to tighten for comfort and positioning off-centre.

Shoulder Wrap

This is a quick trick for so-called French elegance par

excellence. It requires a glorious scarf that goes with a solid-coloured dress.

1. Fold diagonally in half to create a triangle.
2. Place the scarf over one shoulder and pull the two long ends across your body (one behind and one in front) and knot the ends just above the hip opposite the shoulder upon which the scarf rests.

It's very easy and typical in autumn to take our colour cues from the landscape. Heathery and brownish tweeds, deep rust and golden woollens are unimpeachable and these colours usually look too drab or edgy in spring and summer. While these colours are flattering and easy to wear, there is no necessity of banishing bright colour in autumn. Often one bright saturated colour can fetchingly offset the sobriety of other clothes and if you pick the colour of the season (fashion's, not the earth's), you needn't make much more effort to look *au courant.*

MONDAY

Breakfast

65g Grandma Louise's Oatmeal with Grated Apple (www.mireilleguiliano.com)
80ml skimmed milk
½ teaspoon brown sugar
1 slice rye bread, toasted and buttered
Coffee or tea

Lunch

Jarlsberg, Apple, Mushroom Salad (page 186)
1 multigrain roll
1 square chocolate
Non-calorific beverage

Dinner

Skate with Capers (page 177)
Cauliflower Gratin (page 169)
100g green vegetables
125g yogurt
1 pear
1 glass red or white wine

TUESDAY

Breakfast

1 teaspoon soya nuts
2-egg omelette
1 slice wholemeal bread, toasted and buttered
½ grapefruit
Coffee or tea

Lunch

250ml Basic Vegetable Soup (www.mireilleguiliano.com)
1 slice country or wholemeal bread
125g yogurt
1 apple
Non-calorific beverage

Dinner

Macaroni with Spinach and Pancetta (page 175)
120g sprouting broccoli
Mango Carpaccio with Cinnamon (page 250)
1 glass red wine

WEDNESDAY

Breakfast

125g yogurt
1 kiwi
1 small brioche or ½ bagel with butter and jam
Coffee or tea

Lunch

Chicken and Green Bean Salad (page 176)
6 almonds
150g black grapes
Non-calorific beverage

Dinner

Cod with Potato Salad (page 166)
100g spinach
Sautéed Mushrooms (page 82)
Crème caramel
1 glass red or white wine

THURSDAY

Breakfast

2 prunes
125ml freshly squeezed grapefruit juice or ½ grapefruit
125g yogurt
1 fried egg
1 slice wholemeal bread, toasted and buttered
Coffee or tea

Lunch

250ml Green Soup (page 114)
1 slice wholemeal bread
30g cheese
½ papaya
Non-calorific beverage

Dinner

Pork Chops with Apples (www.mireilleguiliano.com)
70g brown rice
Mixed salad
Mousse au Chocolat (www.mireilleguiliano.com)
1 glass red or white wine

FRIDAY

Breakfast

30g cheese
1 slice prosciutto
1 soft-boiled egg
1 slice multigrain bread, toasted and buttered
3 dried apricots
Coffee or tea

Lunch

Buttersquash Soup (page 172)
200g green vegetables
½ banana
Non-calorific beverage

Dinner

Turkey Escalopes with Pesto (page 179)
100g mashed potatoes
Green salad
Pear-Apple Compote with Honey (page 185)
1 glass red wine

SATURDAY

Breakfast

1 slice ham
125ml freshly squeezed orange juice or 1 orange
60g oatmeal with raisins and walnuts
125ml skimmed milk
Coffee or tea

Lunch

Mussels in White Wine (page 178)
1 slice country or wholemeal bread
Mâche (lamb's lettuce) salad with 30g nuts and a pear
Non-calorific beverage

Dinner

Grilled Steak with Wine Sauce (page 181)
1 baked potato with butter or sour cream
Green salad
1 slice Dark and Easy Chocolate Cake (page 198)
1 glass red wine

SUNDAY

Breakfast

125g yogurt
Pears on Brioche (page 190)
Coffee or tea

Lunch (main meal)

Seafood platter (oysters, crab, and clams)
1 slice rye bread with salted butter
200g green vegetables
Baked Apple Aixoise (page 188)
1 glass Champagne or sparkling wine

Dinner

250ml Celeriac Soup (page 228)
80g carrots, sautéed
50g raw fennel
30g hard cheese
½ grapefruit

5

EN HIVER: WINTER PLEASURES

Most of us don't have the choice to sit winter out. The fact is that not every bird gets to fly south. And I confess I wouldn't want to: I love my morning walks in the winter, breathing the cool, crisp air, and I can't imagine living in places without much seasonal variation. When the passing of the year doesn't impress itself upon my senses, I am, in some profound sense, lost.

As the days shorten, other mammals grow fuller coats and change colour. Let's not kid ourselves: winter has an effect on us as well. In the northern climes, including Paris, the U.K. and New York, a point comes when it seems the cold and long hours indoors will never end, when the snows of two months ago are often still piled in the streets, and nothing is left in the cupboard but a few shrivelled root vegetables. Okay, *j'exagère,* but you know the feeling. There is scant comfort in knowing that it's worse elsewhere: Buffalo gets almost two-and-a-half metres of snow a year. Or consider Sweden, an enchanting land in the summer, when the sun rises at 3 a.m., but where in winter there are but four brief hours of grey so-called daylight. No, the real consolation is in knowing what awaits us when it's over: the regeneration of everything in spring. I'm not just looking on the bright side here. I would not trade that thrill, and that awareness of progress—of the fullness of time—for the eternal sunshine of a spotless mind in L.A.

Christmas is celebrated in December less because we believe the Nativity actually occurred then and more as a perpetuation of ancient rites designed to bring some light into the darkness. But once the unwanted gifts have been returned and the last cork of New Year has been popped, we enter a bit of a tunnel. With relatively little light, for those of us in the Northern hemisphere, and even less fresh unfattening food to enjoy—and having perhaps allowed an extra kilo or so to creep aboard during the holidays—we are more vulnerable than ever to getting fat. What can we do to keep it all together? In fact, there is plenty. We need not—and after all, we cannot—spend those months when the slant of light oppresses simply huddled under the duvet with a book, much as a French woman delights in doing that sometimes.

In winter many of us rise in darkness and return home from work in darkness, practically never having seen the light of day. There's a reason nature has designed some animals to sleep through the whole affair. We, however, aren't so lucky—or perhaps we are luckier. Winter's purpose is to clear the decks so nature can start again. Long ago, a person's age would be expressed by how many winters she had on her back. Now technology spares us the worst effects of the elements; the rest is up to us. The trick is to make it as full and energetic a period as it can be.

First, let us acknowledge that humans, like bears and birds, are photoperiodic: we are affected by the duration of daylight. Most of us experience to some degree what has come to be called Seasonal Affective Disorder. In other words, the dearth of light brings us down. And many of us take refuge from the blues in food. *Qu'est-ce qu'on va faire?* One simple solution is to make a point of going outside at midday. If you work in an office, your exposure to light in winter can easily be limited to the fluorescent variety, which is neither flattering nor healthy. Take a little break at noon and soak up what sunshine you can. (A French woman—at least this French woman—will still wear sunglasses to avoid squinting in the glare and crow's feet.) This exposure can help keep our sleep cycles in order—the disruption of these is one of winter's biggest health risks. It also gives you some chance of producing the vitamin D your body requires, although in winter it must be supplemented by tablet and by D-rich foods such as milk, egg yolks, and tuna.

Even on the gloomiest days, a lunchtime promenade will do you good, for the other compensation for the lack of light is to move. Apart from its metabolic and cardiovascular benefits, physical exertion is known to have a stimulative effect on the neurotransmitters that keep our spirits up. Snow sports have become hugely popular in the last few years. Many people I know in Paris and New York track the months of winter by the ski season. But just mention the word "ski" and I imagine not the amazing rush but the prospect of chapped skin in bone-chilling cold, killer trees, and broken bones (mine). Fine for the ski set, not for me, though I do encourage sportier types at least in the less hair-raising cross-country version. Or ice-skating! (In Paris, Rollerblading en masse seems to continue *sans interruption* on weekends through the winter.) Any exercise we undertake for pleasure is a good one. I am told the gym serves as a refuge for some in the winter. But even *sans* skis and treadmill, I find lots of easy ways of getting my heart rate up and working my muscles, overcoming the ever-present temptation to sleep in.

So what do I do? Walking and yoga are my prime winter movements. After the metabolic slowdown of winter sleep, it's important not just to get the body going but to awaken the mind to the body. Feel the connection—it's my French zen thing. Some simple stretching before breakfast can do wonders. In New York, I leave the house by taking the stairs down fourteen floors. That wakes my body up for sure. And when I don't get as much movement in my normal day as I'd like, I make a point of taking the stairs back up . . . often all the way to the fifteenth floor. In winter, the stairs really can be the most efficient and convenient way of elevating not just yourself but your heart rate and mood. And you can avoid hypothermia: New York, for example, can be wickedly cold on winter mornings. On the sub-zero days when I see those morning joggers trailing vapour from their mouths and noses, I have to smile. They don't need to do that to be healthy. I hope they are doing it for pleasure. I imagine these people must be skiers, too.

Though sometimes it is just too cold and windy to leave the house, I do love to walk in the snow . . . especially in New York City. New York with its clear blue winter skies and buzzing streets can become transcendentally quiet when a thick white blanket is first laid down. The traffic disappears (save the large sanitation trucks transformed into ploughs). I look forward to heading out after a blizzard for a long walk. Like walking on the edge of the surf on the beach, trudging through fresh snow is wonderful exercise and, as every kid knows, great fun. As I walk down the centre of big avenues and little side streets, passing fellow travellers, the streetscape feels as it must have centuries ago. Everything is still and clean, and the community becomes a picturesque village of children on toboggans (an odd thing to find in Manhattan, but you do) and neighbours shovelling the pavements . . . eventually some begin to dig out their cars, only to have them partially reburied by the ploughs. Everyone seems in high spirits, even—perhaps especially—those shovellers. The stores slowly reopen, and people share in the wintry gift of a small reprieve from the demands of schedule.

Winter rain is something else, though. It can be awful, and I certainly don't walk in it for pleasure or exercise, though the humid air is wonderful for the skin; on dry winter days, both skin and hair need moisturizing. An excellent homemade beauty mask of *Mamie*'s is always at the ready. She was big on these natural treatments, and in the winter, once a week she'd cut a slice of lemon or grapefruit and rub it on her face first thing in the morning. It was her trick to clarify the top layer of the skin. For my teenage pre-period skin problems, she'd put some parsley juice on a piece of cotton and apply it to troublesome spots. For the oily and dull skin of my cousin, she'd mix some grapes with almonds and apply the paste to her face (use your coffee grinder or a blender to do the mixing), leaving it on for a few minutes and rinsing with cold water. Egg mixtures were some of the most effective weapons in her arsenal. No matter the skin type she'd recommend this one over and over: before a party, mix an egg yolk with a few drops of olive oil and leave the mixture on the face for 15 minutes. Another one was a mixture of an egg yolk, a few lettuce leaves, and 125g yogurt; it tightens the pores and hydrates the skin. Concocting something soothing for your face can make an afternoon at home feel like a day at the spa. (Speaking of spas, massages are cheaper and easier to come by these days, and they can be a great way of pampering yourself.) But in any case, make yourself a jug of lemon water, get out your yoga mat, and after some poses treat yourself to a mask. I have been doing yoga year-round for decades, but in winter I double up at home and love to take classes to expand my practice. In yoga, as in life, one is always learning.

The house gives me another outlet of exertion, this one productive as well as healthly. Even French women with French maids like to *faire le ménage* (do the housework). Other Europeans, too. Recently the *Wall Street Journal* reported that the least effective way to market cleaning products to Italian women is to tout their time-saving convenience. It would seem the Italians know what French women do: convenience has its downside. We are too quick to write off and evade as drudgery activities that keep the blood flowing while giving us a small but satisfying sense of accomplishment. We all need such a sense in this world we've created, where the goals we set ourselves can be so complex.

Finally, I have a little anti-stress winter exercise that makes me feel good physically and mentally, whether I'm at home or at work. Have you ever picked low-hanging fruit from a tree? Apples, cherries, peaches, pears, whatever? Imagine yourself standing under that tree and reaching up as high as you can with one arm to pick a ripe fruit. Are you on your toes? Got it? Great. Now place it in a basket at your feet. Relax and breathe deeply. Now reach up with your other arm and stretch for another fruit, then bend and place it in the basket. Alternate arms until you have filled the basket with twenty or more pieces of fruit. Got more time; need more exercise or escape? Move to a different fruit tree and repeat. Apart from triggering the release of neurotransmitters that create a sense of *bien-être* (well-being), exercises like this loosen tight muscles and bring oxygen-rich blood to the brain, helping to reduce high levels of cortisol, the hormone associated with stress (and not surprisingly with the storage of body fat). For me, just thinking about being outdoors under a fruit tree is a soothing mental vacation in time and space. It's a lot cheaper than Palm Beach, and I can just taste those fruits.

BONNE DÉGUSTATION

Okay, so your blood is flowing. But what's to eat? Even more than in autumn, I need chocolate. If in autumn I feel there should be a prescription drug benefit covering chocolate, in winter I find myself advocating a national strategic chocolate reserve, so convinced am I of its consoling powers. But we still have to observe moderation. Even in winter, or rather in winter especially, we must fashion a plan of nourishment suited to the demands on our bodies, as well as to the limited variety of foodstuffs. Life can't all be treats, but it should still be filled with pleasures, so let me begin with the ones most deeply ingrained in my own psyche.

The first word in winter food worldwide tends to be the dishes served at feasts that have carried over from the earliest pagan celebrations of the solstice. The food is typically elaborate, and these convivial occasions are often the last chance to gather loved ones together until the thaw. The fear that first inspired these rites—fear that the failing light would never return unless we propitiated the gods—has itself mostly faded, but the French have never needed an excuse to pop a cork or share a meal. There are four gastronomic pillars of the typical French holiday menu, especially for Christmas: chestnuts, oysters, turkey, and the ubiquitous *bûche de Noël* or Yule log.

MARRONS

In our kitchen on frosty weekend evenings, my mother would bring out a small wicker basket covered with a cloth napkin under which was a mound of raw chestnuts. We knew we were in for a treat. She would score them with a small sharp knife, and set them in a frying pan on top of the stove to roast as we eagerly waited. For me, that scent in the kitchen was always linked to Christmas and the holiday season, particularly as *Mamie* would often also bake on those evenings. When the chestnuts were ready, the challenge was to peel them while they were still warm without burning our fingers. That danger was part of the fun, and the first kid to cry "*aïe*!" might need the adults to come to the rescue. It often happened to me since I was unable to peel them as fast as I could eat them, the membranes clinging to the flesh, especially in the crevices of the multi-fruited kind.

Later, as a student in Paris, I discovered the big-city version of my childhood Yuletide madeleine: street-corner charcoal braziers in Saint-Germain or the Champs-Élysées or any main intersection, often near cinemas for those leaving the show. We would buy chestnuts freshly roasted, still warm in bags fashioned of layered newspaper. They were neither as good nor as hot as those I remembered from home. But they were a treat all the same, and an affordable one. To this day, whether outside the department stores in Paris, such as the BHV, or on Madison Avenue in midtown Manhattan, it is hard for me to pass up a few warm chestnuts—one of the few truly wholesome street foods.

Of course, there were more elaborate and fancy ways of eating chestnuts as part of celebratory meals. Sometimes they would be proffered in a rich soup, my favourites being a velvety cream of celery finished off with pieces of bacon and roasted chestnuts or the luscious and luxurious little tasting cup of chestnut cream soup. Sometimes the big chestnuts would simply be slow-roasted as a vegetable accompaniment to game dishes, particularly *pintade* (guinea fowl), pheasant, and venison.

But my most cherished discovery of this seasonal delight took place in Provence, where chestnuts are part of the "after dessert". Nowadays big events have "after parties"; but for as long as I can remember, big meals in France have always had the "after desserts" called *petits fours*—bite-sized pastries and chocolates. These would be served with the coffee, which follows dessert. *Marrons glacés,* or glazed chestnuts, are not actually frozen, but they are supremely sweet and delicious, my choice for the queen of after desserts when you are pulling out all the stops. They have become the object of some very opinionated connoisseurship in Paris.

My Uncle Charles gave me a lesson in the art of *marrons glacés,* which he had mastered. Like everything in cooking, the quality begins with the ingredients: impeccable chestnuts come from Torino in Italy (the very best are enormous and of silken texture), or Naples or Collobrières in the French Var, and even the Ardèche, where my uncle had his restaurant in a spa town. The big and perfect specimens that passed muster were boiled till tender and would be ever so lightly dipped in crystallized ice-sugar syrup so as to produce just a patina of glazing while the chestnut within remained *moelleux* (soft). Each would then be wrapped in gold foil. I will confess that very few people make their own, though the quest for perfection can be a long one. I can report my own has ended happily at Stohrer, the high temple of gourmandise in the second arrondissement in Paris; many other chestnut freaks concur. When you bite into one perhaps you'll see stars, as Dom Pérignon claimed when first tasting Champagne—at least I do. A purveyor of similar sublimity is Pierre Marcolini, a world-class *chocolatier*, located down the street from our Paris apartment and now also in New York City (talk about temptation!). Nothing says "I love you" at Christmas like his little four-pack of *marrons glacés.* It's also the gift of confidence in one's appreciation of moderation. They will keep at peak flavour for just a few weeks, but one should never eat more than one at a time. Okay, never say never.

CHESTNUTS AND HONEY

Serves 4

INGREDIENTS

500g chestnuts
2 tablespoons acacia honey
Salt and freshly ground pepper

1. Peel the chestnuts and cook in boiling water until tender, about 20 minutes. Drain and pat dry.
2. Warm the honey in a large pan over medium heat and add the chestnuts, stirring to coat. Stir until they have caramelized slightly. Season with salt and pepper to taste.

N.B. SERVE THIS WITH ANY WINTER BIRD SUCH AS TURKEY, PHEASANT, OR GUINEA FOWL.

CHESTNUT SOUP

Serves 4

INGREDIENTS

500g peeled chestnuts

500 to 750ml beef or vegetable stock

125ml double cream

Salt and freshly ground pepper

15g unsalted butter

2 tablespoons finely chopped parsley

1. Put the peeled chestnuts into a saucepan with 500ml of the stock. Bring to a simmer, uncovered, for 40 to 50 minutes, adding more stock, if necessary, to keep the chestnuts covered.
2. When the chestnuts are tender, drain, reserving the stock. Purée the chestnuts in a food processor or blender. Return the puréed chestnuts to the reserved stock, stirring continuously, and add in the double cream. Season with salt and pepper to taste. Just before serving add the butter and parsley.

THE WORLD OF MY OYSTERS

Did I tell you I love oysters? I mean, I really love oysters and eat them often. And they are good for you—low in calories and high in nutritional value. When I was growing up, we followed the prescription of eating oysters only in months with Rs in them, as that was both when they were harvested and when it was cool enough to ship them safely. Today, with oyster farms and modern transportation, refrigeration, and global shipping, it is possible to eat them year-round. Cold, juicy oysters can be a summer treat, but like a true French woman, I find they speak winter to me (and autumn and spring). Farmed oysters are not significantly inferior to the wild kind—a very different case from, say, salmon. In fact, oyster aquaculture is sustainable and eco-friendly, and so with a fastidious supplier you may do better than with some who troll oyster beds at sea—certainly in the warmer months, when I don't advise eating them raw. Still, oysters are such a staple in late autumn and winter, and such a winter holiday tradition in France—just writing this, I can taste Brittany's fine Claire and Belon varieties on the half shell and see the men on New Year's Eve shucking them by the dozen at temporary stands on Paris market streets—I don't feel the need to eat them except in the natural course of their lives, so long as that ends in my stomach. The French eat them raw or cooked (though the latter is, of course, the only sensible way to use them in a stuffing).

Over the past decade as oyster bars have become more common in restaurants, Americans have come to appreciate oysters more. That's smart: despite such a luscious taste and texture, oysters are not fattening, up to the first couple of dozen anyway. A bit like wine, oysters come in different types and styles typical of their *terroir,* insofar as one can speak of a *terroir*—localized soil and climate—in water. Drawing in countless gallons of local water and nutrients as its sweet flesh plumpens, the oyster is very much a product of where it spawns, and two of the same variety raised in two different locations won't taste the same. In America, there are wonderful kinds from both the East Coast (from Maine to Delaware) and the West. My favourite is the tiny Kumamoto oyster from the Pacific Northwest, which I enjoy whenever I can at

Balthazar, a restaurant in New York's SoHo. Perhaps I should have been born a century ago when New York City was the oyster capital of the world and Restaurant Prunier in Paris had an entire menu with oysters!

In America we still don't have the selection found in France, which is Europe's largest producer, with 200 kinds and a yield of 120,000 tons a year, mostly for domestic consumption. (The connection with French men as great lovers has never been proved, but the concentration of zinc, vital for prostate health, does make me wonder.) Such variety presents delicious possibilities when going to a restaurant with friends; with each person ordering a different kind, everyone can have a *dégustation d'huîtres*—an oyster tasting menu. You can compare flavours between the two basic kinds: on the one hand the *plates* (flat), such as Belons (powerful and *iodées*—tasting of the sea) or Marennes (a more refined taste); on the other hand, the *creuses* (convex), such as Portuguaises, Boudeuses (pouters), and including *les fines* (small and delicate) and *les spéciales* (fleshy).

To test your connoisseurship further, some restaurants offer "boutique oysters" with the name of the grower listed on the menu. My weakness is for Giraudeau, and I'm lucky to be near the wonderful restaurant-brasserie Alcazar in the sixth arrondissement, which becomes my cafeteria during winter stays in Paris and which always seems to carry Giraudeau's offerings on the menu. Regardless of variety, however, oysters are rich in protein, minerals, and vitamins. If you haven't made a place for them in your life, they are a most consoling discovery in winter.

"As I ate the oysters, with their strong taste of the sea and their faint metallic taste that the cold white wine washed away, leaving only the sea taste and the succulent texture, as I drank their cold liquid from each shell and washed it down with the crisp taste of the wine, I lost the empty feeling and began to be happy and to make plans." That's how Ernest Hemingway had them in his memoir of Paris in the 1920s, *A Moveable Feast.* That's how they have been enjoyed for centuries. As far as I am concerned, when serving oysters on the half shell, you can hold the *mignonette* (that's the classic dressing of shallots and vinegar served in French bistros), and if you are serving them warm, the same goes even for the caviar that sometimes dots them. All you need is a few drops of lemon juice (especially if some of the exquisite liquid has been lost), and if your taste runs like mine, a touch of freshly ground pepper. Add some thin slices of rye bread with salted butter and it's a feast. WWHD (What Would Hemingway Drink)? Champagne is festive and always appropriate, Sauvignon Blanc is totally correct, but more often than not I opt for the inexpensive but perfectly matched Muscadet from the Loire Valley.

If your palate is new to oysters, a warm preparation is an easy introduction. They are divine with leeks (as recommended in the leek section); spinach is a close second, but all are easy, so feel free to experiment. If opening them intimidates you more than eating them, your fishmonger will be glad to do it. He will put the oyster and its liquid (liquor) in a container and give you the empty shells if the recipe presentation requires them.

COCKTAIL *D'HUÎTRES*

Serves 4

INGREDIENTS

12 oysters

125ml apple juice

Juice of 1 lemon

1 Granny Smith apple, peeled, cored, and cubed

1. Open the oysters, remove from shells, and drain, reserving their liquor for another use, perhaps a soup (if your fishmonger opens the oysters for you, ask him to give you the liquor, too). Put 3 oysters in each of 4 martini glasses.
2. Put the apple juice, lemon juice, and a few cubes of the apple into a bowl. Mix well and distribute over the oysters. Serve immediately.

N.B. AN OYSTER KNIFE MAKES IT EASY TO OPEN OYSTERS, AND A THICK RUBBER GLOVE MAKES IT SAFE. OYSTERS CAN BE PURCHASED ALREADY SHUCKED.

OYSTER SOUP

Serves 4

Today's cutting-edge chefs are getting very creative with amazing combinations. As always, some work better than others. But the soupe au lait d'huîtres *at Maison de Bricourt in Normandy was an experience worth the detour. And it has inspired this version of mine.*

INGREDIENTS

24 oysters, with their liquor
30g unsalted butter
1 litre milk (regular or skimmed)
1 teaspoon paprika
Salt and freshly ground pepper

1. Open the oysters (see page 223), remove from shells, and poach them in a mixture of oyster liquor and butter over low heat for 3 to 5 minutes, until they swell and their thin edges start curling.
2. Add the milk and paprika and season with salt and pepper to taste. Bring to a boil, then cook over low heat, stirring occasionally, for 10 to 12 minutes. Serve immediately with buttered toast.

OYSTERS WITH GARLIC BUTTER

Serves 4

1. Preheat the grill.
2. Put the butter into a bowl. Press the garlic cloves over the butter and mix well. Add the parsley, season with salt and pepper to taste, and refrigerate.
3. Open the oysters (see page 223) and put them, in their shells, into a grill pan sprinkled with plenty of coarse salt, which will hold them in place. Add about ½ teaspoon of the parsley-butter mixture to each oyster and grill for 1 to 2 minutes. Serve immediately with rye bread.

INGREDIENTS

75g unsalted butter, at room temperature

2 cloves garlic, peeled

4 tablespoons finely chopped parsley

Salt and freshly ground pepper

24 oysters

Coarse salt for grill pan

OYSTERS WITH LEMON ZEST

Serves 4

INGREDIENTS

24 oysters, with their liquor

2 shallots, peeled but left whole

75g unsalted butter, cut into pieces

Coarse salt for grill pan

Zest of 1 lemon

Freshly ground pepper

1. Preheat the grill.
2. Open the oysters (see page 223), remove from shells, and set aside, reserving their liquor.
3. Strain the liquor (you should have 180 to 250ml) to remove any stray pieces of shell. Bring the liquid and shallots to a boil. Continue cooking until reduced by half. Remove the shallots and whisk in the butter. Keep the sauce warm on top of a pan of simmering water or in a double boiler.
4. Put the oysters back into their shells and place them on a grill pan sprinkled with plenty of salt to keep them in place. Sprinkle the oysters with lemon zest, some of the sauce, and season with pepper to taste. Grill until golden, 1 to 2 minutes. Serve immediately with a baguette to soak up the delicious juice.

Let's face it, in winter we find ourselves scraping for fresh vegetables. Passing these months without an arsenal of Italian tomato purée is inconceivable. But as in all seasons, soup is an unsurpassed way of eating a good serving of what is fresh as well as what keeps. Early in winter, for instance, celeriac, a deliciously nutty bulb related to celery, is available for a short time, and I never fail to take advantage. It really is good only in season.

CELERIAC SOUP

Serves 6

As in their mashed potatoes recipe, the women in my family love to experiment with the ratio of potato to celeriac in soup, always in favour of the latter it seems, and, of course, they can't help adding some leeks. When in Provence, we add a drizzle of olive oil for that extra—I'll say it only this once—"je ne sais quoi". *It makes me love this soup even more:*

INGREDIENTS

2 tablespoons olive oil

500g celeriac, peeled and cubed

350g potatoes, peeled and cubed

1 leek, white parts only, sliced

2 onions, peeled and finely chopped

2 shallots, peeled and finely chopped

1 litre vegetable stock

1 bay leaf

Salt and freshly ground pepper

250ml milk (regular or skimmed)

6 slices of day-old baguette, toasted

1. Warm the oil in a large, heavy-based, flameproof casserole and add the celeriac, potatoes, leek, onions, and shallots. Cook for 10 minutes over medium heat, stirring every once in a while. Add the vegetable stock and bay leaf, season with salt and pepper to taste, and bring to a boil.

2. Reduce heat, then cover and simmer over low heat until the vegetables are tender, 15 to 20 minutes. Add the milk, stir well, and cook for another 5 minutes. Serve, placing a warm toasted baguette slice on top of each bowl.

N.B. THE TRADITIONAL. RECIPE CALLS FOR CROUTONS, BREAD PIECES FRIED IN OIL. WE FIND LEFTOVER TOASTED BAGUETTE MUCH LIGHTER AND JUST AS DELICIOUS.

MIXED VEGETABLE SOUP

Serves 4

1. Warm 1 tablespoon of the oil in a large, heavy-based, flameproof casserole. Sweat the onion, add the leeks, and season with salt and pepper to taste. Add the carrots, potatoes, courgettes, chicken stock, and spinach. Bring to a boil, then cover and simmer for 20 minutes, until all the vegetables are tender.
2. Purée in a food mill and serve with a drizzle of the remaining oil and the basil (if using).

INGREDIENTS

2 tablespoons olive oil

1 onion, peeled and chopped

4 leeks, white parts only, sliced

Salt and freshly ground pepper

2 carrots, sliced

225g potatoes, peeled and coarsely cubed

2 courgettes, diced

1 litre chicken stock

250g spinach, washed and chopped

2 tablespoons basil chiffonnade (shredded) for garnish (optional)

N.B. IN THE SUMMER, THIS SOUP CAN BE SERVED COLD. REMOVE IT FROM THE REFRIGERATOR 20 MINUTES BEFORE SERVING. ADD A DRIZZLE OF LEMON JUICE AND REPLACE THE BASIL WITH FRESH MINT OR CORIANDER.

SEA SCALLOPS WITH CITRUS FRUIT

Serves 4

Scallops are another shellfish that intimidates some, but they are amazingly simple to make: the key, in fact, is not to do too much to them. While fresh herbs are still around, I love to sear scallops, adding plenty of fresh sage leaves for flavour. In the dead of winter, though, when there is no sage, but lots of scallops, this preparation is a favourite.

INGREDIENTS

16 sea scallops, rinsed and dried on paper towels

Zest and juice of ½ grapefruit

Zest and juice of ½ orange

Zest and juice of ½ lemon

1 tablespoon honey

4 cardamom pods, crushed

2 tablespoons olive oil

Salt and freshly ground pepper

30g unsalted butter, cut into small pieces

Sea salt

1. Blanch the scallops in boiling water for 1 minute. In a bowl, whisk together the fruit zest and juices, honey, and cardamom.
2. Warm a frying pan over medium-high heat. Add the oil to the pan, season the scallops with salt and pepper, and cook them for 2 minutes on each side. Set the scallops aside on a warm plate and cover with foil.
3. In a saucepan, reduce the juice mixture over medium-high heat for 2 minutes, stirring all the while. Reduce the heat and whisk in the butter a few pieces at a time.
4. Plate the scallops and drizzle with sauce. Sprinkle with a few grains of sea salt.

PRAWN AND TUNA SALAD WITH BANANA AND YOGURT

Serves 4

1. In a salad bowl, combine the prawns and the banana slices with the lemon juice. Add the tuna, almonds, and sultanas.
2. For the yogurt dressing: Combine the yogurt and double cream, mixing well. Add the paprika, dill, and season with pepper to taste.
3. Add the yogurt dressing to the salad bowl and toss gently. Serve chilled.

INGREDIENTS

500g cooked prawns, peeled and deveined

2 bananas, sliced into 5mm pieces

2 tablespoons lemon juice

225g canned tuna in water, drained

60g sliced almonds

120g sultanas steamed for 2 minutes

FOR THE YOGURT DRESSING:

250g plain yogurt

1 tablespoon double cream (or sour cream)

Dash of paprika

1 tablespoon chopped dill

Freshly ground pepper

STUFFED POUSSINS (OR SMALL "FRENCH HENS")

Serves 4

INGREDIENTS

FOR THE STUFFING:

150g brown rice

75g mixed nuts (pine nuts, walnut pieces, whole hazelnuts)

2 tablespoons sultanas

80ml chicken stock

1 tablespoon finely chopped parsley

1 teaspoon dried herbs (chervil and savory or rosemary and thyme)

Salt and freshly ground pepper

2 poussins (600 to 750g each)

Salt and freshly ground pepper

30g unsalted butter, melted

3 tablespoons chicken stock

1. For the stuffing: Bring 500ml water to a boil. Add the rice and cook for 15 minutes. Drain the rice and mix with remaining stuffing ingredients. Season with salt and pepper to taste and refrigerate overnight.
2. Preheat the oven to gas mark 9/240°C. Rinse the poussins and dry them inside and out with paper towels and season with salt and pepper. Stuff the birds loosely with the rice mixture and truss. Put the remaining stuffing aside in a small ovenproof dish.
3. Put the poussins into a baking dish, brush them with the melted butter and season again with the salt and pepper. Bake in the preheated oven for 10 minutes, then baste with the chicken stock. Continue to baste every 10 minutes. After 20 minutes, reduce the temperature to gas mark 4/180°C and put the dish of stuffing into the oven. Roast the birds for another 20 minutes. Serve (half a bird per person) immediately with a tablespoon of stuffing on each side of the poussins as garnish.

N.B. THIS IS A WONDERFUL VALENTINE'S DAY DINNER. WHILE THE POUSSINS ARE IN THE OVEN YOU CAN CONCOCT A LITTLE DESSERT, *ET VOILÀ*, YOU SIT DOWN FOR A CANDLELIT DINNER.

GARLICKY MONKFISH

Serves 4

1. Warm the oil and garlic in a large frying pan over medium heat until the garlic is cooked, but not brown. Add the tomato purée and white wine and mix well.
2. Add the monkfish and cook over medium-low heat for 10 minutes on each side. Season with salt and pepper to taste and sprinkle with the basil. Serve immediately.

INGREDIENTS

4 tablespoons olive oil

4 teaspoons finely chopped garlic

2 tablespoons tomato purée

250ml white wine

500g monkfish

2 tablespoons basil, chiffonnade (shredded)

Salt and freshly ground pepper

SALMON WITH ORANGE *EN PAPILLOTE*

Serves 4

INGREDIENTS

FOR THE MARINADE:

60ml orange juice
1 tablespoon lemon juice
1 tablespoon dry vermouth
2 tablespoons soy sauce
1 tablespoon chopped fresh ginger
Pinch of sugar

Olive oil
4×120g skinless fillets of salmon
Salt and freshly ground pepper

1. Preheat the oven to gas mark 4/180°C.
2. In a small saucepan, combine all the ingredients for the marinade and season with salt and pepper to taste. Bring to a simmer over medium heat until the marinade is reduced by half. Remove from the heat and set aside. Cut 8 large pieces of aluminium foil or parchment paper into squares large enough to cover each fish fillet and leave a 5cm border all around. Lightly brush 4 squares with olive oil.
3. Put a salmon fillet in the centre of each oiled square and drizzle with the marinade. Season with salt and pepper. Place the remaining squares on top of the fillets and fold up the edges to form parcels. Simply double folding each of the four sides is enough to seal each parcel. Put the *papillotes* on a baking sheet and bake for 10 to 15 minutes. Serve with brown rice.

CHICKEN TATIN

Serves 6

INGREDIENTS

8 tablespoons olive oil

1.5kg chicken, cut into pieces

2 tablespoons chopped shallots

2 cinnamon sticks

3 cardamom pods, crushed

1 litre chicken stock

Salt and freshly ground pepper

2 large aubergines, sliced thinly lengthwise

1 teaspoon turmeric

500g basmati rice

50g pine nuts

2 tablespoons sultanas

1 litre yogurt

1. In a large, heavy-based, flameproof casserole, warm 2 tablespoons oil, and brown the chicken on all sides over medium-high heat. Leaving the chicken in the casserole, lower the heat and add the shallots, cinnamon, cardamom, and chicken stock. Season with salt and pepper to taste. Bring to a boil over high heat. Lower the heat to medium, and simmer for another 30 to 35 minutes.

2. Remove the chicken from the casserole and reserve the stock. When cool enough to handle, remove the skin and bones and discard.

3. Warm 4 tablespoons of oil in a large frying pan, and cook the aubergine 5 minutes on each side over medium-high heat. Remove, and pat dry on paper towels.

4. Mix the turmeric with 125ml of the reserved stock. In the frying pan, warm 2 tablespoons of the remaining oil over medium-high heat, and cook the rice, stirring, until the grains are translucent, about 10 minutes. Remove half of the rice,

[continued]

and reserve. Put the remaining rice in the casserole and spread over the bottom, then layer on top of it first half of the aubergine, and then all the chicken. Cover with the remaining aubergine and top with the remaining rice. Pour the turmeric-stock over the rice, then add 1.2 litres of the reserved stock. Bring to a boil, then lower the heat, cover, and cook for about 30 to 35 minutes, or until all liquid is absorbed. Allow to rest 10 minutes.

5. To serve, turn out the chicken tatin onto a wide serving plate, like a tarte tatin. Add the pine nuts, sultanas, and a bowl of yogurt as an accompaniment.

DUCK BREASTS WITH HONEY GLAZE

Serves 4

Today, duck breasts are available in most supermarkets or on the Internet, making a taste of canard *easy and quick. Duck isn't as lean as turkey, but it has less saturated fat than most red meats. Though a rich food—and so not to be overindulged in—it's very digestible and* moelleux *(soft).*

INGREDIENTS

2 duck breasts (4 *magrets*), about 675g

4 tablespoons sherry vinegar

4 tablespoons honey

2 tablespoons chicken stock

Salt and freshly ground pepper

1. Sear the breasts in a frying pan over medium-high heat, about 3 minutes per side. Set aside.
2. Pour the fat out of the pan and reduce the heat to medium. Add the vinegar and scrape up any bits sticking to the bottom of the pan. Stir in the honey and chicken stock.
3. Cut the duck into 1cm strips, return to the pan with the sauce, and cook briefly until done, according to taste. Season with salt and pepper to taste, remove, and arrange on plates. Drizzle the sauce on top.

N.B. YOU CAN USE A SIMILAR SAUCE WITH PORK OR CHICKEN.

DUCK BREASTS SWEET AND SOUR

Serves 4

INGREDIENTS

80ml orange juice
80ml grapefruit juice
2 tablespoons honey
80ml sherry vinegar
¼ teaspoon pepper
250ml veal (or chicken) stock
Salt
1 pear
1 apple
Juice of 1 lemon
¼ teaspoon cinnamon
2 duck breasts (4 *magrets*), about 675g

1. To make the sauce: Pour the orange and grapefruit juice into a small saucepan and reduce by half over high heat. Add the honey, vinegar, and pepper, and stir until all the ingredients are well mixed. Add the stock. Cook, uncovered, over low heat for 15 minutes. Season with salt to taste and set aside.
2. Peel the pear and apple. Core them and slice thinly. Put the slices into a saucepan with the lemon juice. Add the cinnamon and 80ml water and cook over medium-low heat for 15 minutes. Set aside on a warm plate.
3. Remove the skin from the duck breasts and discard. Lightly salt the duck breasts. Warm a non-stick pan over medium-high heat and cook the breasts for 2 minutes on each side. Cover and continue to cook for 8 minutes.
4. Slice the breasts and arrange them in a fan on each dish. Put the pear and apple compote on the side and pour the sauce over everything.

COCOTTE DE LÉGUMES (VEGETABLES) *CROQUANTS*

Serves 4

I discovered this dish in St.-Rémy-de-Provence, the village that inspired van Gogh's Starry Night *vision. One late autumn day, the weather went from T-shirt sunny to earmuff frosty overnight. After an unexpectedly numbing two days, I was ready for something to warm my innards. Walking down Boulevard Victor Hugo, metres from where van Gogh painted* Les Paveurs *(1889), I saw* Cocotte de Légumes Croquants *on the blackboard menu outside the* Café des Arts, *a bistro-style restaurant and bar. A* cocotte *is a cast-iron covered pot, and just the idea of piping-hot vegetables cooking in one drew me in. The dish was delicious, a heart-warming single course for a wintry day's lunch or as part of dinner.*

1. Put the *cocotte* (or large, heavy-based casserole) over medium-low heat. Add the oil and shallots and cook for 2 minutes. Add all the vegetables, fruit, lemon juice, and 125ml water. Mix, season with salt and pepper to taste, and cover. Cook for 50 minutes, stirring occasionally. Some of the vegetables will still be a bit firm (*al dente*) while others will be *moelleux* (soft).
2. Serve piping hot in a soup bowl or perhaps in individual-sized, warmed *cocottes*.

INGREDIENTS

4 tablespoons olive oil
2 medium shallots, peeled and cut in half
1.5kg mixed vegetables (carrots, leeks, thin string beans, fennel, celery, broccoli, squash, and beetroot), peeled, rinsed, and cut into medium pieces
1 pear, peeled and cut in half
1 apple, peeled and cut in half
Juice of 1 lemon
Salt and freshly ground pepper

SHALLOTS *CONFITES EN PAPILLOTE*

Serves 4

A word on shallots. Onions, garlic, shallots, and leeks are all in the same family, but therein lies a world of nuance. For the French, the shallot is "un légume bien de chez nous" *(a vegetable that's very much* us*) since we have quasi-cornered its production (it grows in Brittany, the Loire, the south and southwest). It wouldn't be French if there weren't different varieties to enjoy, from the strongest, which is called* "grise" *and has thick skin, to the "chicken leg", which is longer, more coppery in colour and more subtle in flavour, to the medium-sized specimen with its mild taste and pinkish colour, and finally to the rarest one of all, the small round one. We have recently turned our neighbours in Germany into voracious shallot consumers and are making headway in other countries as well. It's easy to see why: the shallot is low in calories but filled with vitamin C, iron, calcium, selenium, and sulphuric anti-germ components. Besides, it influences and accents a dish's flavour like you wouldn't believe. As the cooks in my family used to say, the shallot adds* "tonus dans vos plats" *(tone). We use it in every way, everywhere: raw and finely chopped in salads or with cooked vegetables, grilled meats, or fresh cheese with fresh herbs. Cooked, it completes classic sauces, is great in an omelette or rice dish, and it can be cooked with butter, a pinch of sugar, and a splash of red wine to accompany fish or white meat. When* confites, *shallots become a delectable mush—in appearance something like baby food, but in taste something else altogether.*

1. Preheat the oven to gas mark ½/120°C.
2. Rub the unpeeled shallots with butter and put them on a large sheet of aluminum foil. Cover with another sheet and fold up all around to seal.
3. Cook in the preheated oven for at least 1 hour. When soft, remove and cut each shallot in half. Serve as a vegetable with a dish such as roast pork; the melted shallot flesh is eaten with a spoon.

INGREDIENTS

500g unpeeled shallots (the long variety is best)

30g unsalted butter, at room temperature

N.B. IN ALSACE, MY GRANDMOTHER WOULD MAKE BIG BATCHES OF THIS DELICIOUS "SHALLOT MEAT". AT LEAST ONCE A WEEK SHE WOULD TAKE IT OUT OF THE FRIDGE BEFORE LUNCH AND THEN SERVE IT AT ROOM TEMPERATURE ON A SLICE OF COUNTRY BREAD INSTEAD OF THE LUNCH CHEESE COURSE. ADD A FEW GRAINS OF COARSE SALT AND ENJOY.

BRAISED FENNEL WITH GINGER

Serves 4

I love fennel and don't see it served in restaurants enough or in many recipes for home. Too bad. High in water content, rich in fibre, and oh so flavourful, it gives a zing to any salad or as a vegetable accompaniment to a main course. Healthy and rich in potassium, vitamins C and E, and beta carotene, an antioxidant, fennel can be consumed raw, thinly sliced, or cooked with a bit of olive oil and shallots or garlic. When picking fennel, look for tender green fronds, a sign of freshness, and always favour thick stem bulbs.

INGREDIENTS

4 fennel bulbs
4 tablespoons olive oil
2 tablespoons finely chopped fresh ginger
Pinch of cumin
180ml white wine
Juice of 1 lemon
Salt and freshly ground pepper

1. Cut the fennel bulbs in half lengthwise. Chop each half into 4 pieces.
2. Warm the oil in a saucepan over medium heat. Add the ginger and cook for ten seconds. Add the cumin and white wine and bring to a boil. Add the fennel pieces and lemon juice, season with salt and pepper to taste, and simmer for 20 minutes over medium-low heat, until the fennel is softened and flavours are blended. Serve warm with most fish or white meats.

BRAISED CARROTS WITH GINGER

Serves 4

1. Wash the carrots and slice thinly. Toss the carrots with the zest and juice of the orange and lemon, the ginger, onions, and oil, and season with salt and pepper to taste.
2. Warm the butter in a saucepan. When it is melted, add all the ingredients except the coriander, and cook over medium-low heat for 20 minutes. Add the fresh coriander and serve.

INGREDIENTS

4 carrots (about 500g)

Zest and juice of 1 orange

Zest and juice of 1 lemon

2 teaspoons finely chopped fresh ginger

2 medium onions, peeled and finely chopped

2 tablespoons olive oil

Salt and freshly ground pepper

30g unsalted butter

2 tablespoons finely chopped fresh coriander

WINTER FRUIT FIX

In winter, "the wise trees", as William Carlos Williams writes, "stand sleeping in the cold". The wise French woman, however, knows this is not an option, much as the duvet may beckon. Still, lovers of fruit—an indispensable element of the French woman's *bien-être*—will find themselves relatively hard-pressed in winter. Never are the pickings slimmer. I still enjoy apples, pears, and bananas that seem to come greener and greener as the days pass (I've waited for up to two weeks for some bananas in a brown bag to ripen). Here is a time when those of us who live in colder climes simply can't go it alone with local produce. In the old days we may have got by with preserved fruit in a jar; there is still a place for that. But I can't survive a whole season without fresh fruit. Without nature's sugar for dessert, my sweet tooth would lead me to a surfeit of pastry temptation. Anyway, I would surely struggle not to get fat *sans fruits.* This does not mean I abandon the seasonality principle. There are still fruits I enjoy only in winter, regardless of how much big-time global agribusiness and marketing wants to make them available year-round. It simply means that I enjoy fruits that aren't the most perishable shipped in from places where they are picked in season. The mainstay of my winter fruit fix is fresh citrus, especially from Florida, and for this I go to the source.

One of America's best-kept secrets is oranges and grapefruits fresh from the groves, not from the supermarket. One winter, some years ago, I had to attend an event in Miami. At the breakfast buffet in my hotel, I rather routinely picked a grapefruit half. To my astonishment, I had never tasted a grapefruit that good. Shiny, juicy, miraculous—a half moon on my plate. I kept squeezing it for the last few drops of juice, marvelling at its difference from all the other grapefruits I'd ever eaten. Being a French woman, I had been under the impression that I was buying *zee best.* Could it have simply been the mesmerizing effect of sitting on the lovely terrace looking at the water and the sun? When the pleasure was recaptured on each subsequent day, I knew this was no placebo effect. It did not take much trouble to discover that the grapefruits came from Indian River and how simple it was to order them.

Many native New Yorkers, it turned out, already knew about this "tradition" of having fruit shipped from Florida, and I have converted dozens of friends to my winter tactic. At first, they are invariably stunned that for about the same price that supermarkets charge you can have fruit that is so indisputably superior. Anyone can order Florida citrus online or by phone. And having spread the good word, I'm now the lucky recipient of several gift boxes from friends, which furnish my citrus cure every winter. The varieties of fresh oranges are all sensational, and the tangelos (a cross between a tangerine and grapefruit), which are in season only a few weeks a year in January, are especially sublime. Serve them on Sunday in place of orange juice or for dessert as an afternoon pick-me-up. (They go deliciously with that other pick-me-up, dark chocolate.) The divine orangey sweetness has, in my experience, been rivalled only by the freshest blood oranges, tasted in Morocco years ago.

ARDÈCHE COFFEE (WITH CHESTNUTS)

Serves 4

Ardèche was where my chef-trained Uncle Charles moved when he married Aunt Mireille. It's also chestnut land, and for a coffee lover this simple winter dessert is heavenly.

INGREDIENTS

4 tablespoons mascarpone (or ricotta cheese)

1 teaspoon sugar

2 teaspoons glazed chestnuts, crumbled

4 scoops coffee ice cream

2 glazed chestnuts, split in half

4 shots freshly brewed espresso or 4 tablespoons strong, hot, brewed coffee

1. Whip the mascarpone and sugar together and divide it among 4 glass dessert bowls. Sprinkle each with the crumbled chestnuts. Add a scoop of coffee ice cream and place half a chestnut on top. Refrigerate.
2. When ready to serve, pour a very hot espresso over each serving.

N.B. YOU CAN BUY GLAZED CHESTNUTS IN SOME CHOCOLATE SHOPS OR VIA THE INTERNET. AN ALTERNATIVE IS AMARETTO BISCUITS FOUND IN SPECIALIST SHOPS.

BANANA MOUSSE

Serves 4

1. Peel the bananas. Mash the bananas with the lemon and orange juice. Add the honey and vanilla essence and mix well. Add the yogurt and mix well.
2. In a separate bowl, beat the egg whites until they form stiff peaks, and fold them gently into the banana mixture. Refrigerate for at least 1 hour before serving.

INGREDIENTS

3 very ripe bananas
Juice of 2 lemons
Juice of 3 oranges
2 tablespoons honey
1 teaspoon vanilla essence
250g yogurt
3 egg whites

COFFEE MOUSSE

Serves 6

INGREDIENTS

4 egg whites
Pinch of salt
250ml double cream
120g sugar
4 tablespoons strong espresso, chilled

1. Beat the egg whites with the salt until very firm, and set aside. Whip the double cream with the sugar. Slowly incorporate the espresso into the whipped cream. Carefully fold the espresso cream into the egg whites.
2. Spoon the coffee mousse into 6 bowls or cups and refrigerate, at least 1 hour before serving.

N.B. I LOVE TO SERVE THIS MOUSSE AFTER DINNER (INSTEAD OF OFFERING COFFEE) WITH FRESH BABY MADELEINES.

HOT CHOCOLATE SOUFFLÉ

Serves 6

1. Preheat the oven to gas mark 4/180°C. Prepare a 1-litre soufflé mould by lightly buttering it, dusting the insides with sugar, and tapping out the excess. Place the mould in the refrigerator.
2. Mix the cocoa powder and sugar in a heavy saucepan and add a little of the milk to make a paste. Stir in the rest of the milk a little at a time. Bring to a boil over moderate heat, stirring constantly. Reduce the heat and cook, still stirring, until the mixture thickens, about 10 minutes. Transfer to a bowl and cool slightly.
3. Stir the egg yolks into the lukewarm chocolate mixture. Stir in the butter.
4. Beat the egg whites until they form soft peaks. Add the salt and beat until stiff. Whisk half of the egg whites mixture into the chocolate mixture. Fold in the remaining egg whites gently with a spatula. Pour into the soufflé mould and smooth the top.
5. Bake on the lower-middle shelf of the preheated oven until puffed and brown, about 18 minutes, which will give you a soft centre. Serve at once with whipped cream.

INGREDIENTS

50g unsweetened Dutch cocoa powder

75g sugar, plus extra for dusting soufflé mould

125ml milk (regular or skimmed)

4 eggs, at room temperature, separated

30g unsalted butter, at room temperature, plus extra for greasing soufflé mould

Pinch of salt

MANGO CARPACCIO WITH CINNAMON

Serves 4

INGREDIENTS

2 tablespoons sugar
Juice of 1 lemon
Fresh mint leaves
½ teaspoon cinnamon
2 ripe mangoes

1. Put the sugar into a small saucepan with lemon juice, 1 mint leaf, and 2 tablespoons water. Bring to a boil and remove from the heat. Stir until the sugar is well dissolved. Remove the mint leaf and add the cinnamon. Let cool.
2. Cut the mangoes into halves, running a sharp knife around the stones to detach. Peel and slice thinly. Arrange the slices in four little serving dishes and drizzle with the sugar syrup. Cover and refrigerate for 15 minutes. Decorate with mint leaves when ready to serve.

. . . . . .

A final word on surviving those fruitless months: consider the pomegranate. It's a loaded proposition. The consumption of the seeds of this fruit cultivated since ancient times constituted Persephone's ill-fated prenup. (With such luck as hers, to say nothing of Eve's travails on account of eating an apple, or whatever it was, it is small wonder the entire female gender has not forsworn fruit.) Looking beyond mythic admonitions, however, the modern French woman loves to toss a handful of sweet juicy pomegranate seeds in a winter salad. Lately, the unrivalled heart-health benefits of pomegranates have become well known—they are loaded with polyphenols, even more so than red wine. As for me, I am captivated by their flavour. Prised from a husk that is utterly inedible, they are a comforting reminder that Persephone's sojourn in the underworld, and ours in winter, is not eternal or even so terrible.

PRÊT-À-CHAUFFER

We must take account of the elements when we put ourselves together in winter. If we let the downside of the season overwhelm us, we can easily get frumpy, hiding under our outer garments and bulky sweaters. A French woman wants to look soignée, pulled together. Her clothes should flatter her shape without obscuring it or baring too much. What goes the rest of the year for cut and quality goes in winter as well: buy to fit, not to billow or constrict, and buy simple basics of quality before all else. Buy chic navies, blacks, beiges and greys, and play colours off against them.

Not surprisingly, I consider winter scarves as much an element of style as of warmth. Obviously, any scarf style can be worn during any season, but in winter I like to keep my neck wrapped, whether wearing the scarf over a dress or blouse or coat. Silk can be remarkably warm, but lambswool and cashmere are my winter fibres of choice. Nowadays a warm cashmere shawl (ideal for a wrap over a coat) has become an affordable luxury item, widely available and no longer forbiddingly expensive.

Neck-Wrap Scarf

If you have a long neck, this choker style is especially elegant (and warm) under a coat and over a sweater, blouse, or dress.

1. Take a rectangular scarf and fold it in half lengthwise once or twice.
2. Put it around your neck with the ends towards your back, wrap it around the front of your neck and around to the back again.
3. Tie it, tucking loose ends under the wrap.

Ascot-Bib Scarf

1. Fold a square scarf in half diagonally to create a triangle.
2. With the point of the triangle hanging under your chin, pull the two ends over your shoulders, crossing the ends at the back of your neck then drawing them to the front under your chin. Tie in front with a simple knot.

Knotless Over-the-Shoulder Wrap

If there's no wind, this wrap works well over a coat to create an extra layer of insulation and especially to cover your throat.

1. Fold a large square or rectangular scarf in half horizontally.
2. Place it around your neck and pull down one end to make it at least fifteen centimetres longer than the other side. Toss the long end up and over your opposite shoulder, making sure the body of the scarf drapes and covers your upper chest and neck. Adjust as appropriate. You can also pin this scarf in front with a brooch or light, ornamental stickpin.

MONDAY

Breakfast

2 prunes
2 scrambled eggs
1 slice wholemeal bread, toasted and buttered
Coffee or tea

Lunch

250ml vegetable soup
125g yogurt
1 grapefruit
Non-calorific beverage

Dinner

Mustard Rabbit (*Lapin*) *en Papillote* (page 266)
Potato-Olive Ragoût (page 167)
Green salad
1 tangerine
1 glass red or white wine

TUESDAY

Breakfast

30g cheese
125ml fruit compote
1 slice rye bread, toasted and buttered
Coffee or tea

Lunch

Chicken breast with tarragon
100g green vegetables
125g cottage cheese
4 dried apricots
Non-calorific beverage

Dinner

Spaghetti carbonara
80g mushrooms
80g carrots
Green salad
Spiced Apples (page 187)
1 glass red wine

WEDNESDAY

Breakfast

1 slice ham
60g oatmeal cereal
125ml skimmed milk
½ teaspoon honey
1 slice multigrain bread, toasted and buttered
Coffee or tea

Lunch

Shrimp or tuna salad
½ bagel
2 clementines
Non-calorific beverage

Dinner

Salmon with Orange *en Papillote* (page 234)
100g spinach
80g potatoes
Pears with Chocolate and Pepper (page 189)
1 glass red or white wine

THURSDAY

Breakfast

½ grapefruit
125g yogurt with 3 tablespoons bran flakes
1 slice multigrain bread, toasted and buttered
Coffee or tea

Lunch

250ml Lentil Soup (page 173)
Mixed salad
2 kiwis
1 square chocolate
Non-calorific beverage

Dinner

Duck Breasts with Honey Glaze (page 237)
Sautéed fennel
125g yogurt
1 apple
1 glass red wine

FRIDAY

Breakfast

125ml freshly squeezed orange juice or 1 orange
1 soft-boiled egg
1 slice wholemeal bread, toasted and buttered
Coffee or tea

Lunch

Turkey sandwich
Green salad
1 pear
Non-calorific beverage

Dinner

Sea Scallops with Citrus Fruit (page 230)
75g brown rice
1 banana flambée
1 glass Champagne or sparkling wine

SATURDAY

Breakfast

1 slice prosciutto
65g Grandma Louise's Oatmeal with Grated Apple (www.mireilleguiliano.com)
125ml skimmed milk
½ English muffin, toasted and buttered
Coffee or tea

Lunch

Salad of chicory with ham
1 slice country or wholemeal bread
1 papaya
Non-calorific beverage

Dinner

Stuffed Poussins (page 232)
100g green vegetables
1 slice carrot cake
1 glass red wine

SUNDAY

Breakfast

30g cheese
2 pancakes with 2 tablespoons maple syrup
125g yogurt
Coffee or tea

Lunch (main meal)

6 oysters
Garlicky Monkfish (page 233)
100g green vegetables
1 large sweet potato
Banana Mousse (page 247)
1 glass Champagne or sparkling wine

Dinner

250ml Mixed Vegetable Soup (page 229)
1 slice bread
125g yogurt
½ grapefruit

ENTR'ACTE: THE FRENCH EAT *WHAT?*

When I was an exchange student outside Boston, some of my classmates and their parents called me "Frenchy". It was a lot easier to remember and pronounce than "Mireille" [meer-RAY], and as they said it with affection I was fine with it. Sometimes, though, I was also referred to as "Froggie" or "our Frog friend, Mireille". It seemed a little weird and it honestly took another twenty years before I made the connection. Other people call the French "Frogs" because, well, we eat frogs, a habit that seems mostly alien and, to some, almost beyond belief. I can just imagine an earlier era when this custom became common knowledge in other countries: soldiers coming back from World War II saying, "And they eat frogs!" *Et voilà. Dis-moi ce que tu manges, et je te dirai ce que tu es.* (Tell me what you eat, and I'll tell you what you are.

Brillat-Savarin was right about most things.)

Well, I do love to eat frogs (we eat just the legs), as do lots of French people. They are delicious simply sautéed in oil, butter, and garlic with some parsley. And we eat snails and fattened goose livers and pigeons and rabbits and sorrel and dandelions, plus a lot more delicious creatures, animal body parts, and plants. Every culture and cuisine has its signifiers.

To many people elsewhere, eating frogs may still be like eating from another planet, and hard to believe. But, as we know, the best food and wine is that most intimately connected with *le terroir*—the land that gave rise to it. And what could be closer to the muddy earth than a frog? There are many other foodstuffs emblematic of foreign gastronomies that give others the willies, even as people have been taking cultivated pleasure in these foods for centuries. This interlude is dedicated to a bit of special pleading for a few of the odder seeming foods of the French, things that I left out of the seasonal programme, recognizing that you have to walk before you can run. I don't expect you to race out and make all these things. The French woman's lifestyle requires only that you maintain your equilibrium by appreciating the best that can be found in your locale. Still, the things I describe here are familiar elements of French fare, and those who are determined enough can find them. The hope is that you understand at least how one woman's "totally gross" might be another's *"très délicieux"*. Anyway, no French woman should be closed to a new experience *en principe.*

When I was growing up, we often had frogs for Sunday supper courtesy of Monsieur Barbier, a large man with a boyishly pink face who was *Mamie*'s supplier of fresh eggs, cheese, and poultry. He'd show up every Saturday, his small truck full of super-fresh food he had collected from farmers in his village and the surrounding area. During frog season, summer and autumn, when he was able to collect enough to supply us, his "special customers", he'd call ahead saying he'd be late. As evening arrived, he'd appear with a basket covered with burlap. It set us salivating. The designation "special customers" was probably his way of letting us know he was favouring us with something in relatively limited supply. His way of marketing his customer service. Anyhow, we liked it.

Little did I know, though, that Monsieur Barbier was doing the "dirty work" himself: catching the slippery creatures and dressing them. For me, the mystery was how he managed to obtain only the parts we ate, the legs. What he delivered under the burlap in his *panier* didn't quite fit with La Fontaine's fable or the princes disguised as frogs in my children's books. My father saw the sense in sparing me such life lessons as how frogs become frogs' legs or how the bunnies I played with would be skinned and cleaned for *ragoût de lapin.* Somehow he always managed to evade my inquisitiveness. And to this day I'm not quite sure how it's done. On the rare occasion when I have a dish of frogs' legs before me (as at New York's *grande dame* La Grenouille, The Frog, an apt enough name for a French restaurant) my mind is fixed only on savouring the succulent little bundles without a thought to the practical considerations. But I do always think of dear Monsieur Barbier . . . *le porteur de grenouilles* (the frog bearer), with his cheerful face. I like to think that by continuing to indulge this pleasure so many years on, I am honouring his frog-catching efforts.

I will not provide more of a recipe for frogs' legs than the sautée mentioned earlier, which works well with the legs plain or breaded. The challenge is not in cooking them, but in finding them. They are not readily available in other countries where I've stayed but curiously I have found traditions of serving frogs and good purveyors in Florida, Georgia, and Northern California.

What I will tell you, however, is where you can enjoy the greatest frog dish on earth. It is in Alsace, at the three-star Michelin restaurant Buerehiesel in Strasbourg. The *schniederspäetle* (a kind of noodle) and frogs' legs *poêlées* with chervil is something any food lover should hope to experience at least once. At Buerehiesel, the culinary alchemists sauté the little drumsticks with oil, butter, parsley, and probably a few other secret ingredients. You pick up the tiny legs with your fingers and the thighs melt in your mouth, exploding with flavour. Why are their frogs so great? The cooking, ambience, and service, sure, but the restaurant seems to have an exemplary purveyor for special frogs fed some fare not to be found in any old pond. (If you are what you eat—and you are—the better or distinctively good your food is fed, the better you and it will be, so think what your food eats is who you are.) In any case, we have been mightily tempted to order a second helping, in defiance of my golden rule of pleasures in moderation. (Then again, everyone has her indulgences—why not frogs?) It is worth mentioning that the famed American wine guru Robert Parker is likewise nuts about this dish at Buerehiesel and has indeed confessed to ordering seconds. His wine pairing, however, and whether perhaps he didn't order them for dessert must remain a matter of speculation.

Readers of *French Women Don't Get Fat* will recall my father's comment when he collected me off the boat twenty-plus pounds heavier after my year in America: *"Tu ressembles à un sac de patates"* (You look like a sack of potatoes). Don't judge: he had many endearing qualities, though tact was not among them. He was generally fair but no flatterer, to be sure, and he always spoke his mind. So when he said something nice, however belatedly, you knew he meant it. It took a year, well after I had regained my former shape thanks to Dr. Miracle, before my father told me *"Tu es à nouveau mon p'tit pigeon voyageur"* (You are again my little homing pigeon). The compliment makes particular sense in my family context.

In addition to his gardening and beekeeping, my father had a third hobby as a member of a *société de pigeons voyageurs* (a homing pigeon fanciers club). We had about sixty birds in a special outhouse, *le pigeonnier,* across a courtyard behind our house. Twice a day he'd go visit and feed them a special mix of organic grains he'd prepared as well as refill their water and make sure their quarters were clean. No matter how tired he was after work, his *p'tits pigeons* got their TLC.

I was allowed, albeit only in his company, to see the tiny eggs, the baby pigeons, the growing ones. He would speak to them, looking each one over to see whether it was ready for its first flight. Some of them would never earn his respect, never make the cut, and he'd joke that they would become *les bâtards* (city pigeons): he meant the fat, shapeless, graceless, lazy birds to be found in cities all over the world; they just eat all day from whatever junk the locals or visitors feed them, and often they grow diseased. Fairly or not, my father had little sympathy for creatures that let themselves go. Living well and in balance was the way to earn his admiration.

To be a *pigeon voyageur* you had to be in shape, lean and nice-looking. *A pigeon voyageur* stood up tall, its plumage neat, its eyes clear and sharp, its moves clean and "in the zone". The difference from the city pigeons was enormous. Early this spring, I was reminded of his distinction as I watched people shuffling out of a cinema on Broadway. To my sadness I saw many women and men lumbering heftily, grazing without a thought, looking for all the world like city pigeons.

A few times as a child I was allowed to watch the birds mating and later lay eggs and take care of their hatchlings. There was a strange beauty in their simple instinctive life. Flying long distances kept them in shape and they could compete for a few years before settling down to bring up a new generation of healthy pigeons. A life of wholesome food, healthful exertion, close to and in sync with the *terroir*.

My father prized his pigeons, but he did not sentimentalize them. He was breeding birds with two purposes: one was the enjoyment of a young *pigeon rôti* (roast pigeon, which today appears more typically as "squab" on the menus of good restaurants). Served with fresh spring peas it is one of the simplest and most delicious meals I have ever had. It was a treat we would enjoy for just a few Sundays each spring, always with great anticipation. Eating the roast pigeon with its little bones meant using your fingers, so this dish was my first exposure to the *rince-doigts*, or finger bowl, which was really more a practical necessity for a simple meal than a formal dining affectation.

Of course, only a few pigeons would be roasted, as I say. My father's real love was the race. From late spring to early summer, he would select the "cream of the flock" for competition, as each member of the pigeon society would do. The pigeons would be sent by train to, let's say, Brest, Biarritz, or Barcelona, where they would rest overnight before being released to fly back home. On Sunday afternoons Dad was often fairly consumed with impatience while waiting for them. Once a bird crossed the threshold of the *pigeonnier* an alarm would click, and my father would hasten to remove the little silver ring around its foot, which he would insert into a special clock that officially registered the exact arrival time. At the end of the season, after all the club's pigeons had made the trip home from a dozen cities across Europe and nearby, the winners were announced. My father, or Justin, as his fellows in the *société* knew him, was always in the top three. It was a great source of pride, as were those trophies I remember, with silver or gold pigeons atop them. It seems odd to some, this intense relation my father had with these birds, some of which we ate. In fact it was quite natural: he loved them as pigeons, not as people, and as kept pigeons they were meant for food or flight.

PIGEON RÔTI

Serves 4

INGREDIENTS

2 tablespoons olive oil

15g unsalted butter

2 shallots, peeled and halved

4 small-medium tomatoes

1 small rasher bacon (about 60g)

4 pigeons (squabs)

Salt and freshly ground pepper

Chopped parsley for garnish

1. Warm a large, heavy-based, flameproof casserole (or heavy saucepan with lid) over medium heat, then add the oil, butter, shallots, tomatoes, and bacon. Cook a few minutes over medium heat. Add the pigeons. Season with salt and pepper to taste.
2. Cover and cook on low heat for 1½ hours. Uncover for the last 10 minutes. You can serve with fresh peas added to the casserole during the final 10 minutes of cooking. Sprinkle with parsley and serve.

RABBIT

Europeans routinely eat rabbit. They are, as everyone knows, prolific little animals, and in the old days a peasant could always catch one even when he did not have a chicken to put into his pot. (It was, by the way, Henry IV, the sixteenth-century French king, who made the chicken-in-every-pot promise, long before it became an American campaign pledge.) Cowboys, as we can observe in Westerns, were routinely shooting rabbits for dinner out on the range. It was less a delicacy than a matter of survival. Today, really since the dawn of animation, rabbits have been given way too much personality and people are skittish about eating Bugs Bunny. Most gardeners who have lost a crop to rabbits, however, have no qualms about settling the score via a fricassée.

Early in my marriage, we hosted a dinner party for some of Edward's friends. I thought I would do something special and went to Little Italy in Manhattan to buy fresh killed *coniglio.* (One thing about New York, if it is grown, caught, or manufactured, you can buy it . . . and just about anywhere people hunt you are bound to be able to score some rabbit.) While the stew was in the pot, Edward, just informed of the surprise I had planned, speculated that the fare might pose a problem for some of the guests, one woman in particular. The French woman's art of useful deception to the rescue: plate in the kitchen, serve in the dining room, and call it a French chicken *chasseur*. I'm pretty militant about truth in advertising, so this was a very rare exception. Fortunately no one caught on and everyone loved it. To this day, I am sure a couple of those guests would swear they have never eaten rabbit.

Rabbit, like turkey, is a lean meat, low in calories and easy to prepare. Mustard, honey, and prunes are some of the classic preparations.

MUSTARD RABBIT (*LAPIN*) *EN PAPILLOTE*

Serves 4

INGREDIENTS

4 pieces of rabbit (legs or loins)

4 tablespoons Meaux or other wholegrain mustard

1 tablespoon olive oil

4 bay leaves

Salt and freshly ground pepper

4 tablespoons port wine

4 sprigs thyme

4 sprigs rosemary

1. Preheat the oven to gas mark 5/190°C.
2. Coat each rabbit piece with a tablespoon of mustard. Cut 8 squares of parchment paper (or aluminum foil), large enough to hold a piece of rabbit and leave a 5cm border all around. Lightly brush 4 squares with oil. Put a bay leaf in the centre of each oiled square, then season with salt and pepper to taste; top with a piece of rabbit and a tablespoon of port wine, then season again; and add a sprig of thyme and a sprig of rosemary.
3. Place the remaining parchment squares on top of the rabbit pieces and fold up the edges to form parcels. Simply double folding each of the four sides is enough to seal each parcel. Put the *papillotes* on a baking sheet and bake in the preheated oven for 45 minutes. Serve by setting each *papillote* on a plate.

N.B. RED OR WHITE WINE CAN BE SUBSTITUTED FOR PORT.

RABBIT WITH GRAPES AND WILD MUSHROOMS

Serves 4

Aunt Annie's husband, Robert, was an avid mushroom picker, and in the fall he'd come home with baskets full of an amazing variety of wild champignons. *With these pickings and some sweet white table grapes, Aunt Annie would whip up her famous rabbit dish for her two favourite nieces, Claudine and me. She'd announce with a wry smirk that "*le chaud lapin*" (literally, hot rabbit) was served. It wasn't until years later that Claudine and I got the joke; she was teasing her adoring husband with the slang expression for "womanizer". But I know Robert was faithful to Aunt Annie, and the mushrooms.*

1. Warm 2 tablespoons of the oil in a heavy frying pan over medium-high heat and sauté the rabbit pieces until they are nicely browned. Remove the rabbit to a side dish while you prepare the mushrooms.

2. In the same pan, sauté the mushrooms and garlic in the remaining tablespoon of oil over medium heat. Add the parsley, season with salt and pepper to taste, and stir. Remove from the pan and set aside.

3. Put the browned rabbit pieces back into the pan along with the shallots and wine. Bring to a simmer and cook for 3 to 5 minutes. Add the stock, season with salt

[continued]

INGREDIENTS

3 tablespoons olive oil
1 rabbit, cut into 6 pieces
675g mushrooms, wiped and sliced (a trio of ceps, oyster and chanterelles works wonders)
2 garlic cloves, peeled and finely chopped
3 tablespoons chopped parsley
Salt and freshly ground pepper
2 shallots, peeled and finely chopped
6 tablespoons white wine
350ml chicken stock

3 tablespoons sour cream
150g halved white seedless grapes
A handful of chives

and pepper to taste, cover, and continue simmering for 20 minutes, until the rabbit is cooked.

4. Remove the rabbit to a warm plate. Raise the heat and add the mushrooms to the cooking liquid. Cook for 5 minutes, then add the sour cream, grapes, and rabbit. Mix and serve, garnishing with chives.

N.B. RICE, POTATOES, OR SOME TAGLIATELLE ARE THE PERFECT ACCOMPANIMENT TO THIS DISH.

. . . . . .

RABBIT LOINS WITH HAZELNUTS

Serves 4

This was another autumn/winter dish made by my relatives in the South of France. It's easy and quick; hazelnuts and spices give the dish an unusual touch.

1. Season the rabbit pieces with salt and pepper to taste. Break the eggs on a dinner plate and beat them with a fork. Mix the hazelnuts, allspice, and curry powder on another dinner plate. Dip the rabbit pieces in the egg mixture, then in the hazelnut-spice mixture.
2. Melt the butter in a frying pan; brown the rabbit pieces for 7 to 10 minutes on each side over medium-high heat. Set aside to rest for 5 minutes.
3. Meanwhile, mix the olive oil and vinegar in a bowl. Season with salt and pepper to taste and toss with the mâche. Serve the salad with the warm rabbit pieces.

INGREDIENTS

4 rabbit loins

Salt and freshly ground pepper

2 eggs

120g hazelnuts, chopped

2 tablespoons allspice

1 teaspoon curry powder

30g unsalted butter

2 tablespoons olive oil

1 teaspoon sherry vinegar

1 pound mâche (lamb's lettuce), washed

CALF'S LIVER

Say liver and I've found you get a funny look from many Americans. It has associations of iron deficiency (children fighting spoonfuls of cod-liver oil). Hannibal Lecter infamously consumed the liver of one of his victims "with fava beans [broad beans] and a nice Chianti" (not a bad pairing).

On the other hand, *foie gras* (French for a fat liver), whether from a duck or goose, cold (*en terrine*) or warm, is regarded as a delicacy. You can now order it at many restaurants in the U.S.A. and across the world. Popularity has created a backlash among the advocates of cruelty-free food who decry the treatment of geese force-fed to fatten their livers. This discontent is perhaps the inevitable result of goose *foie gras*'s having become a commodity. Most liver, however, is simply a by-product of obtaining meat, whether of a chicken or a calf. In America, relatively little of this organ (or any other organs) gets consumed, but in Europe liver is a revered gastronomic tradition. Near our apartment in Paris, a little Italian restaurant named Marco Polo is my regular dispensary for calf's liver Venetian style.

When I grew up, goose liver was reserved for the holiday season, Christmas and New Year's Eve, and occasionally for a very special treat during the year. But Mother was very keen on children eating their slice of calf's liver once a week. It was inexpensive, easy to prepare, and full of nutrients. It is an acquired taste, even for French kids. One of her reliable tricks was to serve it with *haricots verts* (thin string beans) and chicory, both of which we loved. Yvette, our *nounou* (nanny), used to call it *le mystère vert veau* (the mystery green calf), making us believe it was veal.

Liver is an excellent food, not lean, but rich in protein and an excellent source of iron for those who are deficient (as a surprising number of young women are). As it is the part of the calf (or of any creature that has a liver) responsible for the detoxification of the blood, take care in buying it. If possible, the source should be grass-fed and hormone-free.

CALF'S LIVER WITH GREENS

Serves 4

INGREDIENTS

Salt and freshly ground pepper

450g thin string beans

225g chicory, cleaned well and ends trimmed

1 shallot, peeled and finely chopped

5 tablespoons olive oil

1 tablespoon sherry vinegar

1 teaspoon Meaux or other wholegrain mustard

4 slices calf's liver, 80g to 120g each

2 tablespoons flour

1. Bring a saucepan of lightly salted water to boil. Add the beans and boil for 5 to 7 minutes, until tender. Drain and set aside.
2. Cut the chicory into 2cm slices and set aside.
3. In a bowl, whisk the shallot, 3 tablespoons of the oil, the vinegar and the mustard, and season with salt and pepper to taste. Add the beans and toss well.
4. Season the calf's liver with salt and pepper and dust lightly with the flour, tapping off any excess. Warm the remaining 2 tablespoons of oil in a large frying pan and cook the calf's liver over medium heat, 3 to 4 minutes on each side, until they are golden.
5. Add the chicory to the beans and toss well. Serve the liver with the salad (if you have children, cut the liver into small pieces, add it to the salad, and serve in a salad or soup bowl).

IN THE MONEY

In American slang, people sometimes refer to money, their greenback dollars, as "lettuce". In French it's sorrel: *avoir de l'oseille* (to have sorrel), with its tiny coin-shaped seeds, is a colloquial way of saying "to be rich". For me, however, the word has a strictly literal connotation: I love this green of distinctively acidic yet slightly bitter taste, similar to but tangier than spinach. I didn't care for it at first, but since it grew like a weed in my father's garden, my mother found ways of slipping it into dishes, and it has become a cherished taste. Sorrel is in season from late spring to early autumn; though best when fresh, it can be bought in a jar for use year-round. I do wish it were more greatly appreciated elsewhere. It originates in North Asia but is very widely enjoyed in France, where it is used mostly in omelettes, as a great accompaniment to fish (particularly salmon and monkfish), as well as chicken and veal. It's also delicious in bean or lentil soups.

SALMON WITH SORREL

Serves 4

INGREDIENTS

120g sorrel
4×120g fillets wild salmon
1 tablespoon lemon juice
½ teaspoon coarse salt
1 tablespoon olive oil
15g unsalted butter
Salt and freshly ground pepper

1. Wash the sorrel and remove the stems and centre vein of the leaf. Dry in a salad spinner.
2. Warm a non-stick frying pan. Place the salmon in pan, skin-side down, pour the lemon juice over the salmon, add salt, and cook for about 6 minutes over medium heat until the skin is crispy. (Cut a slice to determine the degree of cooking you desire.) Set aside on a warm plate and cover with foil while you cook the sorrel.
3. Warm the oil and butter in a separate frying pan over medium-low heat. Add the sorrel leaves, seasoning with salt and pepper to taste, and turning them over with a wooden spoon until they attain an almost melted, purée-like consistency. Cook over low heat until all the water has evaporated, about 5 minutes.
4. Serve as a side dish to the salmon fillets with some boiled new potatoes.

N.B. IF YOU CAN'T FIND SORREL–A GOOD GREENGROCER WILL ORDER IT FOR YOU–YOU CAN SUBSTITUTE BABY SPINACH LEAVES.

CHICKEN BREASTS WITH SORREL SAUCE

Serves 4

1. To make the stuffing, combine half the sorrel, 2 tablespoons of the shallots, 1 tablespoon of the oil, and season with salt and pepper to taste.
2. Make a pocket for the stuffing by loosening the skin from one side of each chicken breast, leaving it attached on the other side as much as possible. Insert stuffing. Season with salt and pepper to taste.
3. Warm the remaining 3 tablespoons of oil over medium heat in a large frying pan. Arrange the breasts, skin-side down, and cook until nicely browned, about 10 minutes. Then turn the chicken over and continue to cook for 8 to 10 minutes more. Remove the chicken to a warm serving plate and cover with foil while making the sauce.
4. Keep about 1 tablespoon of the drippings from the frying pan. Add the remaining tablespoon of shallots and sauté for a minute or two. Add the white wine and stir to deglaze the pan. Cook until the

[continued]

INGREDIENTS

120g sorrel (or baby spinach), washed and dried

3 tablespoons finely chopped shallots

4 tablespoons olive oil

Salt and freshly ground pepper

4 boneless chicken breasts (with skin)

60ml white wine

60ml double cream

30g unsalted butter, cut into small pieces

wine is reduced and syrupy-looking, about 3 minutes. Add the remaining sorrel. Cook and stir until the sorrel is wilted, about 1 minute. Add 250ml water. Bring to a simmer and cook about 5 minutes.

5. Add the double cream to the sorrel sauce and season with salt and pepper to taste. Pour the sauce into a blender and purée. Return the purée to the frying pan, over medium-low heat, and add the butter a little at a time, until the sauce is thickened and shiny.

6. Slice the chicken breasts on the diagonal and spoon the sorrel sauce over them. Serve with new potatoes or brown rice.

SCRAMBLED EGGS WITH SORREL

Serves 4

1. Rinse and dry the sorrel. Chop coarsely. Warm a frying pan over medium heat. Add the oil and butter. Sweat the shallots for a minute or two. Add the sorrel and stir to melt it.
2. Beat the eggs, and season with salt and pepper to taste. Pour the eggs over the sorrel and keep stirring until the eggs are cooked. Serve on a slice of brioche or toast.

INGREDIENTS

120g sorrel (or baby spinach)

1 tablespoon olive oil

15g unsalted butter

2 shallots, peeled and finely chopped

9 eggs

Salt and freshly ground pepper

6

WINE IS FOOD

Twenty-five years in the wine business, and I am still embarrassed by how much I don't know. Usually, it's no big deal. As Socrates once said: the more you know the less you know. So, forget about any insecurity you may have. There's always more to learn, but you can easily learn enough. The ultimate reality is simple: given a couple of hours and a couple of bottles, anyone can start enjoying wine.

Sure, there is always a greater subtlety of taste to aspire to, always more to say—and professional tasters and wine writers work at doing just that, challenged as they are by the limits of language to convey the experience of a particular wine. Ironically, these critics are concerned with describing the experience for others. Fortunately, as French women we need describe it only for ourselves. And if we get good enough at it, a relationship with wine can bloom, giving us no end of individual memories by which we can mark our days. The attentive palate is always learning, always assimilating new sensations.

In this sense, I begin with the observation that wine is food. Of course, many others say so, quite correctly, on the basis that wine has nutrients, and let's not forget calories—though a small to medium glass (125 to 175 millilitres) has no more than a piece of bread or fruit. But if the French woman's secret is pleasure, and the secret of pleasure is taste, the real magic of wine as food is this: nothing else we consume has so much potential for intensity and variety of taste experience. This is so not merely in wine's own right but in the way it complements the tastes of other things we enjoy, as it is meant to do.

Wine isn't seasonal in the way of other foods whose enjoyment we derive from the cyclical receding and renewal of the same pleasures. With wine, we never know exactly what the experience will be, no matter what we've read or heard. Wine, a "living" thing, keeps changing in the bottle as it ages. Nor is there a correct time of year to savour this or that wine—even if some reds may seem too "big" *en principe* for a hot summer's day or if the Beaujolais Nouveau seems interesting to us only when it has just arrived. I drink wine practically every day, and take it from me: most wine can be drunk any time—especially Champagne.

Wine has a different relation to the seasons, one surprisingly like our own. Even with the strictest requirements of *appellations contrôlées* (exacting standards as to composition and production for this to be called Bordeaux or that Rhône), successive vintages are never the same wine. Wine "grows" seasonally like other foods, starting with the grape-growing cycle, which is subject to the vagaries of nature each year. That's why vintners and drinkers began keeping track of years, and distinguishing them. But such statistical zeal, rather like that of cricket commentators, hardly matters to a basic mindful enjoyment. Great enjoyment doesn't necessarily mean "great" vintages, though those experiences can be among the most rewarding, as well as the most costly. Let's just say that each occasion—even of the same wine—forms its own impressions and memories. And if we can learn to pay more thoughtful attention, not only do the experiences feel fuller as we are having them, but they furnish us with another framework in which to make sense of time and make our years seem fuller as well.

The memory of some bottles can stay with you for life. While the wine doesn't have to be old and rare, a great old bottle can be like a time capsule, capturing in its flavours and aromas the time and place of its creation. Veuve Clicquot's 1955 has long been such a mystical vintage for me. Around the time of my twentieth anniversary of working at Clicquot, I could vividly recall the two times I'd tasted it—both occasions strictly in the line of duty, of course. The first time was in Reims at a very formal tasting in the Veuve Clicquot cellars with our superb cellar master, Jacques Peters, and many "wine experts" on hand. That first taste of the 1955 was a revelation, truly an experience of the classical refinement that makes Champagne the king of wines (and the wine of kings). I was unexpectedly transported to those Sunday mornings when, waking to the smell of my mother's brioche in the oven,

I'd be propelled out of bed by the lure of that first bite. I realized the wine was inciting fantasies of what perfect food I could have with it, though in that setting only thin slices of baguette or crackers were to be had. The second occasion, some years later, was a lunch at Veuve Clicquot's mansion we hosted for some very important guests. The 1955 was one of the wines on the menu, and again it was an epiphany: both uncannily recognizable and yet different somehow from the earlier sensation as I recalled it.

But *jamais deux sans trois:* never twice if not thrice, as the French say. In the autumn of 1999 Jacques asked me very offhandedly where I would be celebrating the last day of the century. Paris, I said, but very quietly at home; we had long resolved to evade the new millennium mania. "Oh perfect," he said. "I will send you a magnum of '55. We only have a few left in the cellar, and I can't think of anyone who would enjoy it more." You can't put a price on friendship! When I announced this at home it was like Christmas in October. Edward and I immediately realized our moral obligation to invite a few of our close friends to New Year's Eve dinner to share the magnum with us.

Shortly before midnight, we eyed the last of the '55 still in the bottle. We grabbed it and antique flutes, and headed down the street, to the Pont des Arts, the very romantic bridge, which at that moment was totally packed with people of all ages and nationalities gathered to watch the Eiffel Tower light display. But as we sipped the last drops of the golden liquid the setting could not have felt more *intime:* it was us, the 1955, and the new millennium. The last taste was even more memorable than the first.

In many countries wine is being consumed as never before. It has proved to be the element of French lifestyle that non-French peoples are most ready and willing to adopt. We have all heard about the healthful and rejuvenating effects of wine *in moderation*. In fact, wine is mankind's oldest medicine, first prescribed by Hippocrates in the fifth century B.C. Long before anyone had the slightest inkling that wine lowers bad cholesterol and elevates the good—before, in fact, cholesterol or anything less obvious than bile was known to affect our equilibrium—wine had recognized health benefits. It was killing pathogens and cleaning wounds before there was any awareness of bacteria. Or viruses: Did you care to know that the tannins in wine help prevent herpes and can speed the healing of fever sores? (Maybe not your problem, but still.) And it's always been known that wine aids digestion.

You can't go anywhere, it seems, without encountering some awareness of the "French Paradox": the French eat fatty foods such as *foie gras* and buttery croissants but have a lower rate of heart disease and live longer than most people in developed countries. The so-called paradox is easily explained by the habit of consuming wine in moderation along with those not-so-heart-healthy fats. The damage of "bad" fat is offset by the anticoagulants and antioxidants in wine. Wine keeps the circulatory system in good repair, and thus keeps the whole body younger. No one disagrees these days, but as recently as the 1970s, experts were burying the salubrious effects of wine. Partly this was due to a lack of understanding of how wine is a benefit. Partly, too, though, it was the legacy of temperance. In many cultures wine was better known not as good health in a glass, but as a debilitating intoxicant, which, despite its pleasures, would destroy even the moderate drinker who, meanwhile, would disturb the peace.

Research demonstrates that women who prefer wine (in moderation, *bien sûr*) to beer, spirits, or abstinence, live a healthier lifestyle and follow better dietary patterns than either abstainers or consumers of alcohol in another form. Moderate wine drinkers live longer than abstainers, are better educated, and enjoy psychological benefits as well. It makes sense: wine is pleasurable and can help people relax and be in a good mood. Plus, it is generally consumed on social occasions, and sociability along with sound eating and drinking patterns is a proven boost to well-being.

Wine, with its many ingredients, including important minerals, can be a tonic in many ways. In many countries as well as France there is a common expression: "An apple a day keeps the doctor away." In Russia. however, they say: "Drink a glass of wine after your soup and you steal a rouble from your doctor."

THE PRESCRIPTION: *MODE D'EMPLOI*

Unlike other, newer medicines, wine doesn't come with a little crimp listing its active ingredients, cautioning about side-effects, or recommending dosage. The prescription is simple. I like the Russian proverb because it sets wine in the context of the table, where it properly belongs. Wine is meant to be drunk always, always, always with food. My French friends visiting New York are still shocked to see women gathered in a hotel lounge or a bar, drinking two or three glasses of Chardonnay on an empty stomach. Wine, being less alcoholic, may not hit you like hard liquor, but it will still go to your head after wreaking havoc on your unprotected stomach with a splash of acid.

I really don't drink except at mealtimes, but if you must have a glass before dinner be sure to have something to nibble with it. It won't throw off your calorific moderation if you choose the right foods and have just a little something. Proteins and fats are best. They slow the absorption process—not only of alcohol but of other foods, preventing overeating as well as tipsiness. For this reason any meal is well started with some slivers of cheese, salami, or some olives, of which you don't need more than four or five. Even a few nuts will do to protect your stomach. And as when one's trying to lose weight, preempt dehydration by drinking a glass or two of water half an hour before going out (alcohol is more than mildly dehydrating and diuretic).

BEGINNINGS

Brought up as a typical French girl of my generation, I started learning about wine at an early age. A family friend taught me at age six how to handle a Champagne flute (by the stem or foot) and on Sundays all the kids got a bit of wine mixed with water, as the ancients enjoyed theirs. By another mixed blessing, I was also introduced to Burgundy relatively early: in those days, the great *grands crus* and *premiers crus* Bourgogne did not cost that much. Now, however, indulging that pleasure can mean quite a hit in the wallet. I learned to locate on the map (and would later visit) all the little villages whose names were legend. My father had instilled in me a love of geography, though funnily enough, his own love was satisfied by books and maps, and he never left France except for one day trip to England that itself became a family legend.

At special meals to celebrate a wedding, a birthday, or just the long Sunday lunch, I would linger around or under the table after dessert listening to heated conversations—or shall I say debates, French men being French men. That's when words such as "silky", "velvety", and "voluptuous" first entered my consciousness, together with the mysteries of the glassware. My parents' dear friend M. Lion, the big lion of a man who first taught me to hold the delicate Champagne glass, warned that any other vessel would break the spell of the magical wine, as in a fairy tale. On one occasion I remember a relative who had graduated from the École Polytechnique explaining rather technically just how the brain reconstructs the bouquet of a wine (or any food for that matter): integrating its look, feel, the context of the tasting, time of the day, and even one's mood. Our memory and many other psychological factors influence the way we judge a wine. Thus, the same wine never tastes the same twice. And compare notes as we might, we never really know how exactly the wine we are sipping tastes to someone else. Nevertheless, I do find that, as a rule, the better the company the better the wine tastes. French women don't drink alone.

And as the poet Paul Claudel observes, *"Le vin est le professeur du goût, le libérateur de l'esprit et l'illuminateur de l'intelligence"* (Wine teaches taste, frees the spirit, and illuminates one's intelligence).

You can't really learn wine from a book: all lessons are in the glass. You learn by tasting. You learn not only what you like but why you like it. Once that's established, you know when to drink it and with what. And along the way you learn about buying and storing, and types and styles, glassware and accessories, and, of course, tasting. Plus there's pleasure in the glass. Pull some corks, pour some glasses, and continue your education. There are some things it helps to know before you remove the cork, however.

The Buy

Before approaching the sometimes bewildering business of choice, let's consider where to buy, and the basic caveat emptor (buyer beware).

Where do I go? Buy from a reputable seller who turns over stock regularly. There are great deals to be had at some large retailers that purchase in huge quantities at top discount or buy close-outs from wineries or distributors trying to raise cash or free up space for new inventory. These outlets are convenient and favour the consumer who knows what she or he wants and is content with some of the more popular brands. For more thoughtful selections, personal attention, and rare bottlings, wineshops and specialist retailers are recommended. And you can find good buys there as well. A knowledgeable shopkeeper will steer you to good vintages, which vary widely by geography (a bad year in the Rhône can be a fine year in Chile) and certainly by year (that year's Bordeaux may be the vintage of the century, while the next year's could be hard to give away—well, relatively hard). Someone who buys professionally can also sometimes point you to good wines in lesser vintages—the star of an otherwise lacklustre year in Napa, say.

If you happen on a wine "promotion" featuring an improbably good price or a questionably exultant rave by the seller, there's a simple test. Buy a bottle. It's not a dot.com stock; the downside risk is small. If you like it, go back for another . . . even a case. *Voilà:* now you are a connoisseur and a collector. Most reputable stores won't steer you far wrong. You know where they live, and they want you back. Of course, taste is always subjective. But once you know each other's palate, any motivated seller and buyer can work together. Plus you'll find that people who work in these stores like wine and like talking about it—with you or anyone. (I know a bunch of guys who drop in each Saturday on their favourite wine shop just to browse and chat.)

Buying direct from wineries, either on-site or via the Internet, is always good for a few *bons mots* at dinner: "When we were in Burgundy, we stopped by the Such-and-Such *domaine* and tried this heavenly little wine. Well, we just had to bring back a few bottles." For many, such chitchat is part of the wine game. Sometimes the stories are quite entertaining, though there are other ways to socialize over a glass that are less self-reflexive. Wine always seems to lubricate the tongue.

How much should I spend? My second piece of advice about buying wine is no more "out there" than the first, but so many people can't seem to get it: price is not synonymous with quality. Truly great is one thing, greatly hyped quite another. There's no reason to get soaked. In today's global economy, with wine from dozens of regions around the world in distribution and new ones coming online each year, and with modern production techniques yielding some amazing results, we are actually living through a time of wine glut, as near a buyer's market as I've seen. For the price of this book, you can easily find a terrific bottle of wine. The "sweet spot" of value I look for now is the quality bottle retailing at between £5.00 and £16.00. No doubt there are decent ones to be had for less, but the odds of finding them are against you, and the cheap disappointments can add up as you taste your way to a winner. I certainly buy and drink wines well above £20 (professional development, right?). Are they "worth it"? Quite often they are, and I have spent years building an experienced palate capable of appreciating subtle traits. But I also know what I'm paying for: the supply-and-demand effect that kicks in when a large segment of the market wants the same product; the middleman who buys and stores the wine until it's old enough to command top dollar and reaching its peak. Of course, top expertise and unique wines also command a premium and do often yield greatness, but after a certain point other factors contribute to cost above any standard of quality.

In the course of my career, I have been the president of one ultrapremium winery in California and chaired the board of another. Both estates produce exceptional wines (if I do say so myself), for a price still within my sweet spot, though at the upper end. But minding the books, I knew that the costs of a bottle were largely buried in the vineyards. Suitable real estate in wine country can make Manhattan prices seem reasonable, as I discovered firsthand when we decided to expand into new acreage and plant more vines. So we borrowed the money.

And guess who is paying the interest and principal on the loan, bottle by bottle?

At least in California there is *some* room to grow. Consider two of my favourite wines, Champagne and red Burgundy. Both are dependent on harvests of Pinot Noir vineyards, some of them postage-stamp small. As there is no immediate prospect of change in the consensus that wines from these regions are among the world's best, the grapes lovingly coaxed to fullness on these little tracts of land are likely to remain the most expensive fruits on earth.

Okay, so what should I get? There are so many choices. Overall, that's a good thing. Huge choice, however, has its downside, too. But learning with wine is trial and error. Again, don't sweat it: you are not picking mutual funds. We begin with the simplest facts: Wines are either sparkling or still. They are white, rosé, or red. They are dry, slightly sweet, or sweet. They are all made from grapes. Here's where it gets a little complicated.

There are dozens and dozens of grape varieties from which wine is made. And those grapes don't even taste quite the same when grown in two different areas of the same vineyard, let alone in two different parts of the world. Furthermore, while great wine is made in the vineyards, there are techniques employed in the winery that can make a huge difference to what ends up in your glass. Some techniques are officially prescribed (those controlled appellations, again): a wine labelled from this region will be not less than x per cent Cabernet Sauvignon, not more than y per cent Merlot, for instance. Yes, as if the dozens of grapes were not mind-boggling enough, the game is further complicated by the fact that some wines are blends (named for place, such as Bordeaux), while others are varietals, named for the grape of which they are mainly constituted, such as Merlot.

Like most people, I'm far more interested in flavour than in production specs, so when choosing, I work backwards from taste, which is also how I advise you to get started if you are a relative novice. Start by buying varietals (one-grape) wines within the price sweet spot.

Get to know the grapes, and you are on your way. Where to start? Let's go to the head of the class: the so-called vinifera, those grapes that dominate and compete head-on for market share in the global wine business.

White grapes: the Chardonnay and the Sauvignon Blanc rule, but don't neglect to try a Pinot Grigio from Italy or a Pinot Gris from Oregon or a Riesling from Alsace.

The reds: Cabernet Sauvignon, Merlot, Pinot Noir, and Syrah make up the lion's share (but that list excludes four grapes found in some of my favourite wines: Zinfandel from California, Grenache from the southern Rhône, Nebbiolo from Piedmont, and Sangiovese from Tuscany).

Once you know a Cabernet from a Pinot Noir, a Chardonnay from a Sauvignon Blanc, you can go on to explore the wines in which different grapes are blended, wines more often named not for grapes but for regions, such as a familiar little blend called Champagne. I mentioned previously that it depends on the Pinot Noir, which is a red grape. You might be scratching your head: Isn't Champagne a white wine? Another French Paradox? Not so much: Champagne typically contains the juice of both red and white grapes, mostly Pinot Noir and Chardonnay. But grape juice is clear;

it's the grape skin that furnishes colour, and only if it's left in contact with the juice (not the case with Champagne).

Incidentally, when you are exploring wines, it helps to keep a journal, recording your impressions of things you've tried. Many wine lovers soak off the labels and paste them in a diary. (Looking back on wine adventures past, one never wonders where all the years went.)

Here's another eye-opener: A wine that is arguably the world's best (and certainly one of the most expensive) is made from a grape I haven't even mentioned: the Sémillon. I am referring to the greatest of all dessert wines, Château d'Yquem [dee-KEM]. Some upscale restaurants offer it on occasion by the glass, making tasting it almost affordable—well, an affordable luxury anyway. If you ever have the good fortune to taste this divine elixir, the last thing on your mind will be what grape it's made from. It's all in the glass, and the more you know . . . well, you know.

A final word about choosing: Palates new to wine often prefer semi-sweet, if not sweet, though they soon acquire a taste for dry wines. Likewise, though white is more often the starting point than red, white wine drinkers often end up as red aficionadas.

Storage

Wine is meant for drinking, not storing. In France, just as in the U.K. and the rest of the world, most wines are consumed within hours of their purchase. Restaurants have to plan ahead, so if you order a bottle of wine and find it costs twice as much as what you've paid for it retail, be advised that not all the restaurateur's mark-up is profit: you are paying for the bottle's acquisition as well as for proper storage to ensure that it hasn't become "cooked" and maderized (spoiled by heat) and is served at the proper temperature. Even so, most restaurants don't carry a large (and costly) inventory of wines but replenish most of their stock weekly or monthly from a distributor.

Operating on a need-to-drink basis, the average consumer buys a bottle (or two if she's having company). Many buy a bottle to bring when invited for dinner (sometimes a better choice of house gift than flowers, which inevitably send the hosts scrambling in search of an empty vase). Discovering a wine you like, you may buy several bottles. But in most cases, you still don't have a storage issue. Most wines for sale are the current release and vintage, meant not to be laid down and aged but to be consumed. Proper conditions for short-term storage are easy: if the room or space is not too hot or cold for human comfort (say, between 10 and 30 degrees Centigrade), the wine will be comfortable, too.

If wines are to be kept for months or even years—you may like to have the same one again on your next anniversary, say—above all keep them in a dark place (light is one of wine's enemies) and protected from sudden, dramatic temperature fluctuations. (The 10- to 30-degree interval is still okay, provided the wine doesn't suffer an unseasonable swing from low to high in a matter of hours.) When in doubt, err on the cold side. Consistent cold down to *near* freezing is not a problem, but high heat can be fatal.

If you are storing a few bottles or more in a closet or cabinet, store horizontally to keep the cork moist and prevent it from shrinking and oxidizing the wine prematurely. You don't need a wine rack, though it can be helpful when trying to remove one bottle without agitating the others at rest. If you find you are regularly holding twenty-five bottles or more, you might invest in a wine refrigerator, or *cave.* There are small countertop models or pricier under-the-counter units which take up the space of a dishwasher. If you find yourself holding 250 bottles, you will probably know this already: you should definitely consider investing in a *cave.* Some of them are as large as an armoire and cost a lot more. It's not cheap, but weigh the cost relative to your investment in the wine: 250 bottles can represent quite an outlay. And with variable climate zones that can be set to suit the ideal storage temperature of any type of wine, these units can provide some peace of mind to the more ambitious collector. We use them, and they keep the whites ready to drink and the reds at a temperature to insure graceful ageing.

The Pour

For me, there's little doubt that some wine-tasting rituals and props enhance the experience, as proper napkins and changing plates for each course can do at the dinner table. Glassware is not a luxury, it's essential. A good all-purpose 250-millilitre glass will do, although you should never pour more than 125 to 175 millilitres into it. Such a "sommelier's glass" is fine for whites, reds, and even sparkling wines. It should be tapered at the top to capture the aromas but without too long a stem, which can cause instability. Moulded glass will do, though crystal can enhance the discernment and appreciation of colour and has a delicate feel on the lips that can also enhance pleasure.

The glass makers and wine magazines tout the benefits of glasses designed for each specific wine type. It's not nonsense: a larger balloon bowl, for instance, does help capture the more abundant bouquets, and there are shapes designed to make the wine flow into your mouth in some optimal way. Most of these refinements have little bearing on the basic enjoyment of wine, though. Yes, a red Burgundy, with its complex aromas, benefits from the big balloon. Yes, the tulip shape of a Champagne flute keeps the bubbles bubbling longer and the bursting bouquet concentrated (so you should *immediately* junk those saucer-shaped Champagne glasses apocryphally said to be modelled on the shape of Marie Antoinette's breasts!). And generally a heavy glass with a long stem feels precarious in my hand. Lately, stemless glasses with bowls of various sizes (larger for reds, smaller for whites) have come into fashion. I rather like them. A nice modern, casually elegant touch, they are our glass of choice in the country.

A word about washing: glassware should of course be clean, but use only the very minimum of detergent, rinse very well, and air dry—don't use a dishcloth reeking of fabric softener. Many a wine experience is doomed by odours already in the glass.

A corkscrew is the one other essential for wine after a glass, though it may not be for much longer. Corks are traditional, of course, but are in short supply and often are flawed or "bad"—up to one in twenty bottles at times—and impart off flavours, sometimes to the point of making the wine unpleasant and unacceptable. Synthetic corks are making good inroads and are effective. Moreover, with so much wine consumed within a year of bottling, screw tops are finding a place, especially among white wines, in the low and middle quality ranges. Fine by me.

The cork and corkscrew, though, are part of the ritual of wine and are standard for fine wines, as they have been for centuries. There's even a rich tradition of collecting corkscrews, notably old silver contraptions that penetrated many a venerable neck (and cork). Modern technology has improved the corkscrew and made the job easier. I advise investing in a good one that should last you for life, even if it doesn't become a collectable or heirloom. What's a good corkscrew? One you find easy to use. It's all about the screw, which is called the worm. It should look like a coil and not a screw, and nowadays the most efficient have a non-stick coating. We generally use one of the lever types, partly because we tend to open bottles regularly, but any model with a good worm works well and easily. There's a certain machismo about the purity of the basic wine waiter's corkscrew—fine if you can handle one with ease—but such considerations don't concern French women.

To Decant or Not to Decant

Before removing the cork, you must make sure you have the serving temperature right. It's not necessarily the same as the storage temperature. And if you are following the 50 Per Cent Solution (see chapter 1) and refrigerating half a bottle, you can't just plop it straight onto the table like a two-litre bottle of Coke (which anyway I hope you are not still drinking). The rules are pretty simple: Champagne and white wines should be chilled to between 5 and 15 degrees Centigrade. Over-chilled wine will not release its aromas, so chill minimally. The rule of thumb with red wines is room temperature (take the half bottle out of the refrigerator half an hour or so before serving), but this centuries-old rule predates central heating and assumes a room temperature of 20 degrees Centigrade. If your room is 25 or 35 degrees Centigrade, serve the wine at a good pouring temperature for reds—the cool, dark place where you've been keeping it—around 15 to 20 is a good target.

Decanting is another ritual about which there are strong opinions. There really are only two reasons to decant: sedimentation and aeration. But my practice runs against orthodoxy in respect to both: I mostly decant younger wines and serve older wines from their bottle.

Decanters are lovely things, of course. They shine and glitter and look good on shelves. But an old wine bottle or a cheap glass decanter or carafe is all you need.

You may have observed a sommelier carefully pouring wine from a bottle while illuminating the neck with a candle (rare nowadays). So mystical, when a little flashlight would work fine—the point being to make sure sediments remain in the bottle and don't make their way into the decanter and your glass and ultimately your mouth. Sedimentary deposition occurs not only in riverbeds; it occurs naturally in big reds as they age and their tannins (the naturally occurring chemicals that account for the astringency of wine) soften. Nothing bad will happen to you if you ingest the sediment, but it can interfere with the pleasure of drinking.

The second reason for decanting is to "awaken" a sleeping wine through aeration. Wine is a living, breathing thing during its time in the bottle and in the glass. It is always changing, especially in the glass. A little oxygen can really open up and release the flavours in a complex wine, as well as mellow the rougher edges of immaturity (again the tannins, necessary for structure but also responsible for harshness: wine can't live with 'em, can't live without 'em).

The problem with decanting very old wines is that they often die in the decanter, oxidizing too quickly, before you can enjoy them. That's why we prefer to stand the bottle up for a day, letting the sediment fall to the bottom; then, after opening, we take care not to pour the dregs into the glass (think of it as decanting straight into the glass). But who has lots of old bottles of wine to decant anyway? It's the big, youngish red wines that most of us uncork and find too rowdy to drink without a few breaths or hours of air. When we were newer to wine, we played the game of tracking the taste of a wine from its first awakening when uncorked through its maturity and finally death, when the air has robbed it of all its most pleasing characteristics. In some sense a wine becomes a different wine at each stage of this life of hours. Talk about the fullness of time.

The Taste

Now we're talking. Here's where it all comes together. All the knowledge about grapes and paraphernalia is but an adjunct to the ultimate business of tasting. In tasting you discover your, well, taste: your personal style and preferences in relation to wine. But this shouldn't be a static pleasure. I know a woman who orders a Sancerre regardless of what she's eating, rain or shine. After the film *Sideways* was released, Pinot Noir became the default wine of many people who had sipped Merlot for years. Never drink wine by default. Knowing what you like is one thing, being closed to new experiences quite another.

As with any aesthetic experience, it does help to be informed and thoughtful about what you are looking for, so you can say not just I like this, but I like this *because.* In that causal link is the difference between the child's and the adult's taste. In helping you become usefully systematic about your wine appreciation, let's *faire simple.* As I and so many others do, you can look for the four classic characteristics: colour, aroma (aka nose), taste, and finish. Each tells you something and is a subsidiary pleasure in the enjoyment of the whole. Nothing teaches you to coordinate the use of your senses like wine tasting. And as the senses are the gateways to pleasure, consider the tasting of wine your total-fitness sensory workout. If you can do it well with wine, you can do it with anything and reap the benefits of sensation rather than quantity. Real wine lovers don't get fat.

Before tasting a wine, examine its *colour* (the appearance and colour is called *la robe*—the dress). Pour a small amount into a clear glass. No matter the colour of the wine, it must be clear, even brilliant, certainly not cloudy or with suspended particles. The clarity of colour is a tip-off to quality, a well-made wine, but also to the type of grape and the age of the wine. You can tell a Pinot Noir, for example, from a Cabernet Sauvignon because it is generally lighter in colour. Its grape skins have less pigment than some of the bigger reds, which can be almost purple when young. If you tilt the glass slightly and set it against a white background, you can get a good sense of the true colour and hue by looking from the deeper centre out to the thinnest edge where the wine laps the glass.

Brilliance, especially in white wines, indicates acidity, without which a wine gets "flabby" (yes, even wine is not immune). Also in white wines, colourlessness indicates immaturity; pale yellow with green overtones suggests a very young to young wine with a good acidity. When a wine is of age, one can expect hues of straw to gold-yellow. Copper-gold also means a mature wine; amber may indicate oxidation, and wine that could well be past its prime.

Among reds, the young'uns are marked by their violet-purple hue; cherry red suggests a wine grown-up enough to drink but one you could keep a while longer; red-orange means the wine is maturing or mature and surely drinking near its peak. Reddish-brown suggests an aged wine fast getting past it, so *carpe vinum.* Brown means a very old wine, which may still please, but it's not a good bet. We've had some very old Bordeaux that had lost perhaps two-thirds of their colour, and the remaining hue was brown indeed, but some of those wines were still showing fruit (the remnants of youth that in good wine are metamorphosed by age into the complexities of bouquet). They were oozing pleasure, not least that of drinking history.

Once you master these colour codes, you'll find they are not nearly as anxious-making as U.S. Homeland Security's. And it's amazing how much you can learn by sight alone.

Another visual element can tell you the amount of alcohol in the wine: we call this looking at its legs. To do this, you swirl the wine in the glass a couple of times (hold the stem between thumb and index finger, and make some little circles on or near the tabletop). Where the lapping wine has coated the inside of the glass it "tears" back down into the bowl. The speed and thickness of those legs indicate viscosity, which means more alcohol. A high-proof Amarone, for instance, will have much more serious legs (thicker, slower) than, say, most Merlot.

Swirling is also the segue to smelling the wine. And aroma more than anything reveals flavour. Tasting is mainly confirmation. (Going to a wine tasting with a head cold is therefore like going to the shoe department without your credit card: you'll never get what you came for.) A little swirl releases the wine's aroma, which you should quickly draw into your nose, either in a long, slow draught or in a few (inaudible) sniffs—don't vacuum the glass, just get enough to bring the aroma in contact with your olfactory organ. First impressions are especially revealing when "nosing" a wine, as when tasting it. With practice you will be able to tell several things from the wine's nose, including its age, complexity, fruit, flavour characteristics, and overall quality. But first and foremost: if the nose gives you pleasure, chances are you will enjoy drinking the wine.

Actually *tasting* wine has its little techniques as well. The key is to take a sip and let it roll throughout your mouth and over your tongue, alighting on as many of your flavour receptors (taste buds) as possible. Do it right and it's like 3-D imaging. Serious tasters do two more things. With the wine in their mouths, they pull in some air through their lips and over the wine to increase vaporization and aeration. Then they sort of chew the wine in an attempt to get at any flavours that might be too subtle or incipient.

Finally, you pick up more flavours through your mouth

and nose as you swallow and again when you exhale. This is to examine the all-important *finish,* and what you look for is *length,* duration of sensation: the more complex the lingering flavours, the longer they persist. Wines with a so-called short finish, such as simple whites, can give pleasure, but for the orgasmic wine enthusiast the real mind-blowing pleasure is in the overtones and complexities, the apprehension of structure, and the experience of length.

At that point, you've tasted the wine and are ready for drinking, so *Santé,* as the French say: to your health!

As I've said, describing experience is one way of augmenting it. It's true you can't *describe* the effect of a sunset upon the senses, or of a wine for that matter. But you can describe the various attributes that contribute to the sensation of what you are drinking. Much pretentious vocabulary arises here. I try to avoid it. Only you and perhaps those with whom you enjoy wine need share a lingua franca. The point is not pretension but to encourage mindfulness by making the experience more conscious, less passive, and thereby more intense. The best things in life can pass you by if you aren't paying attention. It's easier to hold on to a memory if you can remember its parts: if you know the trees by name, you can recall not just a pretty vista but a particular landscape. A great wine will not hit you over the head with its greatness; you have to explore and map it, seek it out where it lurks.

WHEN IN SONOMA, DO AS THE SONOMANS DO

Before agritourism became an "in" thing, Edward and I systematically travelled to many of the world's famous vineyards, continuing the geography game I had begun to play as a girl. The point was not just pilgrimage for its own sake; we wanted to drink the local wines with the local food. It's no coincidence that the two typically work wonderfully well together. Often the locals have been working on these marriages for centuries. And tasting and dining at the source we found a great way to learn not only about wine and food, but also about history and the cultural context that gave rise to the local gastronomic style.

Drinking local is something I recommend highly. If in Sonoma, drink Sonoma; if in Burgundy, drink Burgundy. It's part of the unique pleasure of slipping entirely into the local lifestyle. In this way, we live seasonally even though wine is not really seasonal: summer in Provence is not a time to drink great Bordeaux. There are plenty of choices from among the dozen good wineries surrounding our village and hundreds in the region. Of course we do have our preferences, and uncannily the wines we prefer are always made by the winemakers we like best.

One Provençal speciality I appreciate when in Provence (though rarely in New York or Paris) is still rosé, always served chilled in France whenever the sun is shining and the sea is visible. In the South of France—in Provence or on the Riviera—rosés are the apéritif of choice. Not surprisingly, they are produced in these areas and throughout the southern Rhône Valley. And they go exceptionally well with the olives and other *hors d'oeuvres* the locals traditionally enjoy before a meal. It's a ritual you'll see at all the starred restaurants in Provence but almost nowhere in the middle and north of France.

As with all rules, however, the drink-local principle has its exceptions. We were at a restaurant in Alsace with an incredible selection of local wines, which, though mainly limited to white, do go remarkably well with Alsatian food (and, yes, we did start with a dry Riesling). But looking through the wine list, we noticed a few choice bottles from Bordeaux and Burgundy, some startlingly great vintages and labels—and at prices as close to bargains as such wines come. It was some years ago, but the memory is strong: we picked a '76 DRC Grands Echézeaux. Because most visitors do observe the drink-local rule, wines from outside a region often don't sell and so remain on the wine list a long while, sometimes for years, without a price increase. This was one of those. The price was a blast from the past, although the wine was never drinking better.

When the staff of a good restaurant recognize that you have spotted a terrific value on their wine list, their eyes see differently. A kinship of pleasure is immediately established. We've observed that a good wine choice—even a bargain—can result in super-special treatment, often ending in the exchange of stories and a tasting of a "mystery" glass of wine with cheese or dessert. Ultimately, great restaurateurs are not in it for the money—or at least not *only* for the money.

The wine industry is a hospitality industry as well. We have met so many generous people, some of whom work miracles with food and wine. I'll never forget our first visit to the Tuscan estate of Capezzana. The vineyard and winery near Florence, with its Medici villa, is still one of the grand Old World emblems, where tradition, family, ritual, and seasonality effortlessly entwine into the fabric of life. Sublime art carries the experience well beyond the threshold of civility. The domain is splendid, nestled in the hills, the Duomo of Florence visible in the far distance. We were welcomed by one of the daughters, who served as the oenologist (winemaker) and pizza expert in the small cooking school the family also run. She was eager to show us the cellar, but her brother, the vineyard manager, appeared and wanted first to show us where it all began. No sooner had we set down our bags than we were staring at the majestic plain ringed by olive groves, the pigs in their pen, and stray chickens scratching here and there, as heedless of the history as of the beauty of the chapel where the eldest daughter (head of marketing) was married.

At dinner, the first half hour was spent on the terrace with the count and countess, a couple in their eighties whose stamina and *joie de vivre* would shame most of the young go-getters I know in New York. With great anticipation we headed across the courtyard to the dining room, where the chef, a local, had prepared simple but splendid antipasti and pastas, then meat, accompanied by wines of the property. The food, wine, and setting produced a set of sensations I will never replicate, no matter how many bottles of Capezzana I drink. This is because everything was of the place. On the estate was also a semi-subsistence farm that had produced almost everything we ate. Every member of the family had a job, whether in the fields, in the kitchen, in the smokehouse, or in the office, and each seemed enlivened by his labours. Such a place is a rarity, but rarer still, I reflected, is how the luxury of enjoying such elementally satisfying work—the toil of creating pleasures—is almost as rewarding as enjoying the fruits. The count, though past his toiling days, was a wonderful raconteur, and the countess looked to please in all sorts of subtle ways. The next morning after waking in a room decorated with Della Robbia ceramics, we were met at breakfast by a gorgeous lemon cake made with olive oil, fresh from the oven. I remembered that at dinner we had discussed the pleasures of the French *tarte au citron,* in the course of which exchange the countess had evidently registered that lemon has a magical taste for me.

After a morning soaking in the daylight on the terrace, peering at the Duomo in the distance, there was a lunch of farm-fresh peas, broad beans mixed with prosciutto in a perfect pasta dish, and the culmination: a homemade biscotti and a sip of the estate's *vin santo,* the sweet "holy wine" made since medieval times. The grapes are traditionally pressed during the week before Easter after drying on straw since October. The divine nectar, produced in tiny quantities, matures up to ten years after fermentation and is offered only to honoured guests. A lot of effort and cost. Is it worth it? It is a miracle by any standard of wine.

Not every winery is a Medici estate and palazzo, and my visit to the celebrated Cloudy Bay in New Zealand bears witness to that fact. No aristocrats and no Della Robbias, but lots of sheep. Named after the nearby body of water, Cloudy Bay is in Marlborough, nestled amid a luster of vineyards and open countryside, comfortable, unassuming homes, and relaxed, friendly people. Although many other wineries make beautiful wines, Cloudy Bay still is the point of reference and has even become the stuff of myth. We love the taste—not grassy or overly vegetal like some Sauvignon Blancs but full of exotic fruits, including lychee. This is a New World structure, a combination of power and personality. And there's almost a scrubbed cleanliness to this perfectly made wine. It tastes healthy. Plus it marries exceptionally with food, say grilled or sautéed fish with some fresh asparagus. The purity and flavour of the ingredients in the simple but elegantly cooked meals we had in and around Cloudy Bay, along with the friendliness of everyone we met, is what we drink every time we pull a cork of Cloudy Bay. What a bottle!

Most wine experiences, however, are not in Tuscan villas or on the other side of the world but at home or in restaurants, where variety is more important to encouraging conviviality than the quantity. I was reminded of this recently when out on a "girls' night" in New York, celebrating a birthday. We started with a glass of bubbly. For the main course two of us wanted a white wine and two a red, so I quickly realized that I had to help with the choices, as they were my guests and not as familiar with the bistro's well-chosen list. Of course, the sommelier is a great help for situations like this. But knowing the taste of the two friends who'd ordered the soft-shell crab, I recommended a white from the Loire for one and a Santenay, a red Burgundy that was both light and relatively inexpensive, for the other. A third friend, who loves Italian wine, picked a nice Chianti Classico Riserva from Monsanto that went beautifully with her lamb. As for the birthday girl, she chose to have her quail with more bubbly. I made the choice for some, others chose for themselves, but each tried a new wine and came away with a name to remember on her next visit to the wine store.

I am not alone in the belief that there's a fail-safe wine choice you could always make—depending, of course, on your budget. Champagne, an extremely versatile wine, came to be known as the "wine of kings" because, for centuries, the coronation of French kings took place in the great cathedral at Reims, the capital of Champagne, about ninety minutes northeast of Paris. Ever since, it has reigned as the wine not only of sovereignty but of love, romance, and celebration. Perhaps that status owes something to its natural traces of lithium. (No, it won't cure clinical depression, but it may well help one's mood: imbibers of bubbly get bubbly themselves, and just a glass will do the trick.) For me, Champagne is a state of mind.

For the record, Champagne should *not* give you a headache (though I suppose if you drink it by the litre anything's possible). It's actually the kindest of wines, lowest in histamines and calories while full of healthy minerals. So many people tell me they can't drink Champagne, but upon interrogation it often comes out that they've been drinking something else. Champagne, the one and only, comes from the Champagne region of France. The usual culprit in these "head cases" is sweet sparkling wine from California, Italy, Spain, or even France, but not from Champagne. The low-cost bubbles sometimes get passed off as "Champagne" at big wedding-reception toasts. A glass or two of some of those decoctions of sugar, mediocre grapes, and shoddy vinification would give anyone a headache. A polite sip for the toast is plenty.

By law, real Champagne is the most quality-controlled wine on earth. The white grape Chardonnay and the reds

Pinot Noir and Pinot Meunier are gathered from different villages and even different years to be blended by the cellar master. When the wine in the bottle is from a single, exceptional year, though, that's a vintage Champagne, which is then aged from three to five years before being released. But 85 per cent of all Champagne is non-vintage (or multi-vintage, if you will) and bears no year on the label; the cellar master is not dependent on any one harvest and so can maintain the wine's consistency and quality. Besides the vintage and non-vintage Champagne, a small percentage of a premium vintage goes into what is known as a *prestige cuvée,* such as Dom Pérignon or Veuve Clicquot's La Grande Dame. These are the best bottles the Champagne houses make.

Each house has its style, largely due to the grape composition of the house blend. Some are fuller-bodied, generally indicating a blend that is two-thirds red grapes. A small number of houses use only Chardonnay, and this is called Blanc de Blancs (white from white). Some Champagnes are rosés (that's a Clicquot speciality), which generally include a little red wine in the blend. Champagne's soul, however, is in its famous bubbles, which result from a second fermentation in the bottle. Just before the cork is inserted and the label affixed, the bottle is topped up with reserve wine and sugar; this allows the fermentation to continue and lets the cellar master adjust the sweetness of the wine. Brut is the driest, Extra Dry (despite its name) is a little sweeter, and Demi-sec (half dry) is sweet.

Oscar Wilde said that only those without imagination can't find a good reason to drink Champagne. French women can always think of something.

This shouldn't be the last word in a chapter on wine: it should be the first, second, and third. Pursuers of the *joie de vivre* and the *art de vivre* know this. Wine's essential identity as food is fully realized only in the sacrament of its marriage with other foods. No true lover of wine would content herself with such pleasure as could be had by drinking alone, without food or company. She understands that in the calculus of pleasures, the whole exceeds the sum of its parts. It's a case of 1 + 1 = 11, not 2. But such dividends can be earned only by active management of pleasure.

Some marriages of food and wine are classic and time-tested, others are idiosyncratic, but either way you will know a great experience when you have one. For a classic, try a Sauternes with a blue cheese, preferably Roquefort. As an example of the idiosyncratic, one of my personal favourite discoveries is Champagne and pizza. All types of pizza. I love it. In the spirit of improbable unions that somehow work wonderfully, let's consider the two most basic rules of food-and-wine pairing. Rule One: Drink red wine with meat and white wine with fish and poultry. Rule Two: Forget Rule One. Gastronomic norms are helpful, but they are only derivations of experience, not prescriptions. Nothing can trump the "wow" moment you experience for yourself.

Of course, wine is a limited resource and not cheap. It is indeed possible to choose wrong, or at least to make one choice far worse than another. The French don't believe that all pairings are valid any more than they believe all children are bright. Quality is about degrees of difference. So what follows is not a set of prescriptions but, I hope, a framework allowing you to operate according to individual taste while avoiding common pitfalls. Life's too short for a Shiraz-and-poached-Dover-sole experiment (though it beats any Coca-Cola pairing). For professionals, food-and-wine pairings can get insanely complicated—accounting for grape, region, vintage, and style in relation to each single food item. Then a change of sauce and all bets are off. As in all things, I seek pleasure in simplicity.

The simplest plan is to drink one wine throughout the meal. Select one that goes best with the main course and is at least not wildly at odds with any of the others. (At a restaurant, I recommend you choose your main course, then settle on the wine, *then* decide on your starter—that is, pair the wine to food and then pair the remaining food selections to the wine.) As I write this chapter, I am in Beverly Hills, and yesterday evening I dined at Spago and drank a full-bodied Champagne throughout the meal; it was superb with the duck main course and a fine complement to the fish appetizer. For multi-wine, multi-course dinners, a good rule of thumb is to proceed from light to full-bodied wines, and/or from young to old. So that perhaps means a white wine, then a red (white after red is actually extremely rare and usually comes up because of a cheese or dessert choice). So you might see: Champagne (peerless apéritif), white wine, red wine. Or perhaps, under even fancier circumstances, Champagne, white wine, young red wine, old red wine, dessert wine.

The notion of holding back the older wines upends a rule at least as old as the New Testament. At the marriage at Cana, the best wines were expected to be served first, before the guests got sloshed and could not appreciate them. And so there was general surprise when the wine Jesus made from water was served late in the meal and proved to be better than the wine served earlier. Nowadays we know that pleasures should build as a meal progresses—no anticlimaxes. And drinking too much too soon negates pleasure, though don't hold back your best wine or wine-and-food pairing till your palate is fatigued.

Appetizers and First Courses

White or sparkling wine is usually best with starters. With *antipasto* perhaps a Pinot Grigio, Pinot Gris, or Sauvignon Blanc. With *sushi or tuna carpaccio,* Champagne or Sauvignon Blanc. *Asparagus and artichokes* have a pronounced effect on wine, making it taste sweeter, and so are tricky to pair: try a grassy Sauvignon Blanc with citric overtones, and don't pull out your best bottle with either of these. With *caviar*? Well, Champagne, *bien sûr. Oysters?* Chablis, Muscadet, Champagne, or sparkling wine; depending on the type and style of oyster, perhaps a Pinot Gris or Sauvignon Blanc. Ditto for *clams* (raw or casino). With *crudités,* something like Pinot Blanc, Chenin Blanc, or a light Chardonnay. With *foie gras,* Champagne or sparkling wine, or a late-harvest Riesling or Sauternes. *Nuts or olives?* Champagne or another dry sparkling wine. *Prosciutto and melon* offer interesting possibilities, starting with my favourite, Muscat Beaumes-de-Venise. A Pinot Blanc can go well, too. *Quiche?* Chardonnay, Viognier, Riesling, or sparkling wine. *Scallops* call for Sauvignon Blanc, Chardonnay, sparkling wines, or Sémillon. *Smoked fish* (trout, herring), on the other hand, can marry well with Riesling, Gewürztraminer, Pinot Blanc, and sparkling wine.

Soups call for no wine at all. *Salads* are difficult for wine because of the dressings, especially those that are vinegar-based. Your best bet apart from water is a Sauvignon Blanc, especially if it is a full salad, like a Niçoise.

Say *"pasta",* even in a salad, and I think light Chianti. A pasta salad can also work with a Sémillon or a light red. *Pâtés* marry with a range of wines from Gewürztraminer to sparkling wines to Pinot Gris and Beaujolais. For pasta as a starter or main course, it depends on the sauce and ingredients. If it's a shellfish pasta, a white, for sure, say Pinot Grigio, Pinot Gris, Vernaccio di San Gimignano, Chardonnay, Sauvignon Blanc, or Pinot Blanc. For a pasta with vegetables, a Sauvignon Blanc, Pinot Blanc, Pinot Grigio, Pinot Gris, Vernaccio di San Gimignano, or a Barbera work for me. A cream sauce calls for the acidity of a Chardonnay or Pinot Blanc, among a range of whites. And, *finalemente,* pasta with tomato sauce. Did you say Chianti? Perhaps a Rosso di Montepulciano, Zinfandel, or Côtes du Rhône. (Avoid anything old, because tomato sauces interact too much with wine to permit subtle flavours to survive.)

Red wines are the choice with *cured cold meats,* such as salami, prosciutto, chorizo, and Serrano ham. Ditto beef carpaccio. Try Chianti, Barbera, or, for a bigger red, a Ribera del Duero. (Bigness is full body, depth of flavour, sometimes overpowering for the less experienced palate.) *Lighter cold meats,* such as chicken, marry well with a Pinot Gris, Riesling, Beaujolais, or other light red.

Fish and Shellfish

Lobster cries out to me for Chardonnay from Burgundy or the

Napa Valley. I can also enjoy it with a top Chablis—or Champagne: I couldn't count the number of lobsters we've boiled on a Sunday evening in New York and washed down with bubbly. *Crab* can match with a Sauvignon Blanc as well as Chardonnay and Champagne. *Mussels,* among my favourites, go down nicely with a Muscadet, Pinot Gris, Pinot Blanc, Chenin Blanc, or perhaps a Spanish Albariño. A light and simple Chardonnay, like a Saint-Véran, can work, too, but as with most seafood, a white with a little acidity (or "backbone") meets the challenge for me. With *prawns* try a Riesling, Pinot Grigio, Pinot Gris, Pinot Blanc, or Sauvignon Blanc. For fish of delicate taste such as *red snapper or striped bass,* Chardonnay is more the rule than exception: I'm there nine out of ten times, though, depending on the sauce and accompaniments, a Riesling, Pinot Blanc, or Viognier can work too, as with other white fish. We are red wine partisans, particularly of Pinot Noir, when it comes to everybody's heart-healthy favourite, *salmon* (organic, *bien sûr*). Red's my choice for *tuna* as well, perhaps a Merlot, though you could also consider a Sauvignon Blanc, Pinot Gris, or Chardonnay, in that order. *Swordfish* works for me with the same lineup, though I can also enjoy it with sparkling wine, especially rosé Champagne. As for *sushi,* which I adore, a white such as a Riesling, Sancerre, or Sauvignon Blanc will be fine, but for me nothing beats sparkling wine.

Meat and Poultry

Chicken has the reputation of going well with almost any wine, white or red, but here I have a strong preference for a red from the southern Rhône. Chicken roasted on the spit is one of

Edward's favourite dishes, so we have it regularly in Paris, in Provence, and also at home in New York. We always have it with a Côtes-du-Rhône, a Gigondas, or on occasion a Châteauneuf-du-Pape. Having spent my adult life coming to these preferences, I can't think of a reason to change. Now, if we are sitting in some star-laden gastronomic temple and are served chicken in a preparation that disguises its identity, we would probably set aside our homely preferences and opt for an elegant Chardonnay or more likely a white Châteauneuf-du-Pape.

Any of these whites or a Pinot Noir would be my pick for *poussins. Duck* means red, Pinot Noir being my first choice. Memories of the duck at Paris's La Tour d'Argent with great bottles of Burgundy have pretty much set my standard. Still, lots of people enjoy a Merlot or Cabernet Sauvignon with their duck; and truth to be told, the occasional Saint-Émilion (a Bordeaux combining both those grapes plus Cabernet Franc) has indeed passed my lips at a duck dinner. Ditto Barbaresco. *Pheasant* says Pinot Noir or perhaps a Syrah; and I think I am on to something with rosé Champagne. *Quail* calls for only Pinot Noir. *Goose* can get it on with some bigger red wines, spicy Rhônes first of all. Then there is *turkey:* every Thanksgiving or Christmas you read wine suggestion after suggestion. For Thanksgiving roast turkey, a patriotic California Zinfandel is our pick by a country mile. A Barbaresco is tempting, however, as is a Pinot Noir, if it's turkey for Christmas. A really big white Chardonnay can work, but we prefer that only with straight white-meat turkey, especially in a sandwich.

Veal, like chicken, is wine flexible, and Chardonnay is

recommended, though a light red is understandable. Pork with fuller flavour can sometimes work with a big white, like a white Châteauneuf-du-Pape, but my preference is for a medium-bodied red, such as a Merlot or Spanish Tempranillo. A *light-meat pork dish* can go with a fruity white, such as a German Riesling or a Viognier. Plain *rabbit* calls first for a white, perhaps a Riesling, though with a particularly hearty preparation and sauce, reds from Pinot Noir to Merlot to Syrah can work.

Big reds are the unambiguous order of the day for lamb, beef, venison, and sausage. With *lamb,* I like Bordeaux and Bordeaux blends, Merlots, big Pinot Noirs, Rhônes, and Zinfandel. *Beef* invites me to open up those Bordeaux bottles I've been keeping or the big Napa Cabernet Sauvignons. But a Super Tuscan can be very tempting as well, especially if you've ever had *bistecca fiorentina* (beefsteak). And I challenge you to try Champagne with a grilled steak. It's a real winner. Barbecue also really invites Rhône blends and Zinfandel, which *chez moi* also get the nod for *sausage.* But here's a counter-intuitive sausage tip: try a Riesling. *Venison* and anything gamey call for a Rhône or Zinfandel as well, but we favour Pinot Noir.

Other Main Courses

Are wine pairings with spicy ethnic dishes from cultures without winemaking a waste? Some would say so, but I say nonsense. They can in fact provide some of the most beguiling adventures in taste. For *curried fish or chicken* dishes, try a Riesling if you want white or a Zinfandel if red. Hot *Chinese* dishes marry with sparkling wines, as well as Riesling, Pinot

Gris, Pinot Blanc, or, for a red choice, Merlot. Spicy *Mexican* goes best with, okay, beer. But try a Riesling, Pinot Gris, or Beaujolais. In my experience, *Thai* often marries well with fruity white wines, Riesling or Gewürztraminer, but also a Pinot Blanc or a sparkling wine. *Couscous?* Red as in Merlot or even a Cabernet Franc or Rhône. *Moussaka?* Merlot, Zinfandel, Sangiovese, or Barbera. *Pizza?* You know I love Champagne, but always think first of a Chianti regardless of the topping, and Barbera and Zinfandel are good picks as well.

Cheeses

In the wine business there's a saying: "Buy on apples, sell on cheese". Cheese makes wine look good. Wine and cheese, acid and base, nice marriage. So almost any wine goes with cheese, though some couplings are better than others. Always try local wines with local cheeses. Most people drink reds with cheese, probably because that's what's left in their glass or bottle at the end of a meal when the cheese is served. I belong to the white-wine-with-cheese school and sometimes, though not invariably, switch back to a white for the cheese course after a red wine. So, for *soft goat's cheese,* a Blanc or rosé Champagne, a local white or Sauvignon Blanc, Sancerre, or Chablis; or, if you prefer red, a Pinot Noir or Merlot. For a *hard goat cheese,* a white Burgundy or Chardonnay; or a Pinot Noir, Merlot, Sangiovese, Syrah, or Cabernet Sauvignon. For a *medium cow's or sheep's milk cheese,* Pinot Noir is my pick. For a *hard cow's or sheep's milk cheese,* Cabernet Sauvignon, Syrah, Merlot, Pinot Noir, Barbaresco, Barolo, or Zinfandel is a good match, but so is a great white Burgundy or Chardonnay or a great rosé

Champagne. For *blue and strong cheeses,* sweet wines, such as Sauternes or late-harvest Riesling (*vendange tardive*), Hungarian Tokaji, or Port are perfect.

Desserts

Sometimes a dessert wine *is* dessert. For *apple and other fruit pies* and tarts, try a late-harvest Riesling or a demi-sec sparkling wine. A Sauternes, Tokaji, or *vin santo* might aid and abet your sweet tooth, especially with *berries.* For *melon,* Muscat is great, especially Muscat Beaumes-de-Venise. I don't fancy wine with other fresh fruits or with ice cream. For *creams, custards, and puddings,* many dessert wines work well, from demi-sec sparkling wines to late-harvest Riesling, Muscat, and various ice wines. Those options go for *cakes and biscuits,* as would Sauternes, *vin santo,* and Malvasia di Lipari. Finally there is *chocolate.* If you are going to have chocolate for dessert, you really have to decide whether the mouth-filling sweet isn't enough by itself. If not, try a *vin santo* or a Sauternes, a sweet sherry, perhaps a Tokay or Muscat liqueur. And some people like Cabernet Sauvignon. If your last course was with a full-bodied red, you could do worse than to savour the last drops with chocolate.

THE GENTLE ORDER OF THINGS

In the normal course of food-and-wine pairing, we pick what we want to eat and then find a wine to go with it. When the menu is set, we consult a wine list, the sommelier, or a wine merchant for a suggestion. We might also peruse our stash of bottles to see what's on hand and of an age to marry with what we have in mind to eat. Then there are the wine buffs who, as my husband does occasionally, pick the wine first, then the food. Knowing that great food with a bad wine equals a bad experience, and having suffered the pain of enough meals at great restaurants tarnished by a hasty or inappropriate wine choice, he made his own rule. When we dine out at any restaurant for the first time, he starts by reading the wine list, eyeing it for a few "possibilities" he'd enjoy. Then he reads the menu with an eye to finding food that will pair well with the wine or wines he has in mind. The only problem is that often he *reads* the wine list, cover to cover. So when we are dining tête-à-tête, I have to keep up a monologue until he gets his nose out of the *carte.* Oh, well, I'd rather be with someone who cares too much than with one who cares too little. Plus I have my own rule to fall back on: when in doubt, drink Champagne.

7

RECEVOIR: ENTERTAINING *À LA FRANÇAISE*

Thanks to her great cooking, generous spirit, and seemingly limitless energy, my mother was always opening our house to receive others lavishly. It was typically Alsatian of her, but not so typically French. French women may love to outdo themselves once in a while, especially at feasts to mark special occasions like holidays and birthdays, but in general they like to entertain much more than they care to knock themselves out with preparation. They often gather to share some pleasures, but the gathering together is the primary end and the foremost pleasure.

Entertaining is about creating suitable and inviting occasions. It's about bringing people together. This requires the right mix, a group who can enjoy one another's company.

But most of all—and here's what we all seem to lose sight of—it is about the guests and not about you. It is about giving and not receiving. I know a lot of people panic or obsess over looking and doing their best. We can all become insecure about entertaining at home and sometimes have the feeling that people are coming to judge us. But that's nonsense. Most of them will have made up their minds about you well before they ever show up; if they've accepted your invitation, that already says a lot. Besides, even reluctant accepters still want to have a good time. Nobody shows up determined not to. Really, you've got them from hello.

So relax. You are who you are. Your home is what it is. Entertaining can be a lot of fun. Just remember to be yourself.

In all cultures, holidays call for particular rituals. People have their expectations, and we don't want to disappoint, so we are inclined to go all out to satisfy, whatever the expectation. It's an expression of love. A dressing of fresh cranberries is surely what the Pilgrims had, if indeed they had anything of the sort, and probably what a foodie would want to serve, but I've met people at Thanksgiving dinners who flip out if not provided with the familiar cranberry aspic that slides out of a can. They don't claim it's better; it's just tradition. (*On ne peut pas plaire à tout le monde:* you can't please everybody.)

Entertaining apart from holidays is a much more liberating experience. It is about bringing people together for its own sake. It is about creating a suitable and inviting occasion on one's own terms. Nevertheless, even such unscripted entertaining is still most of all about the guests and about giving. The choices are perhaps subject to more personal discretion and self-expression, but the key to a pleasant atmosphere (as to overall well-being) is, once again, feeling comfortable in your skin. You don't have to be a domestic goddess to send people home satisfied. In fact, the most ingenious exertions can wind up seeming overconsidered and artificial. *Faites simple,* add touches of your own wit, and all will be well. The seasons, more than any food magazine, should be your guide, with formality—whatever that means to you—being reserved for cooler weather.

Of course, entertaining can have various objectives and therefore different styles: we stage one sort of occasion for a small circle of close friends or relatives, quite another for business colleagues or prospective clients. I do both kinds quite frequently. As a professional in the wine business I give small dinners as well as orchestrate grand events for hundreds of guests. In our private lives, Edward and I often find ourselves entertaining several times in a week. It's easiest, though generally costlier, to do it at a restaurant. But doing it at home can be simple and inexpensive, no more trouble than making a meal for ourselves, provided we bear in mind the special circumstances of having others in our midst, adding extra touches to distract and delight. Thoughtfulness, not lavishness, is surely what is appreciated most.

First, there is a matter of self-presentation which matters to French women. Honour the appearance of guests by giving the appearance of a hostess: dress the part. I don't mean a gown and long gloves; but a slightly more festive top, a more eye-catching bit of jewellery, or some snazzy sandals can show your heart is in the right place. In any case, make sure you're put together. It's awkward to sit down with someone who looks like she's been slaving over a hot stove. For this reason, when entertaining, we put a premium on things that can be made entirely or mostly beforehand and served with a minimum of fuss. It's a question of moderating the experience of your visitors so they don't feel like captives to your attempted hospitality. This feeling usually makes the most jovial guest clam up, which is death to any gathering. But we all have our tricks to promote sociability.

A MOVEABLE FEAST

When it comes to home entertaining, everyone knows you shouldn't keep the guests in one configuration for too long. It slows their circulation, making them listless, and conversational clusters form that never seem to break up. Before you know it, you are entertaining several parties of two or three. There are conventions of mingling, but even these can make an event seem predictable or routine: people generally gather and socialize upon arriving in the living room, move to the kitchen or dining room for the main meal, and perhaps return to the living room for coffee or after-dinner drinks. (Mostly gone are the days when the gentlemen finally repaired to the library for cigars and brandy.) There are, however, less conventional ways to encourage circulation, of both people and their blood.

It's primarily a matter of knowing your space and trying to look at it more imaginatively. If you think of space and area arrangements for a party with a fresh eye, you may find you have more "rooms" inside and perhaps outside than you use. In New York, our apartment has more a vertical than a horizontal configuration. There are three levels inside and two outside. Nice but not as grand as it sounds—remember, this is New York. Think of a small house on top of an apartment building. We start the party where the guests are less likely to drift on their own (upstairs) or outside; eventually they find their way back to the more obvious centre of gravity, say, in the living room, or somewhere nearer the entrance downstairs, by which time the party is gathering momentum. Further to guest flow, never leave it to the guests to introduce themselves. Whenever one arrives, I walk him or her to another area. If you wind up parking him with another guest, make sure you have given them something to talk about. ("Jean, this is Anne-Marie. She's a great cook; I love her baked ziti." Or "She's just back from a trip to Mexico." What I do not do is introduce people by, or speak about, their professions. French women don't do that. It is ultimately boring and can be awkward.)

Whenever the season permits, we mix indoors with outdoors; going from one to the other is always an agreeable effect, especially in the country. We greet people at the door, lead them to drinks on the terrace, then to another room for dinner. It doesn't have to be where the dining table usually sits. That can sometimes be moved for the occasion. The point is to make the experience seem progressive, not static.

When dinner is promised but time is short, we might move the gathering from home to a restaurant, which can be a wonderful best-of-both-worlds experience. In Paris and in New York, we have a choice of good places a short walk from where we live. (Even more typically in Provence, "Let's get together" means stopping by a neighbour or friend's house for an apéritif and some nibbles, perhaps meeting some new friends or house guests, then going on to one of the village restaurants.) So we invite the guests to our place for an apéritif: this can be just a glass of Champagne or rosé de Provence and the simplest finger food: olives, melon balls, a few thin slices of salami or prosciutto. The ice is broken, and people are talking, which is harder to achieve when meeting at a restaurant unless everybody knows one another well. You also avoid sitting in a restaurant waiting for your whole party to arrive—nothing less convivial than that (and French people tend to be late). At the restaurant, we go straight to the table, often to a main course, which makes the bill less of a bite than it would be for a multi-course dinner. Sometimes we return home again for coffee and dessert. This is the one kind of eating on the go to which I can relate. The pause between courses is there, so nobody eats or drinks too much. It's also a sensible way to balance the expense of eating out with the time commitment of receiving people at home. Plus we've added some walking to the evening. Remember: *La vie est un mouvement*—literally and figuratively.

CARTE DU JOUR

If you are having people over for a formal dinner, pacing and presenting the experience is everything. Being a good host is not just a matter of what you serve. As in a restaurant, people shouldn't have to sit around twiddling their thumbs wondering what's next. On the other hand, the answer is not to front-load abundance. Your impulse may be to kick things off lavishly with free-flowing spirits and unlimited nibbles, but friends don't let friends eat and drink too much before being seated. (A bunch of groggy adults stuffed with canapés may make for a memorable evening but likely one you would sooner forget.) Consider yourself the manager of everyone's equilibrium for this interval. A drink before dinner does set a tone and can help people relax, but I don't—and suggest you don't—run an open bar before dinner. Offer instead a glass of wine or Champagne. Mineral water should always be offered as well. My mother taught me not to pickle people's taste buds (or your own) before the appreciation of a serious meal and serious cooking effort. (Don't get me wrong, I'm wide open to digestifs and an open bar after the meal, though respecting moderation and balance is at the heart of my philosophy. And remember the 50 Per Cent Solution: Do you really need (or want) a second single-malt Scotch? Is it as pleasurable as the first? Why not have a glass of water instead—it's good for you.)

As you may recall, any time I offer wine, I offer food. No exceptions. Among the starters I like to prepare and pass around before a dinner or at a cocktail party are some traditional French ones that I learned from my family.

GEORGIA GOUDA GOUGÈRES

Serves 8

Gougères, little puffs of cheesy choux pastry, are a classic French offering before a meal. (In France, you can buy them in a pastry shop and reheat them, but they are easier to make than your guests will know—and once you get the hang of choux, you can make your own éclairs or profiteroles as well!) They are best eaten warm and so present a bit of a challenge as to timing. Save them for dinners at which the first course won't be served hot. When I was growing up, we had them at home only when Mamie *or someone else in the family could spare the half hour of preparation time before guests arrived. They always appeared when the occasion called for the popping of a cork: Gougères are judged the perfect accompaniment to Champagne. We had dozens of variations in my family, and one aunt (my least favourite, actually) claimed to make the meanest gougères in town. One day, as a sometimes outspoken if not quite rebellious adolescent, I couldn't help jumping into the fray when my mother and my aunts were debating the matter. Georgia Gouda Gougères, I declared, were the best! As no one had heard of Georgia, much less her gougères, they had no answer to that.*

I hadn't thought of this experience for decades; then I saw the superb film Ray, *about the life of Ray Charles. Between the ages of thirteen and seventeen I was a Sunday school teacher, and after class I would meet up with one or two of my best girlfriends, each of us joined by our respective boyfriend* du jour, *to fix Sunday afternoon plans before heading home for the family lunch. We'd rendezvous for twenty minutes at a large and rather ordinary downtown brasserie near the train station, because it had a jukebox full of English and American music. My pal Simone and I had just started studying English at the lycée, and we enjoyed everything from the Beatles, to Sydney Bechet, and Ray Charles, though at the time the words were Chinese to us. With incessant repetition, however, we could eventually sing many of the lyrics without knowing the meaning. And as adolescents we were convinced that "Georgia on My Mind" was an ode to a beloved girl, not a place (this despite also having begun to study American geography). The owner's wife used to make gougères for her family's Sunday lunch, and since she liked us, she'd send over a little plate of her minis. Her special touch was to use Gouda cheese instead of the more traditional Gruyère. The resulting puffs were great and became our Georgia ("dgoordgeeaa") Gouda Gougères, or GGG.*

Assuming that I was being adolescent and difficult, my aunts challenged me to produce a recipe. Fortunately, the next Sunday, Madame Lemaire wrote it down for me on a little order slip. I never made them myself back then, but the recipe got high marks from the ladies in my family. My own first attempt wasn't until I was gathering recipes for this book and came across Madame Lemaire's order slip. Standard recipes use milk instead of water and usually Gruyère or Parmesan cheese, not the Dutch Gouda, and they omit the shallots and cumin, which may take your guests by surprise.

INGREDIENTS

1 tablespoon olive oil

2 tablespoons finely chopped shallots

90g unsalted butter, cut into small pieces

1 teaspoon salt

180g plain flour

5 eggs

60g Gouda (or half Gouda, half Comté), diced

½ teaspoon cumin seeds

1. Preheat the oven to gas mark 5/190°C.
2. Warm the olive oil in a frying pan. Add the shallots, and cook over low heat until golden. Let cool.
3. Warm 150ml water in a large saucepan, and add the butter and salt. At the boiling point, add the flour all at once, and whisk it with the liquid until a compact, homogenous ball forms. Remove from the heat, and beat in the eggs, one at a time, until the dough is sticky and supple.
4. Add the cooled shallots to the dough. Gently incorporate the cheese and cumin seeds.
5. Make small balls of dough with a heaping teaspoon, and place them 2cm apart on a baking sheet covered with parchment paper. Bake in the preheated oven for 20 to 30 minutes until the gougères are well puffed and golden. Serve lukewarm.

QUICHE LORRAINE

Serves 6 to 8

If French women take something as simple as cheese puffs personally, imagine how passions could fly in the province of Lorraine over versions of the namesake quiche. That's one fray I never entered, though I was ever of the opinion that Mother knew best.

Whenever we had guests for lunch on Sunday between autumn and Easter, Mamie *would give us an early breakfast so she could start her* fameux déjeuner du dimanche: *her classic quiche, which can serve as a starter or the single course at a fancy brunch. You could have it with a mixed green salad, unless you prefer to add steamed broccoli or leeks to the quiche batter. Either way, in Alsace, it was well complemented by a glass of the local white or a light red wine. When quiche became fashionable the word went around that real men didn't eat it. But what I found was that men, real or otherwise, and women too, were not having* real *quiche. The heavy quivering dish often served cold or reheated after sitting for who knows how long in a glass case: this was not the quiche I knew. Here's what real French women eat.*

INGREDIENTS

FOR THE FILLING:

4 eggs

300ml double cream or crème fraîche

120g Gruyère or Jarlsberg cheese (or a mixture of both), grated

Salt and freshly ground pepper

80g bacon or pancetta, cubed

FOR THE PASTRY (PÂTE BRISÉE):

(You can use shop-bought shortcrust or make as follows):

150g sifted plain flour

¼ teaspoon salt

75g unsalted butter, chilled and cut into small pieces

1. Put the flour, salt and butter into food processor bowl and process for about 10 to 15 seconds, until mixture resembles coarse crumbs.
2. With machine still on, pour 60ml iced water in slow, steady stream through feed tube and pulse until dough just holds together. If it is too dry, add more water by droplets.
3. Wrap dough in greaseproof paper, and refrigerate for 1 hour before using.
4. Preheat the oven to gas mark 3/160°C.
5. Roll out the pastry. Line a 20cm tart or flan tin with the dough, cover it with foil, place dried beans or pie weights on top of the foil, and bake for 10 minutes. Remove from oven.
6. Raise the oven temperature to gas mark 5/190°C. Beat the eggs, add the double cream and cheese, and season with salt and pepper to taste.
7. Press the bacon into the prebaked crust, and pour in the egg mixture. Bake for 30 to 40 minutes, until set and slightly golden. Serve lukewarm.

SAINT-JACQUES *TARTINES*

Serves 6

Marraine *Alice, my godmother, was one of those stereotypical French women: thin, chic, with a great sense of style in everything she did, whether it was cooking for the family, entertaining, dressing up, or decorating her home. I spent many holidays during my most impressionable years at her home near Paris. Like my mother, she loved to entertain (*au Champagne s'il vous plaît . . .*); but she had a finer flair for presentation and could set a dazzling table by preparing a few things ahead of time, then adding some plain fresh elements and some store-bought goodies. Her little open-faced sandwiches,* tartines, *are still an inspiration: quartered slices of bread as hors d'oeuvres with bubbly. (Whole slices make a nice lunch.) She thought that conventional sandwiches (with two slices of bread) were too bready (imagine what she would think of our foot-long "submarines") and unattractive: they hid whatever she had prepared as spread, and looked as good as they tasted. Variety was the key to her magic. There would always be a different kind of bread for each* tartine *and three choices, whether she was making canapés or lunch sandwiches: in spring she favoured three fish or seafood choices; in autumn and winter it was a trio of meats or cheeses. For lunch, served buffet style (though not all-you-can-eat,* bien sûr*), there was always the accompaniment of a big bowl of mixed salad. Alice believed that six guests were ideal—not so many that she couldn't manage by herself but enough for lively back-and-forth. Her delicious but unpretentiously elegant* tartines *frequently come to the rescue before dinner is served at our house.*

INGREDIENTS

2 teaspoons sherry vinegar

6 mushrooms, wiped and sliced

10 sea scallops

Salt and freshly ground pepper

4 tablespoons olive oil

1 clove garlic, peeled (if using wooden salad bowl)

120g mixed salad greens

6 slices toasted walnut bread (olive bread is good, too)

1. Pour 1 teaspoon of the vinegar over the mushrooms. Rinse the scallops, pat dry, and season with salt and pepper to taste.
2. Warm 1 tablespoon of the oil in a large frying pan over medium-high heat, and sauté the scallops for 1 minute. Turn over, and sauté one minute more. Remove the scallops from pan, and slice.
3. In a bowl (if using a wooden salad bowl, rub it all over with the garlic clove), combine the remaining vinegar and oil. Season with salt and pepper to taste, and toss with the salad greens.
4. Distribute the salad on the toast slices, and garnish with the scallops and mushrooms. Add pepper to taste, and serve.

N.B. MANY EXOTIC VARIETIES OF BREAD ARE NOW AVAILABLE FROM SPECIALIST BAKERS, HEALTH FOOD SHOPS AND SOME SUPERMARKETS, SO IF THOSE I SUGGEST ARE NOT EASY TO FIND LOCALLY, FEEL FREE TO SUBSTITUTE ACCORDING TO TASTE AND AVAILABILITY.

CRABMEAT *TARTINES*

Serves 6

1. Peel the grapefruit, and separate the segments by taking off the membrane with a knife.
2. Combine the yogurt and paprika. Season with salt and pepper to taste.
3. Distribute the grapefruit and crabmeat on the toast slices. Add some of the yogurt, and serve the rest in a bowl beside the *tartines* so your guests can add more if they wish.

INGREDIENTS

1 grapefruit

250g yogurt

1 teaspoon paprika or allspice

Salt and freshly ground pepper

225g crabmeat

6 slices toasted fig (or sourdough or Poîlane) bread

GOAT CHEESE AND FENNEL *TARTINES*

Serves 4

INGREDIENTS

120g goat cheese
4 slices rye bread
1 fennel bulb, thinly sliced
Salt and freshly ground pepper

Spread the cheese on the bread, top with the fennel, season with salt and pepper to taste, and serve.

LEEK AND SALMON *TARTINES*

Serves 4 hungry people or 8 nibblers

1. Cut 8×2cm-thick slices from the baguette.
2. Top each slice with 1 slice smoked salmon, 1 tablespoon leeks, and a sprinkling of dill.

INGREDIENTS

1 sourdough or wholegrain baguette

8×30g slices smoked salmon

2 leeks, white parts only, boiled and sliced

1 tablespoon finely chopped dill

OPTIONAL: ADD A FEW DROPS OF FRESHLY SQUEEZED LEMON JUICE OR A DRIZZLE OF OLIVE OIL.

PRAWN *TARTINES*

Serves 6

INGREDIENTS

15g unsalted butter

2 apples, rinsed, cut into cubes but unpeeled

Zest and juice of 1 lemon or lime

Salt and freshly ground pepper

1 tablespoon olive oil

18 prawns, peeled and deveined

6 slices dark bread, toasted

1. Warm the butter in a large frying pan over medium heat, and sauté the apple cubes. Add the lemon juice, and stir for a couple of minutes. Sprinkle with a bit of lemon zest and some pepper. Remove the apples from the pan and set aside. Allow to come to room temperature before assembling the *tartines*.
2. In the same pan, warm the oil, and sauté the prawns over medium-high heat, stirring frequently. When the prawns are cooked, after a couple of minutes, add the remaining lemon zest and season with salt to taste. Allow to come to room temperature before assembling the *tartines*.
3. Assemble at the last minute, topping each slice of toast with the prawns and apples.

. . . . . .

As to the main event, the key to a sit-down affair is a well-staged sensory experience. It's less what you serve than how you serve it. Any starter/main-course combination I've described that would be suitable for dinner without guests can also be made for company. Inside the family and out, fresh, simple things always satisfy, so long as you have a variety of foods such as you should want for any balanced meal. With guests, though, the added frisson of thoughtfulness comes in the presentation, often in the finish. A simple squash purée soup can appear much more dramatic presented with 7.5-centimetre cuts of chive, like so many pick-up sticks, for pattern and colour. For thinner soups you might add some kind of won ton, or homemade croutons. I'm not one for drizzling the plate with zigzags of sauce as some chefs will do. But presentation is important. The food must look pleasantly arranged, not as if it had been sloshing around the plate on the way from kitchen to table. Family-style serving, though less formal, can be quite appealing, provided it's a dish that looks good in the serving bowl, for instance, beautifully variegated pasta.

Consider the table setting, too: a perfect context to register the seasons. In summer, especially in the country, I like a splash of colour with place mats which can be mixed and matched for relaxed fun and a personal touch. In cooler weather, I prefer solids, light or dark, and a tablecloth. Try to vary between place mats and tablecloth—the former for a more modern look, the latter for a more traditional look. In either case, do consider cloth napkins when you entertain. It's not that much work, and it indicates a place that has been set with care, as does making sure the glasses and crockery are spotless.

Only on the most formal occasions do I fuss about the formality of setting: setting the table with all sorts of specialized cutlery, matching plates for everything, and so on. Usually I prefer to mismatch on purpose. It is more interesting. And no one is going to report you to the police if you serve white wine and red in the same type of glass, or even in the very same glass for that matter. You don't need every piece in your dinner service to set an elegant table. (Though by all means, if you do buy a complete set of china, make sure it's simple enough to go with different patterns and styles of table linen. Too strong a look can lock you into the same boring table setting for life. And the food on the plate needs to show well.) It can be fun to have different dishware for each course. I like to serve a soup in a slightly mismatched set of inexpensive bowls from a pottery shop, followed by a main course on a more conventional plate. If you have more guests than place settings of one china pattern, you can mix two patterns with a certain purposeful symmetry. If the styles don't clash entirely, you can vary the set as you would the guests, alternating boy, girl, boy, girl, and create a great effect. And you can do it with the napkins as well, to reinforce the statement.

A certain fashion has developed around serving small appetizer soup portions in demitasse coffee cups, which needn't be made of fine bone china either. Ordinary tableware used unconventionally is one way to be playful. Another vessel that I like to conscript for a variety of presentations is the ramekin: It can be used for many things besides *crème brûlée,* from a crab salad to vegetable flan. The portion size is just right for many foods, and don't forget you can get more of them in the dishwasher than you can salad plates. Look at the things you have in your cupboard and use your imagination. If you have little skewers, why not a fruit kebab for dessert instead of a fruit salad? But I'd advise you not to go overboard with cleverness, and do abandon ideas as they become overexposed, particularly novelties invented by caterers: mashed potatoes in martini glasses were never a good idea.

The desire to have people over always occurs to me more frequently than my desire to serve them a dinner of several courses. That's a big job: a lot of work, a lot of time, as well as the added expense. The point of entertaining is really just to receive friends in a relaxed setting and make them feel welcome. You can invent occasions to receive them that don't require you to take the day off to cook.

I don't invite people over just for drinks: even with the best of intentions, it encourages alcohol on an empty stomach. And surprise: I'm not the type to dump a bag of crisps around a bowl of processed (with corn syrup and worse) dip. But I'll always offer a choice of finger foods. I do have favourite alternatives, however, which I stage as sort of open house: the cheese party and the dessert party. Guests are invited to drop by any time between the hours of *x* and *y*. People can come and go, bring children, stay for as little or as long as they like. The parties require little preparation, so you can socialize with your guests. (I tend to do this both with people I've known forever, just to catch up, and with people I am just getting to know, who might not be entirely at ease or congenial over the course of a long dinner; it's more of a hit-and-run, look-and-see type of social affair.) If you want to enlarge your social circle, encourage each invitee to bring a friend. One note of caution, however: In France, if someone accepts your invitation, you can expect one in return and are reasonably obliged to accept it. Not everyone in America lives by that rule—thank goodness—or it would be a strong disincentive to entertain. Like my mother, I would rather entertain than be entertained.

Cheese parties and dessert parties are two types of get-togethers I especially like to throw in winter; on cold Sunday afternoons, they force you out of housebound lethargy and shake off the winter doldrums. If the party is to be held in more than one room, you may want to set up a table in each, varying the selection by room. If you have fewer people or less floor space, setting everything out on one table is fine.

CHEESE-TASTING PARTY

Colette said: "*Un homme qui n'aime pas le fromage ne peut être bien au lit*" (A man who does not like cheese can't be good in bed). I would say there are probably other liabilities as well. Though it doesn't necessarily follow that French men, cheese lovers to a man, are all great lovers, I will say that the French consider cheese one of the foremost gastronomic pleasures. I'd have to wonder about anyone who didn't like it. Certainly it needn't make you fat, if that's the issue.

French women eat cheese all the time, often instead of dessert. Sometimes they eat both (indulgences) and have a light meal the next time (compensations). I find most Americans and British like cheese, or at least some cheeses, though they fear it as fattening or artery hardening. First—my mantra—nothing eaten in proper moderation will make you fat. Second, enjoyed with a bit of wine (see French Paradox, ad nauseam), a moderate amount of cheese is no imminent danger to the cardiovascular system. Besides, I'm suggesting a Sunday-afternoon tasting, not a day-long, ten-cheese feast. A tasting is not a meal; you do it purely for the sensory sensation. If you feel you've thrown your equilibrium off, avoid the stuff for a few days. Reduce your dinner to perhaps just a bowl of soup or some fruit. End of story.

Cheese, of course, is made from cow's milk or goat's milk (sometimes mixed), occasionally ewe's milk, and depending upon ageing is soft, medium, or hard. Some cheeses are soft, creamy, and sweet . . . others are hard, smelly, and sharp, and therein lies the adventure of cheese and of the cheese theme party. There are more than one thousand cheeses made in France alone (as de Gaulle observed, more cheeses than days in the year), but a dozen can make for a full-spectrum tasting party, and as few as six can work fine, too. Some cheeseheads preen like some wine connoisseurs, but no one should feel obliged to cultivate comprehensive cheese expertise. I've met a few, and they are the rarest of birds. Ultimately, it's a fool's errand anyway: you could taste and learn about a thousand cheeses, and there would always be a thousand more you haven't tried. (Cheese is made in many more places and ways than wine.) I'm content to live in my world of about a hundred cheeses. I'm always willing to try a new one, but a hundred is more than enough taste reference points for anyone's palate. So, here are just a couple of dozen or so winners grouped by relative similarity, none of them unduly hard to find. Some have traditional seasons in which they are best or most readily available. Yes, cheeses have their season (what the animal is feeding on when it delivers milk, like lush summer pastures, and then the optimal ageing from that point yield cheese with peak flavours). Otherwise availability is year-round.

Soft Cheeses

- *Brillat-Savarin:* Cow's milk cheese from France, named

after the famous gastronome, it is a sharp triple cream with high fat content.

- *Camembert:* Cow's milk cheese from Normandy. Soft, creamy, buttery, and mild. You can eat the rind or not. That's a question of taste, but most French people do with this cheese. Good all year. Similar to *Brie* (best late autumn to early spring) and *Explorateur,* which can have stronger flavours.
- *Fontina:* Cow's milk cheese, from Northern Italy (the soft version is ripe from spring to late autumn, the harder, mature style is best in winter, four months after summer or autumn milk). It has sweet and nutty, sometimes mushroomy, balanced flavours similar to French *Morbier,* which is (relatively) low in fat, and has a telltale ring of ash in the centre.
- *Gouda:* Cow's milk cheese from the Netherlands, it is mild and tinted yellow, similar to French *Mimolette.* (But Old Gouda is a different ball game—stronger, more orange, tangy and nearer to Parmesan in texture.)
- *Mozzarella:* Cow's or buffalo's milk cheese from Italy, it is sweet, milky, and has a slightly resilient texture. California makes good ones. Must be eaten fresh within a couple of days after it is made. It's made all year round, but in spring when made from the milk of cows that graze on sweet, young grass, it can show off an especially floral, grassy, tangy flavour.
- *Robiola:* A mixed-milk cheese from Italy, it is soft and creamy with a mild, earthy flavour. Similar to *Taleggio.*

Hard Cheeses

- *Beaufort:* Cow's milk cheese from France (late autumn to spring). Firm and sweet, with fruit and nut overtones. Wisconsin offers its own version.
- *Cheddar:* A year-round cow's milk cheese from England, it is complex with flavours going from fruity to sharp. Also made in California, Vermont, Ireland, Australia and New Zealand.
- *Comté:* An easy-to-like cow's milk cheese from France that's hard but buttery with citrus-like trace flavours. Like Parmesan, it comes "aged" and develops a wonderful, nutty taste.
- *Manchego:* Sheep's milk cheese from Spain with sweet to nutty flavours and a salty tang.
- *Parmigiano-Reggiano:* Cow's milk cheese from Italy. Sweet and grassy with fruit overtones.
- *Pecorino:* Sheep's milk cheese from Italy that has a strong flavour with slightly smoky smell. The best known is *Romano.* It is hard and best for grating, but I fancy small bites of it with a sip of wine.

Blue Cheeses

Penicillium fungus is introduced to create blue veining (part of the gastronomy of decay).

- *Bleu de Bresse:* Cow's milk cheese from France with soft, blue veins, supple and sharp. Similar to the Italian *Gorgonzola.*
- *Fourme d'Ambert:* Cow's milk cheese from France. Soft,

strong with some bitterness and grainy texture.

- *Roquefort:* Sheep's milk cheese from France that is creamy with spicy and pungent flavours. (Best spring to late autumn.) Similar blues of this style are made in the United States, Australia, and England.
- *Stilton:* Cow's milk cheese from England. A classic, full-flavoured blue (best late autumn to spring).

Goat Cheeses

- *Chabichou:* Comes from France and is clean and chalky.
- *Chèvre:* Means *goat* in French and refers to a wide range of soft, semi-hard, and hard goat cheeses that can be set on bread or added to salads and omelettes. A range of good, fresh goat cheeses are also made in other countries now too.
- *Crottin de Chavignol:* Comes from France and is rather spicy. (Best late spring to autumn.)

Extreme Cheeses
(well, that's what some of us call them)

- *Vacherin:* Cow's milk cheese from France. Soft and creamy with a smell of mould and resin and a slightly balsamy taste. Delicious. Cheese lovers go nuts for this woodsy, fruity-flavoured cheese over the holiday season; best late autumn to late spring.
- *Époisses:* Cow's milk cheese from France. Soft, rich, strong, and so smelly that I order it only in restaurants, as Edward dislikes it when I keep it in the fridge. It stinks! (Best spring to late autumn.) One of my favourites. *Livarot* is even smellier than *Époisses*, and

Muenster, another smelly one, made in Alsace, is more similar to *Époisses* in taste.

I like to offer cheeses and wines from different countries (though some people prefer to create a spread that is all French, all Italian, all English, or even all American, now that this country has taken a huge interest in cheese that does not come presliced and wrapped in plastic). You can easily get by with a single wine—if so, opt for Champagne, a full-bodied white wine, or perhaps a chilled, dry sherry. If you want things a bit more complex and challenging (at an added cost), select one wine to accompany each individual cheese or grouping. As it is only a tasting, the wine should be poured in very small portions. Put out all the cheese you like, but control the flow from the bottles or you'll have a bacchanal *gratinée* on your hands.

To make the party more of a wine event, you could (1) have a white wine and a red wine; (2) a Champagne, white, red, and sweet dessert wine; or (3) have several whites and reds. Here are some suggested pairings for my favourite cheeses:

Soft cheeses: white wines such as Rieslings and sparkling wines. *Hard cheeses:* full-bodied whites, such as Chardonnay; red wines from light to powerful and complex. Goat cheeses go with either whites such as Sancerre, Sauvignon Blanc, or Chablis, and semi to hard goat cheeses also go with lively reds such as Zinfandel or Sangiovese. Blue cheeses pair well with sweet wines, such as Sauternes, or, as the British know well, with Port.

Even watching what you pour, wine-and-cheese parties

tend to get louder as the party progresses. So, warn the neighbours. Or better yet, invite them, too.

I like to set out the cheeses garnished with vine leaves, on dark plates (black, bottle green) for contrast. To do it *à la française* you'll need some slices of baguette, fresh or toasted; some thick slices of complex multigrain, olive, or nut breads; or crackers or grissini (fine Italian bread sticks). And use only the smallest plates. Finally, not to be nerdish about it, but it helps to put little signs next to each cheese so people take note of what they are tasting as they taste it. If you really want to be obsessive, as your guests are leaving, give them a printout of the wines and cheeses served. You don't want a flood of cheese inquiries by phone or e-mail the next day.

THE DESSERT PARTY

Like the cheese-tasting party, this can be as simple or as elaborate as you choose. You can offer as few as four or five desserts, or more than a dozen (careful with those leftovers). You can make your own desserts (I always make at least one or two myself), you can buy them, or you can even turn it into a potluck or a bakeoff. Professionally, I've held dessert parties for which I've brought in pastry chefs from restaurants who set up individual stations at which they served one or two of their specialities. I must say that invite has a nice response rate. For such occasions, I also set up a beverage station with a selection of dessert wines and dessert (demi-sec) Champagnes, but coffee and tea are really all you need, especially in the afternoon.

My selection always includes a lemon dessert (*tarte au*

citron is sort of expected from a French woman), something airy such as a soufflé (hot or cold), a cake, and a few chocolate desserts (*pots de crème,* mousse, profiteroles), plus a selection of chocolates from different *chocolatiers*. When it fits with my travel schedule, I love to bring back a box from a Paris *chocolatier* like Christian Constant (his ganache cappuccino) or Jean-Paul Hévin (his balao, a caramel ganache in a very dark, slightly bitter chocolate), who do not have stores in New York City. Alternatively, the Internet provides access to some specialist *chocolatiers*. It's the thought that counts (*c'est le geste qui compte*) when the aim is pleasing people.

LAIT DE POULE AU JASMIN

Serves 4 to 6

Here's something that stands out. I can't resist sharing this unusual recipe, as it is a trait of French women to take pride in being a little different, unique in many things. Being "originale" *can be exhausting, until you realize that it's okay to take inspiration from others; just put your own spin on their creations. I devised this dessert after seeing it at a restaurant, but that doesn't make it any less of a surprising treat for my guests. Now it can start a little flurry of admiration at your table, too.*

A few years ago, we were in Paris when the now famous and almost impossible-to-book restaurant Astrance (named after a wild mountain flower) opened. Somehow we had learned that both the chef and the manager came from Arpège, one of our favourite star-sprinkled, special-occasion eateries. So we booked a meal at Astrance during its earliest and starless days. And what a meal—easily two stars, we said, our best meal of the year. Four years later, it had indeed won two Michelin stars, putting it in the major leagues of French gastronomy. (And, happily, we are welcomed back like old friends.) The young chef's technique and creativity are astonishing—a signature unlike anyone's I have seen or tasted. L'oeuf *(egg) is a case in point. After dessert, half an egg carton is brought to the table. Inside are eggshells with their tops guillotined off, as with soft-boiled eggs. The shells are about half full of a pale yellow liquid that looks a bit like* crème anglaise, *though somewhat more liquidy. You pick up the eggshells and drink the cool liquid, delicious with a lingering touch of jasmine. That's what I call finger food! It has huge "wow" factor, whether at a dessert party or after a good meal. I have adapted the recipe and often serve the eggs in a ceramic egg carton I found in Provence—an object of conversation in itself.*

INGREDIENTS

3 egg yolks

2 tablespoons sugar

250ml milk (regular or skimmed)

1 tablespoon cold jasmine tea (rum can also be substituted, as part of the "digestive" notion)

1. Whisk together the egg yolks and sugar until pale and tripled in volume. Add the milk and jasmine tea, while continuing to whisk. It should look like a pale-yellow cappuccino.
2. Serve in empty, prewashed, and dry eggshells.

CHOCOLATE BRIOCHE

Serves 4

1. Preheat the oven to gas mark 3/160°C.
2. Place the brioche slices on a baking sheet and top each with a chocolate bar. Drizzle with 1 tablespoon of the oil, and season with salt to taste.
3. Bake in the preheated oven for 4 to 5 minutes, until the chocolate is molten. Drizzle with the remaining oil and serve immediately.

INGREDIENTS

4×2cm slices of brioche, preferably a day or two old

4 bars (4 squares each) of dark chocolate, preferably more than 60 per cent cocoa

20ml olive oil

Sea salt

CHOCOLATE *MOELLEUX* WITH WALNUTS

Serves 4

INGREDIENTS

150g dark chocolate (above 70 per cent cocoa)

50g unsalted butter, plus extra for greasing moulds

2 eggs, separated

60g plain flour

120g sugar

4 tablespoons fresh walnut pieces, roughly chopped

1. Preheat the oven to gas mark 7/220°C.
2. Break the chocolate into small pieces and melt with the butter in a heatproof bowl over a pan of simmering water. Let cool, then add the egg yolks and flour. Mix well.
3. In a separate bowl, beat the egg whites until they form soft peaks, and incorporate in small batches into the melted chocolate. Do same with the sugar.
4. Butter 4 small individual moulds and fill them halfway with the batter. Add 1 tablespoon of walnuts to each mould and cover with more batter. Bake in the preheated oven 12 to 14 minutes, until a crust has begun to form but the middle is still soft. Turn out onto a serving plate and serve warm.

CHOCOLATE *PETITS POTS*

Serves 4

1. Melt the chocolate in a heatproof bowl placed over a pan of simmering water. Add the milk and mix well. Beat in the butter. Pour the batter into small round moulds or ramekins.
2. Refrigerate for 2 hours before serving.

INGREDIENTS

200g milk chocolate, coarsely chopped

200g dark chocolate, coarsely chopped

350ml milk (regular or skimmed)

90g unsalted butter, at room temperature

COFFEE *PETITS POTS*

Serves 4

INGREDIENTS

250ml milk (regular or skimmed)

125ml double cream

60g sugar

2 shots strong espresso or 125ml strong brewed coffee

75g unsalted butter, at room temperature

1. Combine the milk, double cream, and sugar in a saucepan. Bring to a boil over medium heat. Add the coffee and beat in the butter. Pour into small round moulds or ramekins.
2. Refrigerate for 2 hours before serving.

PUMPKIN *PETITS POTS*

Serves 4

1. Combine the milk, double cream, pumpkin purée, sugar, vanilla, and allspice in a saucepan. Bring to a boil over medium heat. Beat in the butter. Pour into small round moulds or ramekins.
2. Refrigerate for 2 hours before serving. Sprinkle the hazelnuts on top of each mould just before serving. Toasting the nuts brings out their flavour!

INGREDIENTS

250ml milk (regular or skimmed)

125ml double cream

125ml unsweetened canned pumpkin purée (organic is best)

60g sugar

1 teaspoon vanilla essence

¼ teaspoon allspice

75g unsalted butter

2 tablespoons hazelnuts, roughly chopped

While highly chauvinistic, French women are nevertheless flexible about adopting any foreign influence that suits their overall way of living. One of the best inspirations from abroad has been the diversification of breakfast, which is no longer limited to bread, butter, and jam, or croissants. It now extends to cereal and meats, and sometimes even eggs, more like the breakfasts enjoyed in the Anglo-Saxon world. If only for the introduction of protein in the day's first meal, it's a great leap forward. Apart from yogurt and the classic *Café crème*, the French breakfast was typically lacking in protein, which is more likely than carbs are to sustain one until the next meal. While I've loved brunch and even featured it at home for all the time I've lived in New York, it is an innovation of the past decade in Paris, where it is now served at home.

Brunch managed with an eye to portion control—no four-egg omelettes followed with a stack of flapjacks to be had à Paris—actually suits the French perfectly: a variety of quality foods enjoyed at a leisurely pace. In some instances, it is even replacing the Sunday family lunch, which can take up half the day. I don't think the French nation could survive the total loss of that tradition—it's especially vital to the social fabric when the family includes kids. But when it's just grown-ups and outside pressures make the long midday meal impossible, *le brunch* can be a nice alternative.

Some of my favourite brunches are admittedly at hotels, among them the Four Seasons in San Francisco (where the ricotta pancakes are a divine indulgence every once in a great while), le Meurice in Paris (where the selection of croissants and Viennoiseries is unmatched), and La Mirande in Avignon (where one could easily linger till mid-afternoon sampling the variety of Provençal specialities such as *fougasses* and other local breads, or lavender honey and jam selections).

But whatever I know about serving brunches at home, I have learned from American women. I remember a fund-raiser hosted by a vivacious lady in Nashville who served an amazing brunch that was more of a fancy *déjeuner sur l'herbe,* her huge backyard flowing with Champagne; her table laden with grits and peach waffles and a gorgeous spinach soufflé. (I had to ask her: "Are you sure you're not French?") I remember another occasion with some Anglophile friends in New England, a chilly autumn weekend around a fireplace and lots of scones and clotted cream; there may have even been bangers (everything in moderation). At home in New York, I like to combine French and American touches: farm-fresh eggs from the Union Square Greenmarket, homemade yogurt and oatmeal, fresh croissants and brioches from the local bakery. (If they weren't there, I'd bake the brioches as my mother did. Croissants, on the other hand, are hard work, but every so often I am stirred to the challenge.) A small glass of just-squeezed orange juice and freshly ground coffee are the beverages, but neither of these quench thirst, so there's always water on the table. Any time the sun shines, even in autumn, though not in the dog days of summer, we serve the brunch on the terrace. Taking our time, the whole thing is done by one o'clock, which leaves a whole afternoon for museums, reading, a little shopping, or perhaps a walk or bike ride. It is the most relaxing way to entertain, and it isn't even French.

COCKTAIL *DINATOIRE*

Halfway between a full-scale dinner production and a theme party, the *dinatoire* is a very easy and very French way to entertain. It's a sort of dinner buffet, whose name tells guests it's not a sit-down-at-a-dining-room-table affair but more than an apéritif or cocktail in terms of duration and food offerings. *Dinatoire* says you won't leave hungry but advises you not to expect all the formalities of the table. I love the idea, especially during the hectic holiday season when there are so many friends to see and so little time.

The cocktail *dinatoire* is a very Parisian social gesture, but last Christmas, our friend Marie, a worldly and energetic Parisienne, held one in Provence, reminding me once again that with a little imagination less can most definitely seem like more. Marie bought olives, nuts, and a local baker's puff pastry *petits fours salés* (savoury as opposed to the usual sweet *petits fours*), which she served with a glass of Champagne. After a lively apéritif hour, "dinner" was served. By then we were all seated in the living room in chairs and couches beside a glowing fire, and the food was simply placed on the large coffee table in front of us. As it was holiday time, she had opted to serve smoked salmon and some *foie gras* on toasted brioche, both traditional, accompanied by a glass (or two) of Sauternes. All she had to do was toast the brioche slices, apply the salmon and *foie gras*, and arrange them on a tray. We stayed cosily settled—there was no moving this feast—and ate slowly, relishing the conversation, telling stories, laughing, and meeting new people. No silverware necessary.

The first secret to a successful *cocktail dinatoire* is to pick a good wine: not the most expensive, but not the cheapest; something that shows you've put some thought and care into the choice. The second is the food: A carefully curated menu can make an impression out of proportion to the effort. Prepare your speciality and shop carefully for everything else—or buy everything already prepared and arrange it thoughtfully. A little basket of hard-boiled pretty quail eggs is very little trouble and looks inviting. Caviar is a great choice but not within everyone's means or to everyone's taste—a less pricey roe can do nicely. Any handmade produce could be a good choice: something made and acquired with care. The sweets can be fancy or simple, as you like. Dessert at Marie's was a tray of holiday pastries and biscuits. Some people continued with Sauternes, others with coffee or Cognac. Simple, easy, and delicious.

The French have a fancy word for grazing on finger foods: *grignotage.* Nothing new under the sun, really. We owe it all to Spain, the home of tapas, and to Greece, the land of mezze. It's actually a marvellous return to the most elemental satisfactions of eating. Before the fork (which first appeared in the sixteenth century), we all ate with our fingers. *Grignotage* is perfect for an age in which time is shorter and calorific requirements are not what they were when we laboured in the fields from sunup to sundown. A *cocktail dinatoire* is also time elastic, from, say, as little as two hours' duration to the hours and hours of a traditional French dinner.

The small morsels of the *cocktail dinatoire* are certainly in line with the French woman's notion of eating *menu* servings (the French use the word in the sense of an order of little things to be served, not in our sense of a list of options). But this "new" old habit of eating a series of small bites also serves the necessity of taste and variety when the pace of life has made the long leisurely meal more and more the exception than the rule. The French can't all sit down every evening for a longer dinner, much as they continue to relish the custom when they can. In the past thirty years, the average French meal has been reduced to about thirty-four to thirty-six minutes, a third of what it was before (yet this is substantially greater than the American average meal of twelve to sixteen minutes, often consumed while doing something else as well). Abbreviated though it has become, eating in France is not yet a grim and rushed affair. Under the new constraints the French still do not attempt to cram two hours' worth of eating into thirty-six minutes. That interval is simply not sufficient for eating a meal of several full courses properly. Rather than eat faster, the French choose to eat less in the time allotted them. And they are not in danger of starving. They know a shorter menu of high-quality, varied foods can satisfy both the senses and the body's nutritional demands. As I've noted, it takes only twenty minutes of slow, mindful eating for the brain to signal the end of hunger. If the food is good and we are concentrating on its pleasures, healthful satisfaction is still possible.

FINAL TIP

Sometimes entertaining seems like something we hate doing but love having done. The extra work and a little gratuitous anxiety over things that could go wrong can always present enough of an excuse not to bother. When in doubt, just ask yourself—as my mother taught me to do—what's the worst thing that can happen? The cake doesn't rise, wine gets spilled, a guest is rude, the bill is steep, you have to get up an hour earlier, the dog eats your *foie gras*? All relatively minor. Life goes on. Chances are, things will go well, people will have a good time, and you'll feel good about it for some time to come. So go for it. Though it's all about giving, you really do get back more than you give.

À BIENTÔT
A LITTLE FRENCH LESSON

Languages have always been one of my special interests, and I find there is no quicker way to get into a culture than to absorb a bit of its language. Even words that have the same definition in one language can have a very different connotation or nuance in another. And connotation and nuance, that sense of words beyond the totally literal, is where the essence of culture resides. It differentiates even two cultures that supposedly speak the same tongue. As George Bernard Shaw said, "England and America are two countries separated by a common language." Imagine how much a totally different language estranges us from the French.

I obviously believe there are valuable things to be learned from traditional French living. As I have said, a lifestyle is more than a list of habits in isolation; it's a total mind-set and in this case a culture. So if you want to live a bit like a traditional French woman—training yourself to tune in to peak sensory experience, to live in the season, to eat for pleasure and not get fat—being able to get inside the "head" of French culture is a big help.

My first professional training was as a translator-interpreter. I remember one translation class at my university in which we had to learn the rules of cricket. For a French girl, this was as alien as studying a repair manual for a spaceship. We never got to American baseball (I doubt the professor understood it), but the point was that any important part of a culture, in this case sports, infiltrates the language and provides its metaphors. Living in the U.S.A., I appreciate how important baseball is to our American language and culture. I've been to enough games to know what a home run is. (That's when your hotel room isn't ready and they upgrade you to an available suite with an ocean-view terrace, right?) Anyway, the language of whatever preoccupies a people—be it their food, fashion, lifestyle, the arts, sports, even business—is a unique window on their being.

The French are inordinately proud and protective of their language, which for a millennium was the world's language of diplomacy and for centuries the lingua franca for style, fashion, and many of the arts. There is even an official body, the Académie Française, a collection of forty writers, artists, academicians, and politicians (called the *Immortels*) who meet on Thursday afternoons to rule on what's correct language usage and what isn't. But you don't have to learn the language fluently to absorb the lifestyle. As with French portions, a little can go a long way, if you choose well.

In that spirit, here's a little French vocabulary list *à ma façon* useful for all seasons. It is drawn chiefly from words and concepts I have used in this book. Alas, there are no sports metaphors.

Bien dans sa peau [bye(n) dah(n) sah poh]: Healthy French women achieve the state of being "comfortable in one's skin". For all her attention to what she wears and what she eats, a French woman is most defined by her ease in being herself and the attractiveness that comes of her enjoyment of life. French women achieve this state more intuitively than most, but not everyone is successful. The secret of the woman who continues to be *bien dans sa peau* is that she has come to terms with enjoying each phase of her life and adjusting to life's different seasons. Being comfortable with oneself is such an important concept that I want to share another illustration, *une petite histoire*.

Every year we go back to Paris for the year-end holiday season when the Christmas decorations are low-key but lovely and the museums tend to be less crowded and so much more enjoyable. One of our little traditions is that Olivier, who is an inimitable art *conférencier* and the brother-in-law of a friend, gathers a dozen of us at the Musée du Luxembourg at the Sénat to comment on the current art exhibition. In late 2005 and early 2006 we saw the splendid Phillips Collection (Washington, D.C.) of French art from the nineteenth and twentieth centuries. The group attending varies slightly from year to year as some of us can't always make it. For me, it's one of those small pleasures not to be missed. Among the newcomers that year were two women over age fifty. One, Edith, was stunning: slim, full of energy but gently so, with a great haircut, a simple, long black coat, very little make-up, a sense of self-confidence, and emanating an air of serenity and *douceur de vivre*. Her age didn't really matter. She had that *je ne sais quoi* of the mythical French woman. She had adjusted to time and age.

The other, Claudine, was a bit plump, didn't quite look as though she was *bien dans sa peau* and, in her conversation, didn't sound as if she was. She vaguely offered what I believe, that at around fifty, women have to start making choices such as cutting down on food and wine portions, increasing the number of walks and whatever exercise we do, drinking more water, getting enough sleep, and, most important, picking our indulgences . . . but also wearing less and different make-up, deciding what to do about hair colour and style, and giving up certain clothes. In other words, to some extent we have to reinvent ourselves for the next season of life. Claudine knew that but didn't practise it. Being comfortable in one's skin is not simply a question of slim versus plump. Edith however, knew that this season in life is also often a time for new friends, perhaps some new hobbies; the main point is to remain active, curious, enthusiastic, and optimistic. The most positive among us, like Edith, do it almost effortlessly as if one more challenge is welcome. The feeling of well-being is ever so crucial in the way we age and confront the later phases of our life. No *laissez-faire*. No *laissez-aller*.

Bio [bee-Oh]: In their pursuit of quality over quantity French women increasingly select organic (or as they call them, *bio*) foods at markets and shops. Whether organic foods are more nutritious than regular foods is debatable; they are at least as nutritious, but for about the same price—sometimes a bit more, occasionally a bit less if they are local—they spare us ingesting chemical fertilizers and pesticides. And, of course, they are superior to processed foods. *Bio* is as fast a developing market in France as it is in America. But the French are a bit more sceptical about labels; they know that "organic" can mean different things to different governing authorities. If "organic" becomes just a marketing strategy, supply will have to expand to compete with demand, and standards may suffer. That's why we always prefer foods that taste as they were meant to taste. For that, local producers, who are more likely to grow organically, and whose offerings are more likely to be fresh and seasonal, are more reliable than labels. Organic is a good thing but only if we keep it real.

Bonheur [boh(n)-UHR]: French women know happiness is not a matter of luck; it's what you make of your life. This word for happiness is literally "good time". The French way of connecting feeling with time is telling. It suggests something to be cultivated in the course of our hours and days and months and years, how we live in relation to them. The English word *happy* comes from the archaic word *hap*, which means "luck". Interesting distinction.

Bonjour [BOH((N)-zhoor]: A French woman's first word to anyone, be they stranger or friend, is usually *bonjour*, good (*bon*) day (*jour*). The salutation is at the heart of French culture and etiquette, and if you listen the emphasis is almost always on the good side: BON-jour. If you are the sixty-eighth person of the day walking into a small shop, you will be greeted with *bonjour* as were the previous sixty-seven and as will be the sixty-eight who follow. It's an ingrained social ritual, and you must return the store clerk's *bonjour* before anything else, such as asking a question. In New York, complete sentences, let alone verbal niceties, can seem a waste of time to most. (On the other side of the world, credit goes to the Australians who have kept up G'day in a positive spirit.) In France, where the relation to time is different from America, not to observe these customs is considered rude. You have a much better chance of being treated nicely if you say *bonjour* to everyone you meet. If it is evening, *bonjour* becomes *bonsoir*: "Good evening". Only friends use the word *salut*, "hi" and "bye". The farewell matters, too. When you leave a store, don't be surprised if the shop assistant says good-bye, even if she is occupied with another customer. You should not neglect to say, "*au revoir*" ("good-bye", but more literally, "until we see each other again") and always "*merci*". Among friends we also say *à bientôt* ("see you soon"). These pleasant little expressions go a long way in France to help people connect in a friendly and effective manner.

Bricolage [bree-koh-LAZH]: French women (and men) have made an art of making do with what's at hand, whether with one's clothes, or what's in season at the market, or in a storeroom or closet. When I removed a mirror from a wall not long ago, exposing an embedded hook, I had to figure out what to do about that eyesore. I discovered a long-forgotten, old ceramic "art" plate that I had bought years ago but had never found the right place to hang. Now I did, though it was never intended for this sort of wall covering. The ceramic is not the *Mona Lisa,* but guests are repeatedly drawn to it. It covers a blemish as if it were born for that spot and gives the room a fresh, distinctive, and harmonious look.

I love this word, *bricolage,* which comes from the verb *bricoler*, to tinker about, mostly around the house. Though implying somewhat mechanical applications (there's a chain of hardware stores in France called Mr. Bricolage), the word certainly has an extended definition covering how one combines things in the kitchen or even how one puts oneself together in clothes. It has special cultural meaning in that it celebrates a person, *un bricoleur* (masculine) or *une bricoleuse* (feminine), who is creative and imaginative and who puts things together in fresh and original ways. Recently nine out of ten French women admitted to adoring *bricoler*. A friend, for instance, recently made a celebratory, non-edible, birthday cake for her eight-year-old out of flowers from her garden. When I go to the market and the aubergines are in season, I tend to overbuy to capture the moment to the fullest; I come home and then have to figure out how to incorporate them variously into our meals over the next few days. Ratatouille, for certain, but what about using the barbecue to grill them or the vegetable mill to purée them into a spread to start lunch or dinner? Once I went fishing off Long Island and came home with forty-eight mackerels, but that's another story. Sometimes I get really creative and think I've invented a new dish, only to find it on a restaurant menu later. Good chefs are great *bricoleurs*.

Une certaine tenue [ewn sehr-TEHN ten-EW]: A French woman expresses her indefinable flair through that certain something, an added element. It's said we know how to *jouer l'accessoire* (to accessorize). And it's true, the French woman's style has much to do with this knack. But it's not so much the accessories themselves; rather the choice of this (rather than that) as a form of self-expression. As with so many things, less is more. One element—a handbag, a bracelet, even a lipstick—can pull a look together, making it *bien tenu.* Mixing elements, for example, something precious with an item bought from a street vendor, is what stylists and designers do. French women do it for themselves, adding a touch that is entirely individual—sometimes witty and idiosyncratic, perhaps even a little eccentric, but not tacky. It's all about knowing themselves well enough to make the choice self-expressive: this is the French woman's edge.

C'est la vie [seh lah vee]: French women know there is a certain serenity in knowing those things you can change from those things you can't, and French women strive to know the difference. When they use the expression "that's life", it expresses an acceptance, even an embrace, of those things we cannot change, such as getting older and the rhythm of the seasons. But it is also accepting little things. I know when I am in France and at a post office that closes at 5 p.m. and the clerk stops selling stamps ten minutes early (to pack up, of course) or when I show up at the hairdresser for my appointment for a blow-dry and the smiling and chatty *coiffeuse* is an hour behind, I have to tell my American self to stop and think, *"c'est la vie"* (or sometimes, *"c'est la France"*).

Champagne [shahm-PAH-nyuh]: A French woman's eyes sparkle when she hears the word, and even more when she's offered a glass. She will always answer—and here I speak from extensive experience—*"volontiers"* ("gladly", but literally, "most willingly"). Champagne is a state of mind, a very pleasant one. It is made in the Champagne region of France and serves as a mood enhancer the world over. It is at once history and culture and pleasure and celebration, quality and refinement. The sound of a cork popping is magic.

Embracing Champagne as part of French culture starts young in France. Some people in France place a drop on their infant's forehead or behind his or her ears when christened. My first memory of drinking the real thing was when I was six. Recently I had the pleasure of dining at a top French restaurant with a group of six- and seven-year-olds as part of an educational enrichment programme. They all started the meal nonchalantly with a glass of bubbly. I was taken aback for a moment, but then asked a little girl if she liked Champagne, and she said, "It is Champagne d'Enfant, Madame." (Children's Champagne.) The bottle was the same, the label looked just like one on a Champagne bottle, the pop was the same, the glass used was the same as I had for my Champagne, and the bubbles were lively, but the bubbly was nonalcoholic apple cider. It seems these kids always celebrate their birthdays and special occasions with Champagne d'Enfant.

Détox [day-TOX]: French women are very mindful of the process of flushing out the waste products of metabolism that reside in our tissues, aiding our liver in its constant detoxing of our bodies. It's not just hedonism, for example, that makes French women love massages, and it's not only for the tactile pleasure. The vigorous touch of another can stimulate the lymphatic system, loosening stagnant toxins. For this reason, after a massage one is always offered a glass of water. While getting the toxins moving is one thing, nothing flushes them out like the process by which we absorb and eliminate water—again a reason to hydrate plentifully after a massage. And in today's world of preservatives, pesticides, artificial colours, flavours, and sweeteners, we have a lot to flush. The occasional Magical Leek Soup weekend is also as good a detox regimen as you'll find at any spa. (I appreciate professional massages can be expensive, but it's something partners can easily learn to do for each other.)

Eau [oh]: This French woman begins each day with a glass of water and makes sure to have a glass just before going to bed. Water is mythically one of the basic elements, along with fire, air, and earth. It is so vital to the French they denote it with a single vowel sound. French women drink it all day long. It is essential for every bodily process. We absorb it in some of our foods: soup is rich in water and it's known that a meal started with soup is one in which we will typically eat less overall. Some beverages are mostly water, but there is only one way to get enough: drink water itself. And drink it for the taste. (Too many people lose the taste for water by preferring to drink anything but. The idea that a meal might taste better with a diet cola than a glass of water is utterly alien to French women.) Hydration plumps tissue but not with fat. Learning to hold more water not only makes all our bodily processes work better, it also leaves skin clearer and fuller. There is never a time of year not to drink plenty. We lose about two litres of water a day in respiration alone. But in extreme heat and cold, hydration requires more vigilance. As you practise increasing your water intake steadily throughout the day—think six or eight large glasses—your body becomes more efficient at making use of what it was hoarding before. Just see what drinking water does for your breath. Now there are times when I compensate for all the added water by eating a few mildly diuretic foods: leeks, asparagus, cherries, grapes. Stronger diuretics, like any drink with alcohol or caffeine, need to be taken in moderation since they dehydrate and stimulate appetite. Finally, remember that some experiences of hunger are only thirst in disguise. So try answering the sensation with water first.

Entre deux âges [AHN-truh douze ahzh]: French women have a phase in life, literally "between two ages", or of ambiguous age. To be able to appear so is one of the advantages of living like a French woman. Nothing can alter the fact of the number of years you have lived, and some changes with time are inevitable. But how quickly the body ages depends in large part on how you take care of it, especially on what you put into it and whether you keep it moving throughout the day, every month of the year. Ageing gracefully, French women don't suffer the ravages of time too fast, and so they learn to be comfortable with their age. It's an important element of living *bien dans sa peau,* which is the key to feeling good and being attractive. You don't have to be old to be a *grande dame* . . . just great.

Équilibre [eh-kee-LEEBR]: French women know that maintaining balance or a healthy equilibrium is all-important and takes work, though after a while it becomes a continuous, unconscious activity. In terms of food, the notion of equilibrium as it pertains to living like a French woman is the balance between the calories one consumes and those one expends exerting oneself. French women don't aim to "burn" calories. They eat to fuel their bodies in proportion. If they overeat they don't plan to balance by overexerting themselves later. (If they overindulge, they simply eat less later.) Walking and the more intense routine exertion of taking the stairs are the French *équilibriste's* secret agents.

Equilibrium is maintained in several time frames: daily (*quotidien*) balance is, for example, if you have a big fancy dinner, you have a soup or salad for lunch the next day or go for a walk after supper. If you can't square the books the next day, do so by the end of the week. The balance for maintaining weight is weekly (*hebdomadaire*). The yearly equilibrium (*équilibre annuel*) is maintained by observance of the seasons.

But what of the monthly (*mensuel*)? For a stretch of our lives many of us face an added equilibrium challenge. (To some, it can seem a month-long affair every month, from premenstrual syndrome to menstruation to post-menstrual syndrome.) The difficulty of the experience varies for each individual, but French women have traditionally done a few things to ease the symptoms. First, avoid too many carbohydrates at breakfast. Replace orange juice and other sugary things with a bit of protein, such as slivers of ham or prosciutto and a small piece of cheese. For me, yogurt has always been a life-saver, especially when I had more than one a day to ease cramps and control cravings. And something a little counterintuitive: although you may be feeling bloated, do not neglect hydration. Try a large glass of lukewarm water (it's easier to absorb) with a squeeze of lemon first thing when you get up. When you are retaining water, the best way to get rid of it is to add more.

Faites simple [feht sahmpl]: French women know that generally more is less and when you start with quality—keep it simple. In terms of food, "simple" means less preparation and cooking time required, especially when you use marvellously fresh food. In terms of wardrobe, French women are likely to have only a few prime garments per season, but they are quality pieces that can be handsomely dressed up or down with the use of accessories, making it easier to put yourself together.

Joie de vivre [zhwah duh VEEV-ruh]: French women know that a healthy mind and body, taking pleasure in the seasons and in things great and small, are all part of "the joy of living," *joie de vivre* (an expression for which there is sadly no American equivalent). One sure way to maximize your *joie de vivr*e is to become a student of *l'art de vivre,* cultivating an appreciation of balance and gratification in all forms of sensory experience.

Laissez-aller [LEH-say al-LAY]: French women rarely give up on themselves, literally, to let oneself go. They know that it's never too late to be beautiful and that being beautiful is nothing more than maintaining themselves physically and mentally at any given interval of life. Coco Chanel said,

"Nature gives you the face you have at twenty, life shapes the face you have at thirty, but at fifty you get the face you deserve." The fashion industry would like to make us think that a fifteen-year-old girl is the ideal of beauty. Subtext: After that, what's the point? I'm amazed to find lovely young thirty-year-olds in New York who consider themselves past it. Sometimes they make the mistake of trying to seem younger in clothes and styling, but ironically when one appears to be hiding one's years, one only winds up seeming older. Then there's being *figée* (unevolving, frozen) and *coincée* (uptight: we age but our presentation stays the same, for instance keeping the same hairstyle for ten years). French women do make the most of themselves at every age and it's a matter of adaptation—it's up to each of us to construe our own beauty. They believe in *beauté charme:* the total effect beyond just a nice body and a pretty face; it includes the way one talks, smiles, moves, and gestures. If we are confident in feeling energy, depth, and charisma, we naturally transmit the feeling with our body and face. Beauty and its seductiveness are generated from within, not applied from without. As the fox in Saint-Exupéry's *Little Prince* says, "One sees the essential only with the heart. The essential is invisible to the eyes."

La moitié [lah MWAH-tyay]: When being served meat, vegetables, soup, whatever at someone's home or even in a restaurant, French women are apt to tell the person dishing it out, "*la moitié, s'il vous plait*": just give me half of that. It's mainly rhetorical in a French setting, where you are far less likely to get an outsize portion. But in other places, it's a survival tactic. This is the 50 Per Cent Solution in practice.

How much do you want to eat? How much should you eat? How about half?

Nos petits démons [noh puh-TEE day-MOH(N)]: French women, indeed all women, have their little demons, their personal "offenders". They can be foods whose siren song is most likely to mess up our equilibrium. The only answer to their danger is to identify them and to enjoy them with extra care. None should be forbidden; your discipline is not to skip them but to practise eating them mindfully and with focus. For those who are inclined to empty a bag of nuts, for instance, it is an excellent mental yoga practice to eat one nut at a time, up to five, very slowly, until you get to the point where it's simply too boring to contemplate having another one (shelling your own helps in this discipline).

Apart from chronic "offenders" we must also be on guard for cravings, especially at the most hormonally turbulent time of the month. I often answer cravings with a bit of dried fruit, such as figs, apricots, or prunes. Another excellent answer to this faux hunger are the French gherkins, or *cornichons*. Something about the vinegar and spice of these little pickles and their intense hit of flavour, tends to dispel cravings. I find this is true of liquorice as well, a fresh, intense taste that somehow turns off your desire to eat.

I confess to chocolate and bread as two of my demons (not-so-uncommon personal "offenders"), but happily, shopping is not a third. *Nos petits démons* are not limited to food. I don't binge on new shoes or clothes as a pick-me-up (keeping the same size and weight since adulthood helps). But the drill is the same. Know your "offenders" and indulge mindfully and in moderation in order to maintain equilibrium. And if once in a while you succumb to your demons? Congratulations: You are human. Forget the guilt and remember to compensate over time to regain your balance.

Petits riens [puh-TEE ryeh(n)]: French women love their little nothings. A misnomer, really, and all a matter of perception. I love the tiny gifts I receive, incalculably great and incalculably small. It could be a candle, a flower, four chocolates, a nifty magnet for the refrigerator with a clever phrase or picture, a ceramic insect (I did not think that was possible until I got one). In a complex world we have conditioned ourselves not to sweat the small stuff. It's true, you shouldn't sweat small things, but you should enjoy them. I am not speaking of the little irritations we face but about things that seem incidental yet can enhance experience and give pleasure. When it comes to our *petits riens* we don't need to know exactly what they add to the fullness of our experience; we need only to be open to the possibility that seeming trivialities may play a significant role in how we feel overall.

Peu à peu [puh ah puh]: French women appreciate that Rome wasn't built in a day (and neither was France), but rather "little by little". The progress of your life towards peak experiences in all aspects of living will take time. Changes made drastically or all at once are often the sorts of modifications that don't stick. Like New Year's resolutions, they are upheld proudly for a little while, but then we fall back to our old ways. Arrive at your new ways gradually, and you will leave your old ways too far behind for easy return. And if you slip up a bit, you won't feel a failure; you will know how to get back on track because it isn't all or nothing. It's a game of inches.

Plage de temps [plahzh duh tahm(p)]: French women are hedonists without being narcissists, but also pragmatists who understand that a healthy balance of pleasure in life requires a "beach of time", a lovely expression meaning a space of time for oneself to which one repairs on a daily or periodic basis. Sometimes it means making a morning for oneself—I have had to make a practice of scheduling a beach day for myself—or sometimes it can be a half hour or just a few minutes. It can be found in the most unlikely places: when you are stuck in traffic, listening to music, or just doing routine chores. You can let your mind fill up with anxiety or resentments, or with a bit of practice you can learn to head to the beach. The mind is its own place.

De saison [duh say-ZOH(N)]: French women know life would be tedious if it came in only one flavour. Whether fashion, food, or travel, French women anticipate and indulge in what's "in season". It's fun to be "*au courant*" with respect to the latest in food, drink, style. But this does not mean we don't pay proper attention to *les classiques,* whether they be the little black dress or the best of foods that return and give indispensable pleasure year after year. Alas, to define *de saison* properly takes a book (hopefully this one).

Terroir [tare-RWAHR]: French women know it is a combination of soil, sun, and microclimate that makes the same variety of melon from farmer Chassain taste sweeter than that from farmer Dubois. I am mindful of this when I shop locally at the Union Square Greenmarket, where I can choose tomatoes or strawberries from a half dozen vendors, but always seek out the one whose fruit is to my taste. The cultivation of the *terre* (soil, earth) and seasonal weather also have a big impact on quality, which is why wine vintages can vary so much in quality and characteristics from year to year, and from producer to producer, but it all starts with the *terroir*, which imparts distinctive quality to what is cultivated locally on the spot. *Terroir* is virtually a holy word in the world of wine, whether in Alsace, Champagne, Bordeaux, or elsewhere, but especially in Burgundy, vines planted 1.8 metres apart can produce grapes and then wines that are unmistakably different in character and often quality as well. This difference—validated over centuries of harvests—is always registered in the price, sometimes in multiples of five or more from vineyard to vineyard. There is a group of oenophiles who are such militant followers of *terroir* they call themselves "*terroiristes*".

Les vacances [lay vah-KAH(N)s]: French women take their holidays, *les vacances*, very seriously. The French motto is liberty, equality, brotherhood (*Liberté, Egalité, Fraternité*), but along with these inalienable rights, the French add six weeks of holidays. *Bien sûr*. It is a subject and measure of time that shapes their year. Implicit is the deep belief in the need to recharge one's batteries and that self-indulgent "play" is a psychological necessity to well-being. Holidays are so institutionalized in France that the majority of the *citoyens* (citizens) take them at the same time. It used to be that for the entire month of August the main roads leading from Paris had non-stop traffic alerts and long delays. Some years ago the government "asked" large companies to encourage some holidays starting on July 1 or July 15 to keep the economy and traffic flowing, but August is still pretty congested. The winter holidays are fixed by the national school calendar. And I continue to be amazed by how many French people still take their holidays exclusively in France. What's not amazing, in fact it's quite common, is to hear French people on holiday talking about their next holiday.

En vélo [ah(n) vay-LOH]: French women are quite likely to travel *en vélo*, "by bike", but as in China the days of bicycles being a primary means of transportation are greatly diminished. However, French women are terrific at incorporating bursts of physical activity as part of their daily routine (as opposed to going to the gym)—walking, of course, taking the stairs, and even swimming when possible. Today bicycling is still a top recreational activity in France. Go to a sports shop there and see all the special clothing and accessories and, of course, varieties of bicycles in all sizes and prices. It seems everyone lives Le Tour de France (and dresses the part). When I am out for a scenic ride and am huffing and puffing up some gradual climb with my mind on holiday, I am sometimes awakened with the sound in my left ear of the word "*bonjour*", the signal I am about to be passed by some man or woman or *peloton* (pack) on their racing bikes speeding on their way.

Voilà [vwah-LAH]: This is what French women (and men) say when all is said and done, and the thing speaks for itself: here it is, *voilà*, the end of *French Women for All Seasons.* I hope you enjoyed it and benefited from it. And I hope it speaks for itself.

Bonne chance et bonne continuation.

INDEX

accessories, 144, 367 *see also* scarves
"after desserts", 215–16
ageing, 370
air conditioning, 102, 107–8, 144–5
airports, 6–7
Albariño, 313
allergies, food, 48–9
antipasto, 311
appetizers and first courses, wines to drink with, 311–12
apples, 5–6, 182, 183–4, 317
  Baked Apple Aixoise, 188
  Jarlsberg, Apple and Mushroom Salad, 186
  Pear-Apple Compote with Honey, 185
  Spiced Apples, 187
apricots, 140
  Baked, 141
Ardèche Coffee (with Chestnuts), 246
art de vivre, 12, 13, 33, 372
artichokes, 311
asparagus, 47–9, 96, 311
  Asparagus and Cashew Omelette, 51
  Asparagus with Honey Sauce, 52
  Fettucine with Scallops and Asparagus, 53
  White Asparagus with Mayonnaise, *Mamie*'s version, 50
aubergines:
  Aubergine Tapenade, 134
  Curried Lamb with Aubergine, 85
autumn, 153–206

Baked Apple Aixoise, 188
Baked Apricots, 141
bananas, 23–4, 96, 243
  Banana Mousse, 247
  Prawn and Tuna Salad with Banana and Yogurt, 231
Barbecued Duck with Peaches, 128
barbecues, 110–11, 136–7, 315
Barbera, 312, 316

Barberesco, 314, 316
Barbier, Monsieur, 258–9
Barolo, 316
basil, 147
  Pesto, 179
  Steamed Courgettes with Basil, 81
beach holidays, 108, 109
beans *see* green beans
Beaufort cheese, 343
Beaujolais, 312, 316
beauty masks, 105, 211–12
beef, 315
  Grilled Steak with Wine Sauce, 181
beekeeping, 158–61
Beetroot Soup, 115
bien dans sa peau, 12, 31, 32, 363–4, 370
bio, 363–4
Bleu de Bresse cheese, 343
bonheur, 364
bonjour, 364–5
Bordeaux, 290, 299, 303, 315
Bourgogne, 284
Braised Carrots with Ginger, 243
Braised Fennel with Ginger, 242
bread, 94, 96
breakfast, 29–30, 160, 354
bricolage, 365–6
Brillat-Savarin (gastronome), 7–8, 56, 257–8
Brillat-Savarin cheese, 341–2
brioche:
  Chocolate Brioche, 349
  Pears on Brioche, 190
Brown Rice with Peas, 46
brunch, 354–5
buffets, breakfast, 29–30
Burgundy, 284, 289, 294, 303, 314, 316
butter, 94
Buttersquash Soup, 172

Cabernet Franc, 314, 316
Cabernet Sauvignon, 290, 298, 314, 315, 316, 317
caffeine, 95
Cake, Dark and Easy Chocolate, 198–9
calf's liver, 270–1
  Calf's Liver with Greens, 272
Calment, Jeanne Louise, 18–20, 41
Camembert, 342
capers:
  Skate with Capers, 177
Capezzana, 303–5
carbohydrates, 53, 54, 94, 371
cardigans, 144–5
carrots:
  Braised Carrots with Ginger, 243
  Cold Carrot Soup, 118
  Mackerel with Carrots and Leeks, 73
  Sardines with Carrots and Leeks, 71–2
cashews:
  Asparagus and Cashew Omelette, 51
Cauliflower Gratin, 169
cave (wine refrigerator), 293
caviar, 311
celeriac, 227
  Soup, 227–8
cereal, 96
certaine tenue, une, 367
c'est la vie, 367
Chabichou cheese, 344
Chablis, 311, 313, 316, 345
Champagne, 24, 222, 279, 280–1, 289, 290–1, 294, 295, 307–8, 309, 310, 311, 313, 314, 315, 316, 317, 318, 368
  Sea Scallops and Leeks in Champagne Sauce
Chanel, Coco, 372–3
change, 18, 375–6
Chardonnay, 284, 290, 307–8, 311, 312, 313, 314, 316, 345
Charles de Gaulle airport, 7
Château d'Yquem, 291
Châteauneuf-du-Pape, 314, 315
Cheddar cheese, 343
cheese:
  Figs with Ricotta, 143
  Georgia Gouda Gougères, 326–8

Goat Cheese and Fennel *Tartines*, 334
Jarlsberg, Apple, and Mushroom Salad, 186
Leeks Mozzarella, 70
Pear and Goat's Cheese *Papillote* with Yogurt Sauce, 191–2
Potato Gratin à la Normande, 163
Strawberry Soup with Mascarpone, 90
Summer-Vegetable Soup with Cheese, 117
varieties of, 341–5
wines to drink with, 309, 316–17, 345
cheese-tasting parties, 340–6
Chenin Blanc, 311, 313
chestnuts, 214–17
Ardèche Coffee (with Chestnuts), 246
Chestnuts and Honey, 218
Chestnut Soup, 219
marrons glacés, 216–17
Chèvre cheese, 344
Chianti, 312, 316
Chicago, 6–7
chicken:
and Green Bean Salad, 176
Chicken Breasts with Sorrel Sauce, 275–6
Chicken Tatin, 235–6
Chicken with Pastis, 129–30
Roast Chicken with Chicory, 75–6
Stuffed Poussins, 232
wines to drink with, 313–14
chicory:
Roast Chicken with Chicory, 75–6
chillies, 171
Chinese food, 315–16
chocolate, 96, 194–7, 199–200, 213–14, 317, 347
Chocolate Brioche, 349
Chocolate *Moelleux* with Walnuts, 350
Chocolate *Petits Pots*, 351
Dark and Easy Chocolate Cake, 198–9
Hot Chocolate Soufflé, 249
Pears with Chocolate and Pepper, 189
Pears with Ginger and Chocolate Mousse, 193
chrysanthemums, 156
cinnamon:
Grilled Peaches with Cinnamon and Rosemary, 142
Mango Carpaccio with Cinnamon, 250
citrus fruit, 244–5
Scallops with Citrus Fruit, 230
clams, 311
Claudel, Paul, 285
clothes, 90–2, 104, 143–7, 200–2, 251–2, 372
Cloudy Bay, 305–6
Cocktail *D'Huitres*, 223
cocktail *dinatoire*, 356–8
Cocotte de Légumes Croquants, 239
Cod with Potato Salad, 166
coffee, 7, 26, 27–9, 95, 199
Ardèche Coffee (with Chestnuts), 246
Coffee Mousse, 248
Coffee *Petits Pots*, 352
cold meats, 312
cold-water beauty routines, 104
Colette, 157, 340
compotes:
Pear-Apple, with Honey, 185
Rhubarb-Strawberry, 89
Comté cheese, 343
corks and corkscrews, 294–5
corn syrup, high-fructose, 27
courgettes;
Orecchiette with Tuna and Courgettes, 126
Steamed Courgettes with Basil, 81
couscous, 316
crab, 313
Crabmeat *Tartines*, 333
cravings, 374
Crottin de Chavignol cheese, 344
crudités, 311
cucumber, 105

Quick Cold Cucumber Soup, 113
curried dishes, 315
Curried Lamb with Aubergine, 85
cycling, 40–2, 378

Dandelion Salad, 77–8
Dark and Easy Chocolate Cake, 198–9
de saison, 376
decanting, 295–7
dessert parties, 346–53
desserts, 26–7, 88, 139, 196
recipes, 89–90, 141–3, 185, 187–90, 193, 246–50, 347–53
wines to drink with, 317
détox, 368–9 *see also* Magical Leek Soup
diets, 9, 17, 18, 30, 43, 53–4, 183
dinatoire, cocktail, 356–8
diuretics, 370
Dom Pérignon, 308
dressings, 96
Yogurt, 135, 231
duck, 314
Barbecued Duck with Peaches, 128
Duck Breasts Sweet and Sour, 238
Duck Breasts with Honey Glaze, 237

eau, 369–70 *see also* water
Edamame:
Farfalle with Edamame, 174
eggs, 48, 212
Asparagus and Cashew Omelette, 51
Lait de Poule au Jasmin, 347–8
Scrambled Eggs with Sorrel, 277
"elevator" speech, pitfalls of, 16–18
en vélo, 378
Endive, Sautéed, 170
entertaining, 319–59
at brunch, 354–5
at cheese-tasting party, 340–6
circulation of guests, 322–3
at cocktail *dinatoire*, 356–8
at dessert party, 346–52
drinking and, 324–5
finger food recipes for, 326–36
food presentation, 337
restaurants and, 323–4
self-presentation, 321–2
table settings, 337–8
entre deux âges, 21, 370
Époisses cheese, 344
equilibrium (*équilibre*), 12, 13, 31–2, 34, 40, 105–6, 154, 371–2
ethnic food 315–16
Étienne, Christian, 123
exercise, 30–2, 40–2, 106, 156–7, 209–11, 212–13, 378

faites simple, 372
Farfalle with Edamame, 174
fast food, 8
fat, 94
fennel:
Braised Fennel with Ginger, 242
Cold Fennel Soup, 116
Goat Cheese and Fennel *Tartines*, 334
Salmon with Fennel *en Papillote*, 74
fettucine:
Fettucine with Scallops and Asparagus, 52
Leeks Fettucine, 67
Fiddlehead Ferns, 57–9
Spaghetti with Fiddlehead Ferns and Prosciutto, 57–8
50 Per Cent Solution, 21–6, 28, 95, 325, 373–4
Figs with Ricotta, 143
finger foods, 326–36 *see also* cocktail *dinatoire*
first courses and appetizers, wines to drink with, 311–12
fish and shellfish
wines to drink with, 311, 312–13
see also names of specific fish and shellfish
Florence, 54–5
Florida, 245
flowers, 38–40, 93, 148, 156
foie gras, 270, 311
Fontina cheese, 342

food aversions and allergies, 48–9
Fourme d'Ambert cheese, 343–4
fragrances, 105
free weights, 31, 157
french fries, 162
French language, 360–79
"French Paradox", 282
frogs, 257–60
fructose, 27
fruit, 96, 138–40, 196, 244–5, 250–1
  Sweet-and-Sour Fruit-and-Vegetable Salad, 125
  see also names of specific fruits
fruit juices, 11, 27

gardening, indoor, 147–8
Garlicky Monkfish, 233
Georgia Gouda Gougères, 326–8
geraniums, 148
Gewürztraminer, 311, 312, 316
Gigondas, 314
ginger:
  Braised Carrots with Ginger, 243
  Braised Fennel with Ginger, 242
  Pears with Ginger and Chocolate Mousse, 193
glassware, 293–4
glycaemic indexing, 54
goat cheese, 316, 344, 345
  Goat Cheese and Fennel *Tartines*, 334
  Pear and Goat Cheese *Papillote* with Yogurt Sauce, 191–2
goose, 314
  liver, 270
Gopnik, Adam, 26
Gouda, 342
  Georgia Gouda Gougères, 326–8
grapefruit, 96, 245
grapes, 289–91
  Rabbit with Grapes and Wild Mushrooms, 267–8
green beans:
  Chicken and Green Bean Salad, 176
  Green Beans with Tomatoes, 80
Green Soup, 114
Grenache, 290
grignotage, 357
Grilled Peaches with Cinnamon and Rosemary, 142
Grilled Steak with Wine Sauce, 181
grills, 136–7
gym, 30–2

hair care, 104, 211
hazelnuts:
  Rabbit Loins with Hazelnuts, 269
health, wine and, 282–3
heat, summer, 101–2, 105–6, 108
herbal tea, 95
herbs, growing, 147
holidays, 101, 108–10, 155, 320, 377–8
honey, 158–61
  Asparagus with Honey Sauce, 53
  Chestnuts and Honey, 218
  Duck Breasts with Honey Glaze, 237
  Pear-Apple Compote with Honey, 185
Hot Chocolate Soufflé, 249
housework, 212–13
Houston, 102, 136

impatiens, 148
indoor gardening, 147–8

Jarlsberg, Apple, and Mushroom Salad, 186
jasmine tea:
  Lait de Poule au Jasmin, 347–8
jewellery, 144
joie de vivre, 12, 13, 372

laissez-aller, 372–3
Lait de Poule au Jasmin, 347–8
lamb, 84, 315
  Curried Lamb with Aubergine, 85
  Rack of Lamb Persillade, 86
leeks, 62–3
  Leek and Salmon *Tartines*, 335
  Leek and Spinach Quiche, 66
  Leeks Fettucine, 67
  Leeks Mozzarella, 70

Mackerel with Carrots and Leeks, 73
Magical Leek Soup (Broth), 62–4
Oysters on Steamed Leeks, 65
Prawn and Leek "Mimosa", 68
Sardines with Carrots and Leeks, 71–2
Sea Scallops and Leeks in Champagne Sauce, 69
Vichyssoise (Cold Leek and Potato Soup),120
Lenten fast, 42–3
Lentil Soup, 173
Livarot cheese, 344
liver, 270–1
Calf's Liver with Greens, 272
lobster, 312–13
longevity, 18–21

Macaroni with Spinach and Pancetta, 175
Maccioni, Sirio and Egi (restaurant owners), 60
Mackerel with Carrots and Leeks, 73
Magical Leek Soup (Broth), 62–4
makeup, 105
Malvasia di Lipari, 317
Manchego cheese, 343
mango, 96
Mango Carpaccio with Cinnamon, 250
maple syrup, 161
marigolds, 148
markets, 43–4, 103, 139
marrons *see* chestnuts
mascarpone:
Strawberry Soup with Mascarpone, 90
mashed potatoes:
Mashed Potatoes (*Mamie*'s version), 164–5
Ultra Rapide Mash, 168
masks, beauty, 105, 211–12
massage, 212, 369
mayonnaise:
White Asparagus with Mayonnaise, *Mamie's* Version, 50
meat and poultry
wines to drink with, 313–15
see also specific type of meat or poultry
melon, 317
Soup, 119
menstruation, 371–2
menus, 94–6
for autumn, 203–6
for spring, 97–100
for summer, 149–52
for winter, 253–6
Merlot, 290, 313, 314, 315, 316
metabolism, 31
Mexican food, 316
milk, 96
Mireille's Simple Tomato Salad, 124
Mixed Vegetable Soup, 229
moitié, la, 373–4
Monkfish, Garlicky, 233
moussaka, 316
mousse:
Banana Mousse, 247
Coffee Mousse, 248
Pears with Ginger and Chocolate Mousse, 193
Mozzarella, 342
Leeks Mozzarella, 70
Muenster cheese, 345
mullet:
Red Mullet with Spinach *en Papillote*, 127
Muscadet, 222, 311, 313
Muscat, 317
Beaumes-de-Venise, 311, 317
mushrooms, 158
Jarlsberg, and Apple and Mushroom Salad, 186
Rabbit with Grapes and Wild Mushrooms, 267–8
Sautéed Mushrooms, 82
mussels, 313
Mussels in White Wine, 178
Mustard Rabbit (*Lapin*) *en Papillote*, 266
mutabilité, 93

Nebbiolo, 290
New England, 154–5
New York, 3, 5, 26, 41, 47, 48, 93, 122, 156, 210, 211, 221, 283–4, 306
nos petits démons, 374–5
nuts, 296, 311, 374 *see also* names of specific nuts

olives, 311
  Potato-Olive Ragoût, 167
omega-3 fatty acids, 72
Omelette, Asparagus and Cashew, 51
onions:
  Spring Peas with Button Onions, 47
orange juice, 11
  Salmon with Orange *en Papillote*, 234
oranges, 244, 245
Orecchiette with Tuna and Courgettes, 126
organic foods (*bio*), 363–4
overeating, 6–7, 8
overweight, 7, 8–9, 32
oysters, 219–22, 311
  Cocktail *d'Huîtres*, 223
  Oyster Soup, 224
  Oysters on Steamed Leeks, 65
  Oysters with Garlic Butter, 225
  Oysters with Lemon Zest, 226

pancetta:
  Macaroni with Spinach and Pancetta, 175
Pappardelle with Spring Vegetables, 60–1
Paris, 3, 8, 41, 47, 49, 156, 220, 347, 362
Parker, Robert, 260
Parmigiano-Reggiano cheese, 343
parsnips, 171
pasta, 53–7, 96
  Farfalle with Edamame, 174
  Fettuccine with Scallops and Asparagus, 53
  Leeks Fettuccine, 67
  Macaroni with Spinach and Pancetta, 175
  Orecchiette with Tuna and Courgettes, 126
  Pappardelle with Spring Vegetables, 60–1
  Spaghetti with Fiddlehead Ferns and Prosciutto, 59
  wines to drink with, 312
Pastis, Chicken with, 129–30
pâtés, 312
peaches:
  Barbecued Duck with Peaches, 128
  Grilled Peaches with Cinnamon and Rosemary, 142
pears, 96, 182–3, 184
  Pear and Goat's Cheese *Papillote* with Yogurt Sauce, 191–2
  Pear-Apple Compote with Honey, 185
  Pears on Brioche, 190
  Pears with Chocolate and Pepper, 189
  Pears with Ginger and Chocolate Mousse, 193
peas, 45
  Brown Rice with Peas, 46
  Spring Peas with Button Onions, 47
Pecorino cheese, 343
peppers, 171
  Tricolour Peppers, 131–2
Pesto, 179, 180
  Turkey Escalopes with Pesto, 179–80
petits démons, 374–5
petits fours ("after desserts"), 215–16
petits pots:
  Chocolate, 351
  Coffee, 352
  Pumpkin, 353
petits riens, 375
peu à peu, 375–6
pheasant, 314
picnics, 111
pigeon, 261–3
  Pigeon Rôti, 264
pine nuts:
  Spinach with Sultanas and Pine Nuts, 83
Pinot Blanc, 311, 312, 313, 316

Pinot Grigio, 290, 311, 312, 313
Pinot Gris, 290, 311, 312, 313, 315–16
Pinot Meunier, 308
Pinot Noir, 289, 290, 297, 298, 308, 313, 314, 315, 316
pizza, 309, 316
plage de temps, 376
plancha, 137–8
pleasure, 6, 9–10, 12, 33, 34, 38, 95, 184, 214, 279, 309, 372
Poire Williams, 183
pomegranates, 250–1
pork, 315
Port, 317, 345
portions, 21–6, 55, 95, 96
positive emotional outlook, 33
potatoes, 96, 161–2
  Cod with Potato Salad, 166
  Mashed Potatoes (*Mamie*'s Version), 164–5
  Potato Gratin à la Normande, 163
  Potato-Olive Ragout, 167
  Ultra Rapide Mash, 168
  Vichyssoisse (Cold Leek and Potato Soup), 120
poultry and meat:
  wines to drink with, 313–15
  see also specific type of poultry or meat
poussins, 314
  Stuffed, 232
prawns, 313
  Prawn and Leek "Mimosa", 68
  Prawn and Tuna Salad with Banana and Yogurt, 231
  Prawn *Tartines*, 336
prosciutto, 311
  Spaghetti with Fiddlehead Ferns and Prosciutto, 57–8
protein, 49, 94, 354, 371
Provence, 19, 41, 42, 49, 93, 110, 122–3, 161, 302, 323–4
Pumpkin *Petits Pots*, 353

quail, 314
quiche, 311
  Leek and Spinach Quiche, 66
  Quiche Lorraine, 329–30

rabbit, 265, 315
  Mustard Rabbit (*Lapin*) *en Papillote*, 266
  Rabbit Loins with Hazelnuts, 269
  Rabbit with Grapes and Wild Mushrooms, 267–8
Rack of Lamb Persillade, 86
ramekins, 338
recipes:
  autumn, 163–70, 172–81, 185–93, 198–9
  for dessert party, 347–53
  finger foods, 326–36
  spring, 46–7, 50–3, 58–61, 63–83, 85–6, 89–90
  summer, 113–20, 124–36, 141–3
  for unusual foods eaten in France, 264, 266–9, 272, 274–7
  winter, 218–19, 223–6, 228–43, 246–50
Red Mullet with Spinach *en Papillote*, 127
redcurrants, 6
resistance training, 31, 157
Rhône wines, 302, 312, 314, 315, 316
Rhubarb-Strawberry Compote, 89
Ribera del Duero, 312
rice, 96
  Brown Rice with Peas, 46
Ricotta, Figs with, 143
Riesling, 290, 311, 312, 313, 315, 316, 317, 345
rince-doigts, 48, 262
Robiola cheese, 342
Roquefort, 309, 344
rosemary:
  Grilled Peaches with Cinnamon and Rosemary, 142
roses, 148
Rosso di Montepulciano, 312

Saint-Émilion, 314

Saint-Jacques *Tartines*, 331–2
Saint-Véran, 313
saison, de, 376
salads, 312
  Chicken and Green Bean, 176
  Dandelion, 77–8
  Jarlsberg, Apple, and Mushroom, 186
  Potato, Cod with, 166
  Prawn and Tuna, with Banana and Yogurt, 231
  Salmon-and-Spinach, 79
  Sweet-and-Sour Fruit-and-Vegetable, 125
  Tomato, Mireille's Simple, 124
salmon, 313
  Leek and Salmon *Tartines*, 335
  Salmon-and-Spinach Salad, 79
  Salmon with Fennel *en Papillote*, 74
  Salmon with Orange *en Papillote*, 234
  Salmon with Sorrel, 274
Sancerre, 297, 313, 316, 345
Sangiovese, 290, 316, 345
Sardines with Carrots and Leeks, 71–2
sauce:
  Champagne, Sea Scallops and Leeks in, 69
  Honey, Asparagus with, 53
  Sorrel, Chicken Breasts with, 275–6
  Wine, Grilled Steaks with, 181
  Yogurt, Pear and Goat's Cheese *Papillote* with, 191–2
Sautéed Endive, 170
Sautéed Mushrooms, 82
Sauternes, 309, 311, 317, 345
Sauvigon Blanc, 222, 290, 305, 311, 312, 313, 316, 345
scallops, 311
  Fettuccine with Scallops and Asparagus, 52
  Saint-Jacques *Tartines*, 331–2
  Sea Scallops and Leeks in Champagne Sauce, 69
  Sea Scallops with Citrus Fruit, 230
scarves, 91–2, 145–7, 201–2, 251–2
Scrambled Eggs with Sorrel, 277
Seasonal Affective Disorder, 209
seasonality, 34–6, 121
  and wine, 279–80
self-presentation, 321–2
Sémillon, 291, 312
Shallots *Confites en Papillote*, 240–1
Shaw, George Bernard, 360
shawls, cashmere, 251
shellfish *see* fish and shellfish
shopping, 374
Skate with Capers, 177
skin care, 104, 211–12
snacks, 95
snow sports, 209
sorrel, 273
  Chicken Breasts with Sorrel Sauce, 275–6
  Salmon with Sorrel, 274
  Scrambled Eggs with Sorrel, 277
Soufflé, Hot Chocolate, 249
Soups, 96, 111–12, 171, 227, 312
  Beetroot, 115
  Buttersquash, 172
  Carrot, Cold, 118
  Celeriac, 227–8
  Chestnut, 219
  Cucumber, Cold, 113
  Fennel, 116
  Green, 114
  Lentil, 173
  Magical Leek (Broth), 62–4
  Melon, 119
  Mixed Vegetable, 229
  Oyster, 224
  Strawberry, with Mascarpone, 90
  Summer-Vegetable, with Cheese, 117
  Vichyssoise (Cold Leek and Potato Soup), 120
Spaghetti with Fiddlehead Ferns and Prosciutto, 57–8
Spiced Apples, 187
spinach:
  Leek and Spinach Quiche, 66
  Macaroni with Spinach and Pancetta, 175

Red Mullet with Spinach *en Papillote*, 127
Salmon-and-Spinach Salad, 79
Spinach with Sultanas and Pine Nuts, 83
spring, 37–100
Spring Peas with Button Onions, 47
squash, 171
Buttersquash Soup, 172
stairs, 210, 371
Steak, Grilled, with Wine Sauce, 181
Steamed Courgettes with Basil, 81
Stilton, 344
stock, 111
Strasbourg, 260
strawberries, 87–8, 105, 121
Rhubarb-Strawberry Compote, 89
Strawberry Soup with Mascarpone, 90
stress, 21, 154, 157
Stuffed Poussins, 232
style, personal, 33–4
sugar, 26, 27, 28, 160
sugar substitutes, 28
sultanas:
Spinach with Sultanas and Pine Nuts, 83
summer, 101–52
Summer-Vegetable Soup with Cheese, 117
sun, exposure to, 103–4, 209
sushi, 311, 313
Sweet-and-Sour Fruit-and-Vegetable Salad, 125
sweetness, 26–9, 88 *see also* honey; maple syrup; sugar
swimming, 106
swordfish, wines for, 313
Syrah, 290, 314, 315, 316

T-shirts, 143
table settings, 337–8
tangelos, 245
tartines:
Crabmeat, 333
Goat's Cheese and Fennel, 334
Leek and Salmon, 335
Prawn, 336
Saint-Jacques, 331–2
tea, 95
Tempranillo, 315
terroir, 220, 258, 376–7
Thai dishes, 316
three-meal-a-day, 94
time, 8, 34–6, 364, 376
Tokaji, 317
Tokay, 317
tomato sauce, 122
tomatoes, 121–3
Green Beans with Tomatoes, 80
Mireille's Simple Tomato Salad, 124
travel, 108–10
Tricolour Peppers, 131–2
trousers, 143–4
tulips, 39–40
tuna, 311, 313
Orecchiette with Tuna and Courgettes, 126
Prawn and Tuna Salad with Banana and Yogurt, 231
turkey, 138, 314
Turkey Escalopes with Pesto, 179–80

Ultra Rapide Mash, 168

vacances, les, 377–8 *see also* holidays
Vacherin cheese, 344
veal, 314–15
vegetables, 54, 56, 111–12, 171
Cocotte de Légumes Croquants, 239
Green Soup, 114
Mixed Vegetable Soup, 229
Pappardelle with Spring Vegetables, 60–1
Summer Vegetable Soup with Cheese, 117
Sweet-and-Sour Fruit-and-Vegetable Salad, 125
Vegetables with Yogurt Dressing, 135
see also names of specific vegetables

vélo, en, 378 *see also* cycling
venison, 315
Vernaccio di San Gimignano, 312
Veuve Clicquot, 280–1
  La Grande Dame, 308
Vichyssoise (Cold Leek and Potato Soup), 120
vin santo, 317
vineyards, 301–2, 303–5
Viognier, 311, 313, 315
vitamin D, 103–4, 209
voilà, 379

walking, 31, 40, 106, 156, 209, 210, 211, 371
walnuts:
  Chocolate *Moelleux* with Walnuts, 350
wardrobe *see* clothes
water, 31, 94, 95, 105, 106, 284, 325, 369–70, 372
  bottled, 11
Watercress Coulis, 133
weight control, 21–6, 95, 194, 371
weight loss, 9, 13, 18, 34
White Asparagus with Mayonnaise, *Mamie*'s Version, 50
Wilde, Oscar, 308
wine, 24–6, 95, 222, 278–318, 345, 377
  for appetizers and first courses, 311–12
  buying, 286–91
  for cheeses, 316–17, 345
  corks and corkscrews and, 294–5
  decanting, 295–7
  for desserts, 317
  drink-local principle, 301–3
  for ethnic dishes, 315–16
  50 Per cent solution and, 24–6
  for fish and shellfish, 312–13
  as food, 279
  glassware for, 293–4
  grape varieties, 289–91
  health benefits, 282–3
  for meat and poultry, 313–15
  mode d'emploi, 283–4
  pairing with food, 309–18, 345
  price, 287–8
  serving temperature, 295–6
  storing, 291–3
  tasting, 297–301
  terroir, 377
  vintages, 280–1
winter, 207–77

yoga, 31, 157, 210, 212
yogurt, 95, 105, 371–2
  Pear and Goat's Cheese *Papillote* withYogurt Sauce, 191–2
  Prawn and Tuna Salad with Banana and Yogurt, 231
  Vegetables with Yogurt Dressing, 135

Zinfandel, 290, 312, 314, 315, 316, 345